Library of
Davidson College

Senate Elections

Senate Elections

Alan I. Abramowitz and Jeffrey A. Segal

Ann Arbor

THE UNIVERSITY OF MICHIGAN PRESS

Copyright © by the University of Michigan 1992
All rights reserved
Published in the United States of America by
The University of Michigan Press
Manufactured in the United States of America

1995 1994 1993 1992   4 3 2 1

A CIP catalogue record for this book is available from the British Library.

To my parents, Jack and Isabel
A. I. A.

To Christine and Michelle
J. A. S.

Preface and Acknowledgments

The central argument of this book is that Senate elections are now much more competitive than House elections and that, because of this, the Senate has been more responsive to shifts in the national political climate than the House of Representatives. Obviously, this is not what the framers of the Constitution intended. However, this role reversal can be explained by several trends that have affected Senate elections since the 1960s: partisan dealignment and the growth of interparty competition in many states once characterized by one-party domination; the continuing attractiveness of the Senate for many ambitious politicians; a dramatic increase in campaign spending; and increasing use of television advertising by both challengers and incumbents. All of these trends have affected Senate elections much more strongly than House elections. The result has been a striking discrepancy in the outcomes of these contests—only 5 percent of House incumbents have been defeated, compared with 20 percent of Senate incumbents. Even though only one-third of all Senate seats are contested every two years, the Senate, because of its more competitive electoral environment, has actually experienced a higher rate of turnover in its membership than the House of Representatives. Just as important, in recent years, the division of seats between the parties has been much closer in the Senate than in the House. This has contributed to two changes in party control in the Senate since 1980.

We focus our attention primarily on Senate elections since 1974, because information about campaign spending was not available before this year. However, we also discuss the outcomes of earlier Senate elections and, in chapter 4, we propose and test a model that explains the outcomes of Senate elections for the period since the end of World War II.

The electoral environment has had important consequences for the style of leadership and decision-making processes of the Senate. In the House of Representatives, the Democratic party appears to enjoy semipermanent majority status and the overwhelming advantage of incumbency insulates most members from the effects of national political tides. As a result, there is little incentive for cooperation between the majority and minority parties and little reason for individual members to weigh the interests of their party along with those of their own constituents. In the Senate, in contrast, the realization that national issues can affect both the political survival of individual members and party control of the Senate has contributed to a consensual style of leadership and a stronger sense of collective responsibility for policy outcomes.

The Plan of This Book

In chapter 1, the Senate's rejection of President Reagan's nomination of Robert Bork to the Supreme Court in 1987 is used to introduce the relationship between Senate elections and Senate politics. While many factors contributed to the Senate's rejection of Bork, we argue that almost all of these factors were related to the changing character of Senate elections and the results of the 1986 Senate elections. The impact of the 1986 Senate elections on the rejection of Robert Bork by the Senate in 1987 illustrates the way in which the Senate's electoral environment shapes its internal decision-making processes.

Against this backdrop of political pressure, we compare the present Senate to that envisioned by the framers of the Constitution. Concern about the tyranny of the majority led the founders to create an upper chamber that would be more deliberative than the lower chamber, and not as subject to majoritarian pressure. This was accomplished by providing for the selection of Senators for terms of six years by the state legislatures. Finally, we examine the movement that culminated in the passage of the Seventeenth Amendment and the direct election of Senators.

In chapter 2, we use national survey data to analyze the attitudes and behavior of voters in Senate elections. The data come from the regular 1986 and 1988 National Election Studies conducted by the Center for Political Studies at the University of Michigan and a special Senate Election Study conducted by the Center for Political Studies in 1988. We have chosen to analyze these two elections because of their contrasting results—in 1986, seven incumbents were defeated as the Democrats gained eight seats to regain control of the Senate; in 1988 only three incumbents lost and the net shift in party control was only one seat. In addition, these two elections allow us to compare voter attitudes and behavior in a presidential election year with voter attitudes and behavior in a midterm election year. Data from the special Senate Election Study are used to examine the effects of differences in state population on voters in the 1988 Senate elections.

Chapter 3 examines the process by which Senate candidates are nominated and the factors affecting these nominations. After reviewing differences among states in the procedures used to select Senate candidates, we turn to an in-depth examination of the six primaries since 1974 in which elected incumbents were defeated: William Fulbright (D-Arkansas) in 1974, Clifford Case (R-New Jersey) in 1978, and Jacob Javits (R-New York), Richard Stone (D-Florida), Donald Stewart (D-Alabama), and Mike Gravel (D-Alaska) in

1980. While we examine a number of factors that contributed to the defeat of these incumbents, we pay particular attention to the role of ideology in several of these contests. In addition, because of the impact of primaries on general election contests, we systematically examine factors that have influenced incumbents' primary margins since 1974.

In chapter 4, we propose and test three statistical models of Senate election outcomes. The first model is concerned with explaining (and predicting) the national outcome of the Senate election—that is, the net seat gain or loss for each party; the second and third models are concerned with explaining the outcomes of individual Senate contests. We use the results obtained for our aggregate and individual seat models to make predictions about the 1988 and 1990 Senate elections. Although our predictions are fairly accurate, lending support to the basic models, we attempt to explain why our models failed to correctly predict the outcomes of several individual races in 1988 and 1990. The errors produced by our statistical models point to the importance of certain unmeasured (and perhaps unmeasurable) factors in Senate elections, such as campaign effort and skill. These are considered in greater depth in our case studies of four 1986 Senate campaigns in chapters 6 and 7.

Our case studies of Senate campaigns as well as our statistical analyses of Senate elections underscore the crucial role of money in today's media-based Senate contests. Chapter 5, therefore, examines who gives this money and who gets it. We describe trends in Senate campaign spending since 1974, the first election for which accurate information on campaign finance is available. Even after controlling for inflation, there has been a dramatic increase in campaign spending in Senate elections. We examine trends in spending by Democratic and Republican incumbents, challengers, and candidates for open seats. This makes it possible to determine what kinds of candidates have been helped or hurt by the increase in campaign spending. We also explore what kinds of contributors (individuals, party committees, PACs, and the candidates themselves) give money to what kinds of candidates (Democratic and Republican incumbents, challengers, and candidates for open seats). We pay particular attention to two controversial issues: the influence of PACs, and the extent of self-financing by Senate candidates. In the final section of this chapter, we evaluate recent proposals for reforming Senate campaign finances in light of the findings presented in chapter 4 regarding the impact of campaign spending on election outcomes.

Chapters 6 and 7 explore the character of modern Senate campaigns by means of an in-depth examination of four 1986 Senate campaigns: the Cranston-Zschau contest in California, the D'Amato-Green contest in New York, the Hawkins-Graham contest in Florida, and the Abdnor-Daschle contest in South Dakota. There is no such thing as a typical Senate campaign, and even four campaigns in the same year cannot do justice to the variety of candidates and circumstances found in Senate contests. However, these four campaigns illustrate many of the characteristics of modern Senate elections and some of the variations on these characteristics. Our analyses of these four 1986 Senate campaigns use personal interviews with several of the candidates and their top campaign advisors, results of exit polls conducted by ABC News in all four states, and newspaper accounts of key campaign events. Because of the crucial role played by television advertising in modern Senate campaigns, we also provide a detailed description and analysis of the television advertisements used in these four campaigns.

In our concluding chapter, we summarize the main findings presented in the book and discuss the implications of these findings for the role of the Senate in the contemporary U.S. political system. Contrary to the intent of the framers of the Constitution, the Senate has developed, in recent years, into a legislative chamber that is highly responsive to the shifting political mood of the nation—perhaps more so than the House of Representatives. This surprising development is a direct result of the volatile electoral environment of the upper chamber. While most members of the House of Representatives are relatively secure and insulated from the effects of national political forces, senators exist in a much more uncertain electoral environment.

There are many people we would like to thank for their contributions to this book. Numerous participants in Senate elections granted us time for interviews, including Senators James Abdnor, Bob Graham, and Paula Hawkins, candidates Mark Green and Ed Zschau, and Senate aides Roy Greenaway (Alan Cranston), and Peter Stavrianos (Tom Daschle). Julian Kanter of the Center for Political Communications at the University of Oklahoma provided the political commercials used in chapters 6 and 7 that were transcribed, in part, by Christine Segal. Yen Giang and Kimberly Nelson provided invaluable research assistance, and the Public Records Office at the Federal Elections Commission was always cheerful, prompt, and efficient in handling requests. Greg Haley provided valuable assistance in analyzing data from the National Election Studies. Albert Cover provided helpful comments and suggestions on several chapters. Chapter 4 is based on two articles originally published by the authors in the *Journal of Politics* and the *American Political Science Review*. Chapter 5 is a revised version of an article originally published in *Legislative Studies Quarterly*. We thank these journals for permission to use this material in the book.

Part of the book was written while Jeffrey Segal was a fellow at the Law and Social Science Program, Northwestern University, on sabbatical leave from SUNY at Stony Brook. Support for this project was also provided by a research grant to Alan Abramowitz from the Emory University Research Committee. All three institutions are thanked for their support.

Contents

Chapter

1.	Introduction	1
2.	Voters in U.S. Senate Elections	27
3.	Primary Elections	49
4.	Explaining Senate Election Outcomes	93
5.	Money in Senate Elections: Who Gives It and Who Gets It?	123
6.	Incumbent Winners in Senate Campaigns in the Television Age	145
7.	Incumbent Losers in Senate Campaigns in the Television Age	185
8.	Conclusions: Senate Elections, Senate Politics, and Electoral Accountability	227

Appendixes:

Appendix A	243
Appendix B	244
Appendix C	246
Index	247

CHAPTER 1

Introduction

"We lost this nomination on November 4, 1986."
—Tom Korologos, White House lobbyist.

President Ronald Reagan nominated U.S. Circuit Court Judge Robert Bork to the Supreme Court on July 1, 1987. The campaign in the Senate against Bork actually began a few days before his nomination was announced. On the day Associate Justice Lewis Powell resigned, Senator Joseph Biden (D-Delaware), chairman of the Senate Judiciary Committee and Democratic presidential aspirant, declared that he would resist any effort by the administration to "impose an ideological agenda upon our jurisprudence."[1] Senator Paul Simon (D-Illinois), also on the Judiciary Committee and also seeking the presidency, proclaimed, "If the President appoints an ideologue . . . then there's going to be delay. . . . The Senate might very well reject a nominee."[2] Senate Majority Leader Robert Byrd (D-West Virginia) stated four days later that the nomination of Bork "would be inviting problems."[3] Even the interest groups were attempting a preemptive strike against Bork. Ralph Neas, executive director of the Leadership Council on Civil Rights, predicted that "A Bork nomination . . . would most likely precipitate the most controversial and confrontational battle of the Reagan years."[4]

Though the battle against Bork began in the days before his nomination, the campaign for Bork actually began ten months earlier in Reagan's 1986 campaign to retain Republican control of the Senate. The Republicans had gained control of the Senate for the first time since the Eisenhower administration in Reagan's 1980 landslide victory over Jimmy Carter. They were able to

---

1. Gerald Boyd, "White House Hunts for a Justice, Hoping to Tip Ideological Scales," *New York Times*, June 30, 1987.

2. Boyd, "White House Hunts."

3. Jonathan Fuerbringer, "Byrd Says Bork Nomination Would Face Senate Trouble," *New York Times*, June 30, 1987.

4. Gerald Boyd, "Bork Nomination Weighed by President," *New York Times*, June 30, 1987.

control the Senate because twenty-four of the thirty-four seats at stake in the election were held by Democrats, President Carter had the lowest popularity ratings of any modern president, and the economy was in shambles.[5] Thus, the Republicans won twenty-two of the seats, the Democrats won twelve, and majority control passed to the Republicans.

Partisan control of the Senate is crucial to any president's legislative agenda. Members of the president's party are more likely to vote for him than are members of the opposition party. In addition, majority control brings with it the chairmanships of all the legislative committees and subcommittees, which are crucial to the passage of legislation. An adept chairman can easily manipulate when a proposed bill will be considered and even if the bill will be considered. The chair can determine when proponents of the bill can speak and when opponents will speak. Republican control of the Senate was pivotal in Reagan's first-term legislative victories—slashing tax rates, cutting domestic programs, and strengthening the Defense Department.

The 1986 Senate featured fifty-three Republicans and forty-seven Democrats. Though Reagan's popularity was high, twenty-two of the thirty-four seats at stake were held by Republicans. In an attempt to prevent the Democrats from winning more than fifteen of the seats and thus becoming the majority party, Reagan campaigned more actively in the midterm election than any president in recent history.[6] Reagan's campaign speeches focused on the need for a continuing conservative majority to keep taxes low, domestic spending low, and "Star Wars" spending high. He also emphasized the Senate's role in confirming judicial appointments. Stumping for Senator James Broyhill (R-North Carolina), Reagan blamed liberal judges for the nation's drug problems and warned that the problem would get worse if the Democrats took control of the Senate.

> The proliferation of drugs has been part of a crime epidemic that can be traced to, among other things, liberal judges who are unwilling to get tough with the criminal element in this society. . . . We don't need a bunch of sociology majors on the bench. What we need are strong judges who will aggressively use their authority to protect our families, communities and way of life; judges who understand that punishing wrongdoers is our way of protecting the innocent; judges who do not hesitate to put criminals where they belong, behind bars.[7]

The survival of law and order was dependent on Republican control of the Senate and, thus, the Judiciary Committee.

---

5. See chap. 4.
6. R. W. Apple, "A President's Limits," *New York Times*, November 5, 1986.
7. "Reagan Aims Fire at Liberal Judges," *New York Times*, October 9, 1986.

Today, Senator Strom Thurmond and Jim Broyhill are in a majority on the Senate Judiciary Committee, overseeing judicial appointments. Without Jim Broyhill and a Republican Senate majority, that job will be turned over to Teddy Kennedy and Joe Biden. . . . You can strike a blow against drugs, thugs and hoodlums by casting your vote for Jim and keeping him as a force for law and order in the United States Senate. The future of our country, its safety and security is in our hands.[8]

Similar comments were made during other speeches, including campaign swings to Missouri and Alabama.

While the voters might have heard President Reagan's message, they did not heed his advice. The Democrats won a resounding victory on November 4, winning twenty of the thirty-four elections, thus taking a fifty-five to forty-five Senate majority. The Democratic victories were particularly stunning in the South. Aided by huge majorities among black voters, Democrats took over Republican seats in Alabama, Florida, Georgia, and North Carolina.[9] With these victories, Senator Edward Kennedy (D-Massachusetts) assumed the chair of the Labor and Human Resources Committee, leaving the Judiciary Committee chair to Senator Joe Biden.

On July 1, 1986, the day Bork was nominated, liberal interest groups, including People for the American Way, The Women's Legal Defense Fund, The Alliance for Justice, and the National Abortion Rights Action League (NARAL), announced opposition to the nominee. Ted Kennedy became the first senator to state his opposition to Bork and set the tone for the accusations and counteraccusations that were to follow.

Robert Bork's America is a land in which women would be forced into back alley abortions, blacks would sit at segregated lunch counters, rogue police could break down citizens' doors in midnight raids, writers and artists could be censored at the whim of government, and the doors of the federal courts would be shut on the fingers of millions of citizens.[10]

Joe Biden, chairman of the Judiciary Committee, was in a little more precarious situation. In November, 1986, Biden told the *Philadelphia Inquirer* that if a well-qualified conservative like Bork were nominated for the Supreme Court, "I'd have to vote for him, and if the groups tear me apart, that's the medicine I'll have to take."[11] As interest-group opposition to Bork

---

8. "Reagan Aims Fire."
9. Lena Williams, "Blacks Cast Pivotal Ballots in Four Key Senate Races, Data Show," *New York Times*, November 6, 1986.
10. James Reston, "Kennedy and Bork," *New York Times*, July 5, 1987.
11. Larry Eichel, "Judiciary Post to Gauge Biden's Presidential Chances," *Philadelphia Inquirer*, November 16, 1986.

quickly mobilized, the medicine started to appear more and more bitter. On July 7, Biden began privately announcing that he would oppose Bork.[12] Given Bork's previous FBI investigation when he was nominated for the U. S. Court of Appeals for the District of Columbia, and given his unanimous confirmation by the Senate Judiciary Committee and the full Senate for that position, hearings on Bork could have begun almost immediately. Biden, using his power as chairman of Judiciary to his advantage, decided that hearings on Bork would not begin until September 15, all but guaranteeing that Bork could not be confirmed before the start of the Court's term, the first Monday in October. The move also allowed liberal interest groups, which were already in opposition, to mobilize their supporters. A successful campaign against Bork would depend on grass roots opposition, but by July 22 only 12 percent of the U.S. public was opposed to Bork, with the overwhelming majority unsure.[13]

Through the summer, more and more liberal groups announced opposition to Bork. The AFL-CIO announced its opposition on August 17, and on August 31 the American Civil Liberties Union dropped its fifty-one-year-old policy against involvement in Supreme Court nominations and joined the opposition to Bork. Bork supporters, however, were far from silent and, at the grass roots level, appeared initially to be better organized. By the beginning of September, the Judiciary Committee had received over 33,000 cards and letters on both sides, with negative letters only starting to catch up with positive ones. A sample letter from Dr. Robert Gant's *Christian Voice* made clear what Senators knew all along: the vote on Bork would have direct electoral consequences.

> As my representative in Congress I demand you confirm Judge Bork to this appointment. Since the 1930's this nation has been burdened with a liberal majority on the Supreme Court. No longer will I stand for it. Either vote yes for Bork or count yourself one vote short in the next election.[14]

Soon, however, liberal groups began to gain the upper hand. By September 11, such groups had raised over $6,000,000 to fight Bork.[15] This money started to find its way into full-page newspaper advertisements. NARAL

---

12. Kenneth Noble, "Biden Vows to Lead Fight Against Bork's Confirmation," *New York Times*, July 9, 1987.

13. E. J. Dionne, Jr., "Senate Should Consider the Opinions of High Court Nominees, Poll Finds," *New York Times*, July 24, 1987.

14. Kenneth Noble, "Bork Backers Flood Senate with Mail," *New York Times*, September 2, 1987.

15. Richard Berke, "Bork as a Bonanza," *New York Times*, September 11, 1987.

claimed that "we're just one vote away from losing our most fundamental rights . . . one Justice away from *in*justice."[16] Planned Parenthood had this to say about Bork: "State controlled pregnancy? It's not as far fetched as it sounds. Carrying Bork's position to its logical end, states could ban or require any method of birth control, impose family quotas for population purposes, make abortion a crime, or sterilize anyone they choose."[17] The campaign even made its way into television, with film star Gregory Peck denouncing Bork on behalf of People for the American Way.

Despite these efforts, opposition to Bork did not begin to crystallize until the Judiciary Committee hearings began. At the start of the hearings, 14 percent of the country supported Bork, 13 percent were opposed, and 66 percent could not or would not say, according to the *New York Times*.[18] After a week of televised testimony, during which time Bork hoped to put fears of him as a radical rightist to rest, opposition to his nomination had doubled. Twenty-six percent of *New York Times* survey respondents stated that they had an unfavorable opinion of Bork, while only 16 percent had a favorable opinion.[19]

In the Senate, Reagan would be able to count on the overwhelming support of Republicans, and the overwhelming opposition of Northern Democrats. The key to Bork's confirmation lay in the hands of Southern Democrats, who traditionally voted conservatively. But Southern Democrats were not oblivious to the results of the 1986 Senate elections. According to Steven Roberts of the *New York Times*, the president lobbied for Republican senatorial candidates in 1986

> in part to make sure that if he had the chance to name a Supreme Court justice, his choice would be confirmed. But the voters then returned the Senate to Democratic control, and as a result, many lawmakers feel that they have been insulated from the political costs of opposing the President's choice.[20]

Southern Senators in particular were pressured by black voters to oppose Bork. Senator John Breaux (D-Louisiana), who won an upset victory in 1986,

---

16. "What Women Have to Fear From Robert Bork," advertisement by National Abortion Rights Action League, *New York Times*, September 13, 1987.

17. "Robert Bork's Position on Reproductive Rights," advertisement by Planned Parenthood, *New York Times*, September 13, 1987.

18. Robin Toner, "Poll Finds Most Undecided on Bork," *New York Times*, September 15, 1987.

19. Philip Shenon, "Poll Finds Public Opposition to Bork is Growing," *New York Times*, September 24, 1987.

20. Steven Roberts, "White House Says Bork Lacks Votes for Confirmation," *New York Times*, September 26, 1987.

told the *Times* that "many Southern Democrats were elected by black votes and that his black supporters were making the Bork vote a 'litmus test' issue. 'You can't vote maybe.'"[21]

On October 6, the Senate Judiciary Committee voted nine to five against Bork. The Senate rejected Bork by a vote of fifty-eight to forty-two on October 23. Included in the vote against Bork were Democrats Terry Sanford of North Carolina, Richard Shelby and Howell Heflin of Alabama, and John Breaux of Louisiana. All were elected in 1986, and each owed his election to black voters, for none received a majority of the white vote.[22] The list of Southern Senators against Bork even included John Stennis of Mississippi, one-time leader of the Southern segregationists.

One cannot understand the defeat of Robert Bork without understanding the nature of Senate elections. Despite the apparent luxury afforded by the six-year term, the volatility of recent Senate elections (which contrasts with the relative tranquility of recent House elections) has resulted in an increased concern with reelection among senators. This heightened concern with reelection has enhanced the influence of constituency groups, lobbying organizations, and PACs, which contribute a large proportion of the funds needed to wage expensive, media-oriented campaigns. All of these factors were evident in the Senate's consideration of the Bork nomination: liberal interest groups waged an effective public relations campaign against Bork; black political leaders and civil rights groups targeted moderate-to-conservative southern Democratic Senators whose reelection might depend on strong support by black voters. The Reagan administration tried to launch a counterattack, but a lame-duck president whose popularity had been diminished by the Iran-Contra scandal lacked the clout necessary to persuade moderate Democratic and Republican Senators to support his nominee.

For better or worse, this is not the system envisioned by the framers of the Constitution. We turn now to the original purpose of the Senate, and the original reasons for the election of Senators by state legislatures.

The Senate in the Constitutional Convention

The framers of the Constitution arrived in Philadelphia determined to produce a political system strong enough to govern, yet not so strong as to invite tyranny. Most of the decisions made at the convention about the structure of government can be seen as part of a plan to give the people enough power to rule on the one hand, but to protect against a tyranny of the majority on the

---

21. Roberts, "White House Says."
22. Robin Toner, "Saying No to Bork, Southern Democrats Echo Black Voters," *New York Times*, October 8, 1987.

other. The creation of a Senate served the dual purposes of protecting against the rash judgments of the popularly elected branch, and protecting the small states against the encroachments of the large ones.

The Virginia Plan

The first plan presented to the Constitutional Convention was the Virginia Plan. The Virginia Plan, supported by the larger states, created three branches of government. The legislative branch consisted of two houses, with the lower house elected directly by the people, and the upper house chosen by the lower house out of persons nominated by the state legislatures. Representation in both houses would be proportional either to taxes paid or free inhabitants. The legislature had broad powers, including the right to veto state laws, and the power to select the executive and the judiciary.

Debate on the Virginia Plan began on May 30, 1787. On May 31, the question of bicameralism passed, with Pennsylvania being the only dissenting state. Given the powers that were to be granted the national legislature, the creation of a deliberative upper chamber indirectly chosen was seen as necessary to check the impulsiveness of a single branch chosen directly by the people. As George Mason of Virginia declared, "the mind of the people of America . . . was unsettled as to some points: but . . . in two points it was well settled. 1. in an attachment to Republican Government. 2. in an attachment to more than one branch in the Legislature."[23]

The method for selecting the legislature was also taken up on May 31. The convention was virtually unanimous in its support for popular elections of the lower house. On June 7, John Dickenson of Delaware first proposed that the Senate be chosen by the respective state legislatures. Implicit in this proposal is that each state would have at least one Senator. Thus, either proportional representation would be eliminated, or the Senate would grow tremendously in size. Though James Madison strongly objected, the convention, voting by state, approved Dickenson's proposal unanimously.

Election of the Senate by the state legislatures did not answer the question of state equality versus proportional representation. David Brearly of New Jersey opened with the position of the small states.

> The idea of a national government as contradistinguished from a federal one never entered into the mind of any of the states. If the states are as states still to continue in union, they must be considered as equals. . . . New Jersey will never confederate on the plan before the committee. I

---

23. Max Farrand, *The Framing of the Constitution of the United States* (New Haven: Yale University Press, 1913), 74.

would rather submit to a despot than to such a fate. I will not only oppose the plan here, but on my return home will do everything in my power to defeat it there.[24]

After proportional representation in the lower house passed, Roger Sherman of Connecticut moved that each state should have one vote in the upper house. "Everything depends on this; the smaller states will never agree to the plan on any other principle than an equality of suffrage in this branch."[25] Nevertheless, the convention voted six to five against equal representation. Each state, though, was guaranteed at least one senator.

A few secondary issues were approved with less controversy. Members of the lower house would have to be twenty-five years old, with thirty the requirement for the more stable, upper chamber. Three years was set as the term of office for the lower house, with seven the requirement for the upper house. Again, this would make the Senate less responsive to the exigencies of the day.

The New Jersey Plan

As the convention progressed, the small states grew increasingly fearful of the power of the larger states in the new national government. According to historian Max Farrand, "the climax was reached when proportional representation was voted for the upper house. . . . This action . . . served to unite the opposition."[26] On June 15, William Paterson of New Jersey presented a plan for a federal government as a substitute for the all but approved Virginia Plan. The New Jersey Plan, as it came to be called, consisted of nine amendments that would strengthen, but not effectively change, the Articles of Confederation. The national legislature would remain unicameral, and each state would retain its one vote.

James Wilson of Pennsylvania decried the proposed unicameralism. "Is there no danger of legislative despotism? Theory and practice both proclaim it. If the Legislative authority be not restrained, there can be neither liberty nor stability; and it can only be restrained by dividing it within itself."[27] On June 19, the convention chose the Virginia Plan, with bicameralism, proportional representation in both houses, and indirect election of senators over the confederacy advocated by New Jersey. The vote was seven to three, with Maryland divided.

---

24. George Bancroft, *History of the Formation of the Constitution of the United States of America*, vol. 2 (Littleton, Colo.: Fred B. Rothman, 1983), 32.
25. Bancroft, *History*, 33.
26. Farrand, *Framing*, 84.
27. Farrand, *Framing*, 254.

The Connecticut Compromise

With the Virginia Plan in place, small compromises were made. The lower house term was decreased to two years; the upper house was decreased to six. Yet opposition to previously supported resolutions was increasing, especially those concerning representation in Congress. Luther Martin of Maryland later reported that the convention was "on the verge of dissolution, scarce held together by the strength of a hair."[28]

On June 29, William Samuel Johnson of Connecticut proposed what soon became known as the Connecticut Compromise.

> The fact is that states do exist as political Societies, and a Government is to be formed for them in their political capacity, as well as for the individuals composing them. Does it not seem to follow, that if the states as such are to exist they must be armed with some power of self-defense? . . . In one branch the *people* ought to be represented; in the *other*, the *States*.[29]

Madison remained unalterably opposed to such a plan. Equal representation of the states involved "a principle which was confessedly unjust, which could never be admitted, and if which admitted must infuse mortality into a Constitution which we wished to last forever."[30] After the convention again rejected equal representation in the upper house, Oliver Ellsworth beseeched the delegates to compromise. "On this middle ground, and on no other, can a compromise take place. If the great states refuse this plan, we shall be forever separated."[31]

On July 2, five states voted for equal representation, five against, and Georgia, previously aligned with the large states, split. The Connecticut Compromise was defeated by an equally divided vote.

"The convention was now at a standstill."[32] To break the deadlock, a committee was formed with one member from each state. Crucially, Georgia was represented by Abraham Baldwin, the delegate who voted for equal representation. The convention adjourned for three days while the committee worked to develop a compromise. On July 5, the committee presented its report, calling for proportional representation in the lower house and equal representation in the upper house. After continued debate, the latest compromise was accepted by a vote of five to four, with Massachusetts divided

---

28. Bancroft, *History*, 58.
29. Farrand, *Framing*, 461–62.
30. Farrand, *Framing*, 464.
31. Bancroft, *History*, 62.
32. Farrand, *Framing*, 97.

and two-thirds of the New York delegation abandoning the convention in protest, thus leaving the state without a vote. The large states finally acceded, for on the next day, when Gouverneur Morris of Pennsylvania called for a reconsideration, he could not find a second for his motion. Representation in the Senate would be by the states. As the senators represented the states, there was little further discussion about how they should be selected; representatives of the states would be chosen by the states.

The Political Theory of the Framers' Senate

Virtually everything about the framers' Senate was designed to keep it protected against the majoritarian winds of the day. We start with the very reason for its existence. The most power in the newly formed government belonged to the legislature; the formal powers of the president were few and, for the most part, subject to the approval or override of Congress; and the judiciary "has no influence over the sword or the purse. . . . It may truly be said to have neither force nor will, but merely judgment."[33] On the other hand, all legislative powers belonged to Congress, and such power had to be tempered. "Why did you pour that coffee into your saucer?" asked George Washington of Thomas Jefferson. "To cool it," replied Jefferson. "Even so," said Washington, "we pour legislation into the senatorial saucer to cool it."[34] According to Madison, "the necessity of a senate is not less indicated by the propensity of all single and numerous assemblies to yield to the impulse of sudden and violent passions, and to be seduced by factious leaders into intemperate and pernicious resolutions."[35]

The second branch would not only check rampant majoritarianism, but tyranny as well.

> It is a misfortune incident to republican government . . . that those who administer it may forget their obligations to their constituents, and prove unfaithful to their important trust. In this point of view, a senate, as a second branch of the legislative assembly, distinct from, and dividing the power with, a first, must be in all cases a salutary check on the government. It doubles the security of the people, by requiring the concurrence of two distinct bodies in schemes of usurpation or perfidy, where the ambition or corruption of one would otherwise be sufficient.[36]

---

33. Alexander Hamilton, *The Federalist* No. 78, in *The Enduring Federalist*, ed. Charles A. Beard (Garden City, N.Y.: Doubleday, 1948), 332.

34. Farrand, *Framing*, 74.

35. James Madison, *The Federalist* No. 62, in *The Enduring Federalist*, ed. Charles A. Beard (Garden City, N.Y.: Doubleday, 1948), 263–64.

36. Madison, *Federalist*, No. 62, 263.

The peculiar aspects of the Senate—six-year terms, limited size, older members, unlimited debate, and representation by the states—all served the countermajoritarian interests better than a second branch popularly elected (as originally proposed by the Virginia Plan) could. Again we turn to Madison, who, at the convention, was arguing for even longer terms for senators.

> The second branch, as a limited number of citizens, respectable for wisdom and virtue, will be watched by and will keep watch over the representatives of the people; it will seasonably interpose between impetuous counsels; and will guard the minority who are placed above indigence against the agrarian attempts of the ever-increasing class who labor under all the hardships of life, and secretly sigh for a more equal distribution of its blessings. The longer the members of the senate continue in office, the better will these objects be answered.[37]

The characteristic of the framers' Senate that interests us most is election by the state legislatures. As stated earlier, once the decision was reached that the Senate should represent the states, election by the state legislatures was only natural. We turn to Madison one last time.

> It is equally unnecessary to dilate on the appointment of senators by State legislatures. Among the various modes which might have been devised for constituting this branch of government, that which has been proposed by the convention is probably the most congenial with public opinion. It is recommended by the double advantage of forming a select appointment, and of giving to the state governments such an agency in the foundation of the federal government as must secure the authority of the former, and may form a convenient link between the two systems.[38]

Thus, it is clear that the House of Representatives was to be the democratic branch, its members elected directly by the people and answerable to the people at two-year intervals. The Senate, on the other hand, with its members elected by the state legislatures at six-year intervals, would be far more stable and far less subject to fleeting majoritarian concerns.

Today, we see a picture almost opposite that envisioned by the Founding Fathers. The reelection rate among members of the House is about 95 percent. In the 1988 election, less than 2 percent of House members seeking reelection were defeated. Because of the advantages of incumbency—name recognition, the ability to raise campaign funds, the opportunity to do constituent

---

37. Bancroft, *History*, 56.
38. Madison, *Federalist* No. 62, 261.

casework—members of the House of Representatives are largely invulnerable to shifting political tides. Senators are now similarly elected by the people, yet they are not nearly so well insulated as their House colleagues. Due to the higher saliency of Senate races, Senate challengers tend to be relatively better known and better financed than House challengers. With more media attention and less impact of casework, the campaigns are more likely to be issue oriented. While senators still have an incumbency advantage, the reelection rate among senators is much lower than among representatives. Since the end of World War II it has averaged 78 percent. Thus, in 1980, as Reagan won a landslide victory, he was able to bring the Senate into Republican control, even though only one-third of the Senate seats were contested in that (or any) election year. In the House, where every seat could be contested, Democratic incumbents won 90 percent of their races, leaving the lower house firmly in Democratic hands. Today, the Senate is the branch of Congress that is more strongly tied to the sway of national political issues.

We now examine the election of Senators by state legislatures and the movements that led to the Seventeenth Amendment, which provides for the direct election of Senators.

Senate Elections Through 1912

Procedure

Article I, section 4 of the Constitution provides that "The Times, Places and Manner of holding Elections for Senators and Representatives, shall be prescribed in each State by the Legislature thereof; but the Congress may at any time by Law make or alter such Regulations, except as to the Places of choosing Senators." It was not until July 25, 1866, that Congress first acted to regulate the election of Senators. Legislation increasingly became seen as necessary, for the Constitution does not state whether the election should be by joint or concurrent vote. The problems of concurrent voting, where each house of the state legislature votes separately, with the separate approval of both necessary for a senator's election, is obvious. If the houses are controlled by separate parties, or by different factions of the same party, deadlock can ensue, leaving the state without full representation in the Senate. Yet the contemporary practice was for concurrent election, which was considered the correct application of the Constitution.[39]

As documented by George Haynes,[40] one of the earliest scholars of

---

39. Joseph Story, *Commentaries on the Constitution*, 5th ed. (Boston: Little, Brown, 1891), 523.
40. George Haynes, *The Election of Senators* (New York: Henry Holt, 1906).

Senate elections, the effect of this procedure was a great deal of mischief: the Tennessee legislature could not agree on a second Senator throughout the entire Twenty-seventh Congress; California failed to elect a Senator in 1851, 1855, and 1856; and Indiana did not send a second Senator to the Thirty-fifth Congress until three weeks were left in the session. The persons chosen for the remainder of the current term and the term to follow, however, were chosen under conditions of dubious legality. The election was made by a joint session of the Democratically controlled legislature, but state law required concurrent votes. Further, a legal quorum of the Indiana State House was not present. Nevertheless, the U.S. Senate accepted the credentials of the new Senators. In the following election, both houses of the legislature came under Republican control, and the Republicans, claiming the Senate seats were legally vacant, elected two new Senators. The U.S. Senate, controlled by the Democrats, refused to accept the new elections.[41]

Further escapades took place in New Jersey in 1866. The election of Senator Stockton was challenged on the grounds that he was elected by a plurality, whereas state law required a majority. By a vote of twenty-two to twenty-one, with Stockton casting the decisive vote, the Senate accepted Stockton's credentials. The Senate quickly reconsidered the wisdom of allowing Stockton to vote in his own case, and three days later Stockton was unseated.[42]

In an effort to prevent such future shenanigans, a unified voting procedure was recommended to the Senate by the Judiciary committee. The bill provided that if the concurrent votes of the legislature do not choose the same person, the legislature shall meet in joint assembly every day until a single person receives a majority. The bill passed the Senate by a vote of twenty-five to eleven, and it passed the House without debate.[43]

The reform did not solve the problems of deadlocked legislatures and unrepresented states. According to data gathered by Haynes, between 1891 and 1905 no fewer than fourteen Senate seats went unfilled.[44] In 1895, Delaware deadlocked after 217 ballots over 114 days. In 1899, Utah deadlocked after 164 ballots in 52 days. Florida elected Wilkinson Call on the 75th ballot, which occurred on the 35th day. But not even early ballot victories signaled harmony, for they often masked extremely contentious caucus battles. For instance, in 1898, Turley was elected by the Florida legislature on the 7th ballot. Yet it was not until the 145th ballot of the Democratic caucus that he was nominated. It took the 1903 North Carolina Democratic caucus 61 ballots

---

41. Haynes, *Election*, 21–22.
42. Haynes, *Election*, 23.
43. Haynes, *Election*, 24.
44. Haynes, *Election*, 38–39.

to nominate Overman, who was promptly and overwhelmingly approved by the joint assembly the following day.[45]

Election Outcomes

Though the indirect election of senators was intended to mediate majoritarian influences, there was little difference in the outcome of Senate and House elections through 1912, at least as far as the dominant political parties were concerned. In the first national election, in 1788, George Washington, a Federalist, was elected president. The Federalists not only controlled the House, where they won thirty-eight of sixty-four seats, but the Senate as well, where they won seventeen of twenty-six seats. In 1790, the first midterm election, a longstanding tradition was established: the president's party lost seats in Congress. In the House, the Federalists lost one seat while the opposition, soon to be called the Democratic-Republicans, gained seven. In the Senate, the Federalists again lost one seat while the opposition gained four.

Washington's reelection in 1792 provides the first aggregate evidence of ticket splitting: Washington overwhelmingly won the electoral vote, but the voters sent a fifty-seven to forty-eight Democratic-Republican majority to the House. In keeping with the framers' hope that six-year terms would lead to greater stability in the Senate, the upper house remained in Federalist control.

Such stability would not be the rule in future Senate elections. In 1800, when Thomas Jefferson and the Democratic-Republicans defeated John Adams and the Federalists, not only did the House switch to Democratic-Republican control, but the Senate did as well. In the House, a sixty-four to forty-two minority turned into a sixty-nine to thirty-six majority; in the Senate a nineteen to thirteen minority became an eighteen to thirteen majority. There was as much turbulence in the Senate elections, even though only one-third of its seats should be at stake. One prominent reason for the turbulence was the refusal of early senators to serve out full terms of office. For example, of the twenty-eight senators first elected to six-year terms of office between 1789 (class 1) and 1793 (class 3), fourteen resigned early and one was expelled. Thus, over half the seats were, in fact, at stake every two years.

The Democratic-Republicans remained in control of the presidency, the House, and the Senate until 1824, when John Quincy Adams's coalition party defeated the Jacksonians in a split election and won control of all three. In the 1826 midterm election, the Jacksonians took control of the House and the Senate. Minorities of 105 to 97 (House) and 26 to 20 (Senate) became majorities of 119 to 94 and 28 to 20 respectively. The Democrats, as the Jacksonians became known, took control of the presidency in 1828 and retained control there and in both houses of Congress until the Whig sweep in 1840. Repeating

---

45. Haynes, *Election*, 41–42.

a familiar story, the Whigs won control of the presidency and House in 1840, and the Senate as well. In short, through 1840, neither the six-year term nor indirect elections prevented the Senate from being any less mercurial than the House. And as far as the U.S. party system was concerned, the Senate was in lockstep with the House and president; it offered no protection against the passions of the day.

Somewhat greater stability followed in subsequent years, aided by senators who were more likely to serve out their terms. The Whigs lost their House majority in 1842, but held their Senate majority until 1844. The Whigs regained control of the House in 1846, but the Senate did not follow. The Republicans were a plurality of the House in 1854 but did not capture the Senate until 1860. The Republicans controlled the presidency, the House, and the Senate through 1874, when the Democrats took the House. From then until 1894, Congress was mostly split: the Democrats typically controlled the House while the Republicans, who controlled malapportioned state legislatures, typically controlled the Senate. This was followed by solid Republican control until 1910, when the Democrats won the House. The Senate and the presidency followed two years later, the last time state legislatures elected the Senate.

Of the sixty-three Senates elected by state legislatures, fifty-one matched the party chosen to run the House by the people. Even when party systems changed, as from Federalist to Democratic-Republican, the change in the Senate was often immediate, despite the fact that only one-third of the Senate seats are scheduled to be at stake in any election. Occasionally, as in 1858 and 1910, the state legislatures lagged two years behind the people in bringing the new, dominant party into control. But in only one period, from 1874 through 1894, did the House and Senate represent substantially different interests. Thus, judging by party control, the Senate was largely representing majoritarian concerns even prior to the passage of the Seventeenth Amendment.

Popular Election of Senators

The Movement Toward Reform

The first resolution to call for a constitutional amendment to provide for the direct election of senators came from Congressman Storrs of New York. On February 26, 1826, Storrs proposed that "the Constitution of the United States be so amended that senators be not appointed by legislatures, but chosen by the electors in each State having the qualifications requisite for electors in the more numerous branch of the state legislature."[46] The resolution was quickly tabled. Seven similar House resolutions were proposed and

---

46. Haynes, *Election*, 101.

tabled between 1829 and 1855. Two of these were sponsored by Andrew Johnson of Tennessee, who was later to succeed Abraham Lincoln as president.[47] While president, Johnson again proposed direct election of not only senators, but the president and vice president as well, with federal judges serving twelve-year terms. These are not proposals that a popular president could easily get passed. Johnson, never elected on his own, a Union Democrat elected vice president with a Republican president, faced a Republican Congress that had impeached him and had come within one vote of removing him from office. He had little hope of having his amendments enacted.

To amend the constitution to provide for the direct election of Senators would require the support of two-thirds of the House and Senate and three-quarters of the state legislatures. These were unlikely groups to support such a change. Every Senator owed his election to the current mode of operation, and state legislatures cannot generally be counted upon to give up power voluntarily and vest it in the people. The popular election of senators would and did require the support of two large-scale political movements: the Populist movement of the 1890s and the Progressive movement of the early 1900s.

The Populist Movement

The latter third of the nineteenth century in the United States saw fundamental changes in the economic and social bases of society. Huge trusts, particularly in oil and steel, dominated the economic horizon. Railroads, telegraphs, and telephones made the world a smaller place in which to live. Industries in the United States were dependent on not just local, or even national, but international markets.

On the farms, the quality of life was deteriorating rapidly. Prices of agricultural products declined continuously from the early 1870s through the 1890s.[48] Railroads set monopoly prices for shipping goods to market. Steps purportedly aimed at improving farm conditions, such as the Homestead Act, which provided free land to farmers, were "a triumph for speculative and capitalist forces, and it translated cheap or free land into a stimulus for more discontent than it could quiet."[49]

As farm prices continued to decline through the early 1890s, farmers created a new political organization in 1892, the Populist party. While the party's economic platform advocated nationalization of the railroads, price supports and farm credits, and a graduated income tax,[50] its political planks

---

47. Haynes, *Election*, 101–2.
48. Richard Hofstadter, *The Age of Reform* (New York: Knopf, 1955), 51.
49. Hofstadter, *Age of Reform*, 55.
50. Arthur Link and Stanley McCormick, *Progressivism* (Arlington Heights, Ill.: Harlan Davidson, 1983), 18.

included the initiative, referendum, and the direct election of senators.[51] With little support from urban reformers, known as Mugwumps, the party gathered 9 percent of the popular vote in the 1892 election.

The event that unified the reform movements was the depression of 1893–94. Three to four million people were out of work, yet President Cleveland stood by his belief that it was not the role of the federal government to aid those in distress. On the other hand, Cleveland did believe it within the role of the federal government to use force to break up strikes, as with the Pullman strike in 1894, and to use force to protect the nation's capital against protesting marchers.[52] Under these conditions, urban reformers began to see that they could gain support for their political objectives if they expanded their goals to include the needs of the poor.

This fusion of reform interests culminated in the election of 1896. The Democrats absorbed the Populist party and ran William Jennings Bryan for president. The Republicans were able to label the Democrats as radicals, and the result was not only a Republican landslide, but a realigning election that left the presidency in Republican hands until 1912, when Democrat Woodrow Wilson won with only 42 percent of the popular vote. The Populist party died, but populism and reform did not die with it.

The Progressive Movement

Despite the defeat of the Populists at the polls, the plight of farmers was alleviated by a dramatic rise in crop prices during the late 1890s and early 1900s. "The American commercial farmer entered upon the longest sustained period of peacetime prosperity he has ever known."[53] But there was no corresponding increase in the quality of urban life. Pittsburgh, for instance, due to its impure water supply, had one of the highest rates of typhoid, dysentery and cholera of any large city in the world.[54] Political scandals rocked New York, Pittsburgh, and San Francisco. Reform movements sought and gained power in New York, Detroit, Cleveland, and Jersey City. Reform spread to the state governments and took control in Wisconsin, Iowa, South Dakota, Alabama, Georgia, and Mississippi.

Teddy Roosevelt, who became president in 1901 upon the assassination of William McKinley, pursued a most limited Progressive agenda during his first term. There were efforts at trust-busting, for which Roosevelt gained renown, but such efforts actually increased under President Taft, who suc-

---

51. Hofstadter, *Age of Reform*, 108.
52. Link and McCormick, *Progressivism*, 18.
53. Hofstadter, *Age of Reform*, 109.
54. Link and McCormick, *Progressivism*, 29.

ceeded Roosevelt.[55] It was not until after the election of 1904 that Roosevelt became squarely allied with the Progressives. Under his leadership, Congress passed legislation regulating the railroad and meat packing industries, and also passed the Pure Food and Drug Law. Roosevelt also pushed for procedural reforms in government, creating administrative agencies staffed by experts that purportedly would arrive at objective, scientific decisions that were devoid of "politics."[56]

These two broad areas of interest, substantive reform and procedural reform, marked the Progressive movement. Mayor Pingree of Detroit (1890–97) typified those interested in substantive reform. Under his administration, the city improved welfare services, regulated utility and trolley companies, and redistributed Detroit's tax burden.[57] Alternatively, Mayor Strong of New York (1895–97) represented those most concerned with procedural reforms. These forces pushed for the secret ballot, the initiative and referendum, primary elections, antilobbying laws, civil service reform, and administration by experts.

The area of government most in need of reform was the legislative branch. A consensus existed among Progressives that "the legislative branch of government, particularly at the state level, was the least capable and most corrupt branch and ought to be restrained. This attitude was not new to the progressives; many Americans of the late 1800s had considered legislators to be partisan, parochial and selfish men."[58] We need look no further than scandals over the legislative election of senators to prove the point.

Between 1890 and 1905 there were charges of bribery in the election of senators from seven states, Ohio, California, Montana, Utah, Delaware, Pennsylvania, and Connecticut. In Ohio, California, and Montana, legislative investigations concluded that votes for Senate seats had been bought, though Ohio Senator Hanna, leader of the country's conservative forces, was absolved of any direct knowledge of the alleged bribery. A Senate committee concluded that Senator Clark of Montana bought at least eight votes through "illegal and corrupt practices." Clark resigned his seat, but, following prompt reelection by the Montana legislature, he returned to the Senate without incident. The Speaker of the House in California resigned after being charged with accepting campaign funds from a Senate candidate, all the while stating that he was unpledged in the Senate race. In Utah, one member was "improperly approached" about his vote in the Senate election, but charges were never filed. Nor were charges filed in Delaware, Pennsylvania, or Connecti-

---

55. Arthur Ekirch, *Progressivism in America* (New York: New Viewpoints, 1974), 143.
56. Link and McCormick, *Progressivism*, 36.
57. Link and McCormick, *Progressivism*, 29.
58. Link and McCormick, *Progressivism*, 60.

cut, despite widespread allegations of bribery.[59] In 1912, William Lorimer (R-Illinois) was expelled from the Senate by a fifty-five to twenty-eight vote on the basis of bribery stemming from his 1911 ninety-ninth ballot election.[60] Given the corrupt nature of Senate elections and an environment hospitable to political reform, the time was ripe for a Constitutional amendment.

The States Take the Lead

While the Constitution of 1787 invested the state legislators with sole authority to elect Senators, nothing prohibits state legislators from acting as mere delegates in the process, faithfully electing the candidate preferred by the people. An imperfect but useful analogy to today is readily apparent. While the ultimate choice of the president rests in the electoral college, the electoral college by custom, though not law, is bound by the choice made by the people. Much as voters today choose slates of candidates for the electoral college based on who they support for president, voters quickly began choosing state legislators based on who they supported for the Senate. The people of Illinois, in voting for a Democratic legislature in 1858, selected the party publicly committed to Stephen Douglas over the party publicly committed to Abraham Lincoln.[61]

Notwithstanding this situation, legislative elections, with numerous issues confronting the people, are often a poor method of communicating popular desires on any particular issue. More direct methods were called for. In 1875, the voters of Nebraska passed a constitutional amendment providing for a preferential poll for Senator among the voters of the state. It must be noted, though, that it was not until 1904 that the legislature actually elected the person who received the most votes in the straw poll.[62] Unperturbed by the results of the Nebraska model, Nevada passed similar legislation in 1899, followed by Oregon in 1901. In Oregon's next election, Governor Geer received 57 percent of the popular vote, but on the forty-second ballot the legislature elected a man who received not one popular vote. Yet by 1911, buoyed by the reform movement, over half the states provided for popular election polls, with some attempts to require legislators to abide by the results.[63]

While the states were attempting to bring about the direct election of

---

59. Haynes, *Election*, 51–59.
60. Congressional Quarterly, *CQ Guide to Congress* (Washington D.C.: Congressional Quarterly Press, 1982), 634.
61. Haynes, *Election*, 133.
62. Haynes, *Election*, 141–43.
63. Haynes, *Election*, 145–48; Alan Grimes, *Democracy and the Amendments to the Constitution* (Lexington, Mass.: Lexington Books, 1978), 76.

Senators through ordinary legislation, they also realized the need for a Constitutional amendment. By 1911, two-thirds of the states had passed propositions that, in one way or another, called for an amendment to provide for the direct election of Senators. In 1903 alone, fourteen states called for a Constitutional Convention to do so if Congress refused to take the lead.[64] Behind these initiatives was a highly supportive public: referenda on state ballots in California, Nevada, and Illinois showed popular approval between five and fourteen to one.[65]

Congressional Action

Increasingly, the House of Representatives passed resolutions calling for a Constitutional amendment. While the Fifty-third House responded favorably by a vote of 141 to 51, the majority in the Fifty-fifth House was up to 185 to 11, and in the Fifty-sixth House, 240 to 15. But such resolutions did not receive even a simple majority in the Senate.

In April, 1911, Congressman Rucker (D-Missouri) proposed the following resolution (H.R. 39).

> The Senate of the United States shall be composed of two Senators from each state, elected by the people thereof, for six years; and each Senator shall have one vote. The electors in each State shall have the qualifications requisite for electors of the most numerous branch of the State legislatures.
>
> The times, places and manner of holding elections for Senators shall be prescribed by each State by the legislature thereof.[66]

The seemingly innocuous second paragraph would deprive the federal government of the right to regulate Senate elections, a right the Constitution clearly gave it over house elections. The purpose of the paragraph was clear: it was devised by Southern Democrats to help prevent the national government from interfering with electoral devices that, despite the Fifteenth Amendment, barred blacks from voting. The "race rider," as it was called, badly split the Progressives. Republicans would not vote for the amendment if the race rider were attached, and Southern Democrats would not vote for the amendment if the rider were not attached.

House debates show little opposition to the concept of popular Senate elections itself. Congressman Adair (D-Indiana) declared that "wealth, plutocracy, and subserviency to the interests will no longer be the qualifications

---

64. Haynes, *Election*, 108–9.
65. Haynes, *Election*, 106.
66. *Congressional Record*, 62d Cong., 1st sess., 1911, 47:203.

necessary for a Senator, but rugged honesty, recognized ability, admitted capacity, and wide experience will be required."[67] Congressman Hobson stated that "only men of reactionary temperament can harbor misgivings."[68] Reform was essential because, "in the blocking of legitimate reform, no agent has been more effective than the U.S. Senate."[69] "It cannot be denied that the method of election by the smaller number who compose a legislature invites corruption from great moneyed interests seeking to secure or to hold unmolested . . . power."[70] Congressman Sulzer (D-New York), who had introduced similar resolutions each year for the previous seventeen years, continued the attack on the upper house.

> The United States Senate is the last bulwark of the predatory trusts. Here is the citadel of every unscrupulous monopoly. And more and more the special interests of the country, realizing the importance of the Senate, are combining their forces to control the election of Federal Senators through their sinister influence in State legislatures.[71]

The Republicans eagerly joined the attack. Congressman Norris (R-Nebraska) denounced the great combinations of wealth controlling the Senate and nullifying the will of the people. "The evils of the present system are so great and so apparent that it seems to me this change ought to appeal to every reasonable citizen."[72] Congressman Foster (R-Vermont) noted that, despite the concerns of the Founding Fathers, the people had proven themselves competent to elect the president, and they ought to be given the same chance to chose their Senators.

Controversy, though, was sharp over the race rider. Congressman Young (R-Michigan) proposed an amendment that would remove the rider, and Southern Democrats quickly attacked the motion. "I think there are many of us who will under no circumstances vote for this resolution with that amendment upon it," threatened Congressman Bartlett (D-Georgia).[73] While arguments were typically couched in terms of "states' rights," Congressman Sherley (D-Kentucky) spoke most candidly.

> We in the South have had confronting us a very grave and very serious problem—a problem that, according to the best judgment of the southern

---

67. *Cong. Rec.* 47:208.
68. *Cong. Rec.* 47:210.
69. *Cong. Rec.* 47:211.
70. *Cong. Rec.* 47:211.
71. *Cong. Rec.* 47:226.
72. *Cong. Rec.* 47:230.
73. *Cong. Rec.* 47:208.

people, involved the supremacy of the white people in those States. Out of much turmoil, out of much that might not have been defended in the cold forum of law, has now come a solution that has been upheld by the courts, and that to-day is making for the future prosperity and safety of the entire land. We are not willing, many of us, to endanger that status, believing it to be most vital, by giving a power as to elections more extensive than now belongs to the Federal Government.[74]

Republicans, on the other hand, universally favored Congressman Young's motion to strike the race rider. Congressman Morgan (R-Oklahoma) argued that the rider could well defeat the entire amendment. When the vote on Young's amendment came, no Republican voted against it and only a dozen Democrats voted for it. With Democratic control of the House, Young's motion was defeated 189 to 123.[75] The House then passed Rucker's original resolution 296 to 16.[76]

With Progressivism on the rise throughout the country, even the Senate was favorably inclined to amending the election process, if only a consensus could be reached on the race rider. Senator Borah (R-Idaho) sponsored the Senate version of the amendment, which included the rider. Senator Bristow (R-Kansas) quickly offered an amendment to the Borah resolution that would retain federal control over Senate elections.

The debate in the Senate was almost entirely over the Bristow amendment. As in the House, there was little opposition to the concept of direct election of senators.[77] Needless to say, there was none of the Senate bashing that so delighted the House. While the debate over the amendment was, as in the House, couched in terms of states' rights versus federal power, the real issue was again race. Senator Bacon (D-Georgia) repeatedly accused supporters of the Bristow amendment of succumbing to "racial influences" and "racial pressures."[78] Senator Bristow responded with an attack of his own. "The controversy which the Senator from Georgia has been carrying on here for months against this amendment has been because of racial prejudice that exists in that section of the country."[79] Undaunted, Bacon continued his attack on "racial insistence and influence."[80]

The vote on the Bristow amendment was a tie, forty-four to forty-four. The vice president cast the deciding vote in favor of the amendment. Six

---

74. *Cong. Rec.* 47:240.
75. *Cong. Rec.* 47:241.
76. *Cong. Rec.* 47:242–43.
77. *Cong. Rec.* 47:1482–90, 1535–47, 1735–43, 1879–1925.
78. *Cong. Rec.* 47:1908, 1909.
79. *Cong. Rec.* 47:1909.
80. *Cong. Rec.* 47:1909.

Republicans voted with the Democrats against the measure, and only one Democrat voted with Bristow for the measure.[81] The vote on the amendment itself easily achieved the necessary two-thirds majority, by a vote of sixty-four to twenty-four.[82]

As the proposed amendment passed the House and Senate in two different forms—the House version with the race rider, the Senate version without—the resolution was sent to a House-Senate conference committee in an attempt to settle the differences. The Senate showed no inclination to back down, and, at first, neither did the House. The first vote on accepting the Senate version was defeated 171 to 111.[83] Finally, one year later, under pressure from voters for direct elections, the House acceded to the Senate's position by a vote of 238 to 39.[84]

With two-thirds of the states already on record in favor of the amendment, there was little concern over its ultimate passage. It is interesting to note, however, that the Progressives received help from an unlikely ally, the big-city Democratic machines. The reason for these strange bedfellows is quite simple; the state legislatures were malapportioned to favor rural (i.e., Republican) interests over the cities. For instance, in Rhode Island, 7 percent of the population could elect over 50 percent of its upper house.[85] Thus, they were far more Republican than the states they represented. The opportunity for the election of Democratic Senators was much greater with popular voting than with election by the Republican-dominated legislatures. In New York, for example, the ratification resolution was introduced in the State Senate by Robert Wagner of New York City, who also represented the interests of Tammany Hall. All twenty-two members of the Tammany-controlled New York City delegation voted for ratification. An identical pattern was followed in the State Assembly: the resolution was introduced by a Tammany Democrat and received almost unanimous support from the machine politicians. Similar stories took place throughout the Northeast.[86] With machine Democrats uniting with progressive Republicans against the old-line Republicans, the amendment swept through the country.

Within one year it had the requisite three-fourths support. The states that failed to ratify were Alabama, Delaware, Florida, Georgia, Kentucky, Louisiana, Maryland, Mississippi, Rhode Island, South Carolina, Utah, and Virginia. Louisiana eventually ratified the amendment two years after it went into

---

81. *Cong. Rec.* 47:1923.
82. *Cong. Rec.* 47:1924–25.
83. *Cong. Rec.* 47:2433.
84. *Cong. Rec.* 47:6367.
85. John D. Buenker, "The Role of the Urban Machine," in *The Progressive Era*, ed. Arthur Mann (Hinsdale, Ill.: Dryden Press, 1978), 98.
86. See Buenker, "Urban Machine," 94–107.

effect. Utah and Delaware were the only states that actually rejected the amendment; the rest never acted upon it. The inaction stemmed largely from the Southern states, which would not ratify without the race rider, and Rhode Island, which was so malapportioned that the Machine-Progressive coalition could not break the strength of the old-line Republicans.

TABLE 1.1. Incumbent Defeats, 1914–90

Year	Primary Election Defeats	General Election Defeats	Total Defeats
1914	2	0	2
1916	3	8	11
1918	0	5	5
1920	3	7	10
1922	3	9	12
1924	4	4	8
1926	4	6	10
1928	1	5	6
1930	4	2	6
1932	4	8	12
1934	1	8	9
1936	1	5	6
1938	2	5	7
1940	5	2	7
1942	3	7	10
1944	5	4	9
1946	4	4	8
1948	1	7	8
1950	4	4	8
1952	2	7	9
1954	0	4	4
1956	0	5	5
1958	0	8	8
1960	0	1	1
1962	0	3	3
1964	0	2	2
1966	2	1	3
1968	4	4	8
1970	0	4	4
1972	1	5	6
1974	1	2	3
1976	0	8	8
1978	1	6	7
1980	4	10	14
1982	0	2	2
1984	0	3	3
1986	0	6	6
1988	0	3	3
1990	0	1	1

On May 31, 1913, Secretary of State William Jennings Bryan certified that the resolution to provide for the direct election of Senators had attained the requisite approval of two-thirds of Congress and three-fourths of the state legislatures. On November 3, 1914, the citizens of the United States directly chose their Senators for the first time. The people, intoxicated with their newly gained power, promptly returned to the Senate twenty-four of twenty-six senators seeking reelection. Two Senators were denied their party's nomination, but not one legislatively chosen incumbent was defeated in the November elections.

This insulation did not last. In the 1916 election, three incumbents were denied their party's nomination and the voters rejected eight more in the general elections. The number of defeated incumbents from 1914 through 1990 are presented in table 1.1.

Defeated incumbents range from a low of one in 1960 and 1990 to a high of fourteen in 1980. Four Senators were defeated in a primary election in 1980. No Senator lost a primary since then until Alan Dixon (D-Illinois) lost in 1992. The ten incumbents defeated in the 1980 general elections were largely Democrats defeated in the Reagan landslide. Similarly, voters rejected twelve incumbents in 1932, the year Franklin Roosevelt swept into office. Off-year elections can be hard on incumbents too, as was 1942, when Democrats suffered large defeats. The best years for Senators were 1960–66, when an average of just over two incumbents per year lost reelection bids. The early 1960s insulation from electoral sanction, though, is today more parallel to House elections, where reelection rates are over 90 percent, than to Senate elections. Despite the 1990 results, electoral competition is more the norm in Senate elections than in House elections.

Summary

We have seen that the authors of the U.S. Constitution developed a political system that would allow the people to rule but also protect against a tyranny of the majority. The most democratic branch of government was to be the House of Representatives, whose powers would be checked by a more reflective, less democratic Senate, whose members would be chosen by the various state legislatures.

Pressure to democratize the Senate, which first started in the 1820s, increased with each revelation of a purchased Senate seat and every deadlocked legislature that could not choose a Senator. The movement toward direct election of Senators, spurred on by the Progressive reform era, culminated in the passage of the Seventeenth Amendment in 1913.

Reelection rates of incumbent Senators have varied tremendously since 1914: only one incumbent was defeated in the 1960 elections; fourteen were defeated in 1980. On average, about two-thirds of Senate incumbents win reelection, compared to over 90 percent in the House of Representatives. The advantages House incumbents have over Senate incumbents have thus made Senate elections more responsive to the will of the people than House elections. This, of course, is the opposite of what the authors of the Constitution envisaged.

We begin our more thorough examination of modern Senate elections in chapter 2, which examines voting behavior in Senate elections.

CHAPTER 2

Voters in U.S. Senate Elections

In this chapter we will examine the attitudes and behavior of voters in U.S. Senate elections. First, we examine voter turnout in Senate elections. We will attempt to determine who votes in Senate elections, and how Senate campaigns themselves affect voter turnout. Then we turn our attention to candidate choice in Senate elections. We will attempt to explain why, in recent years, Senate elections have been much more competitive than House elections. We will also attempt to explain why competition in Senate elections varies from state to state and over time.

To address these questions, we will analyze survey data collected by the University of Michigan Center for Political Studies in 1986 and 1988. We will analyze data from the regular 1986 and 1988 American National Election Studies (NES) to compare voting behavior in Senate and House elections. Then we will analyze data from a special 1988 Senate election survey to examine the effects of differences in states' populations on voters in Senate elections. The special Senate election survey used telephone interviews with approximately equal numbers of eligible voters in all fifty states. This design does not permit direct comparisons between voters in Senate and House elections because it greatly overrepresents voters in sparsely populated, rural House districts. The special survey does, however, provide more accurate data for comparing Senate voters in large and small states because it includes a large number of respondents from less populous states.

The 1986 and 1988 elections provide a clear contrast in terms of competition for Senate seats: in 1986, seven of twenty-eight incumbents seeking reelection were defeated and several others experienced close calls; in 1988, only three of twenty-six incumbents seeking reelection were defeated and very few of the twenty-three successful incumbents won by narrow margins. In both years, however, over 98 percent of House incumbents were reelected and the vast majority of these incumbents won in landslides—over 85 percent crushed their challenger by a margin of at least 20 percentage points.

Voter Turnout

Voter turnout in the United States is always substantially higher in a presidential election year than in a midterm election year. Since 1972, turnout in presidential elections has ranged between 50 and 55 percent of the voting-age population, while turnout in midterm elections has ranged between 35 and 40 percent of the voting-age population. The importance of the presidential contest along with the intense media coverage received by presidential candidates brings out a large number of voters who are not sufficiently motivated to turn out in other types of elections.[1] To remove the influence of the presidential race on voter turnout, we analyze turnout in a midterm election year, 1986.

Just over half of the respondents in the 1986 NES claimed to have voted in the midterm election. As is generally the case, the reported turnout was substantially higher than the Census Bureau's estimate of the actual turnout of eligible voters, which was around 37 percent. This gap is a result of differences between the NES sample and the entire population of eligible voters (people who are homeless or institutionalized are not included in the NES sample) as well as some overreporting of turnout by respondents. However, the difference between actual and reported turnout should not have much effect on our findings regarding the factors associated with voter turnout. Previous studies have reported very similar findings using either reported turnout or a validated turnout measure based on the actual voting records of respondents included in the NES sample.[2]

Who voted in 1986? Generally, we would expect the same demographic characteristics associated with turnout in presidential elections to be associated with turnout in a midterm election. The two demographic characteristics that have been consistently found to influence voter turnout in the United States are education and age.[3] Education increases both interest in politics and political information. Therefore, people with more formal education should be more likely to vote. The results shown in table 2.1 strongly support this hypothesis. College-educated respondents were almost twice as likely to vote in 1986 as those with only a grade school education.

Many studies of voter turnout in the United States have found a strong association between turnout and age. Younger citizens are generally less interested in politics and much less likely to vote than their elders. Turnout generally increases until citizens reach retirement age, when turnout drops off slightly. However, the rate of turnout remains much higher among the elderly than among voters in their teens and twenties. The data in table 2.1 are consistent with this pattern. Less than one-third of 18–29 year-olds reported voting in the 1986 midterm election, compared with over two-thirds of voters

---

1. See Herbert Asher, *Presidential Elections and American Politics*, 4th ed. (Chicago: Dorsey Press, 1988), 49–59.

2. John P. Katosh and Michael W. Traugott, "The Consequences of Validated and Self-Reported Voting Measures, *Public Opinion Quarterly* 41 (1977): 61–80; see also Raymond E. Wolfinger and Steven J. Rosenstone, *Who Votes?* (New Haven: Yale University Press, 1980).

3. Wolfinger and Rosenstone, *Who Votes?*, 13–60.

TABLE 2.1. Reported Turnout in 1986 by Demographic Characteristics

Characteristic	Percentage Reporting Voting	N
Age		
18–29	30	551
30–49	52	874
50–69	71	514
70 or over	66	232
Education		
High school only	38	454
Some college	56	502
Graduated college	72	430
Sex		
Male	53	951
Female	52	1,223
Race		
White	53	1,802
Black	50	332
Region		
North	57	1,472
South	44	702

Source: 1986 National Election Study.

between 50 and 69 and almost two-thirds of voters over the age of 70. The most elderly group of voters turned out at more than twice the rate of the youngest group.

In addition to education and age, we examined the effects of three other demographic characteristics on voter turnout in 1986—sex, race, and region of residence. Neither sex nor race had much impact on turnout: men and women voted at about the same rate and blacks were only slightly less likely to report that they had voted than whites. There was, however, a noticeable gap in turnout between respondents living in the South (defined here as the eleven states of the old Confederacy) and those living in the rest of the nation. Turnout among southerners was about 13 percentage points lower than turnout among northerners. Although poll taxes, literacy tests, and other legal barriers to voting were eliminated in the South during the 1960s, the region retains a less participatory political culture than the rest of the nation. In addition, southern states still tend to have more restrictive voter registration requirements than states outside of the region.[4]

In addition to these demographic characteristics, previous studies have

---

4. Wolfinger and Rosenstone, *Who Votes?*, 61–88.

found that citizens' motivation to vote is affected by their degree of partisanship. Strong partisans generally take a greater interest in political campaigns and turn out at a higher rate than weak partisans or independents. Similarly, citizens who have strong ideological convictions may be more concerned about the results of congressional elections and, therefore, more motivated to vote.

The data shown in table 2.2 support both of these hypotheses. Strong partisans were more than twice as likely to turn out in 1986 than pure independents. Similarly, although less dramatically, respondents with strong ideological convictions (those who placed themselves at positions 1, 2, 6, or 7 on the seven-point liberal-conservative scale) turned out at a higher rate than respondents lacking such convictions (those who placed themselves at position 4 on the scale or who indicated no ideological preference). Almost two-thirds of the strong liberals or conservatives reported voting in 1986, compared with less than half of the moderates and indifferents.

Citizens' motivation to vote may depend upon the nature of the campaign as well as their personal characteristics and attitudes. In a presidential election year, all citizens are exposed to basically the same national campaign. In a midterm election such as 1986, however, the nature of the campaign varies considerably from state to state and from House district to House district. The greater the degree of competition between the parties and the greater the

TABLE 2.2. Reported Turnout in 1986 by Partisanship and Ideological Intensity

	Percentage Reporting Voting	N
Partisanship		
Low	27	298
Moderate	51	1,254
High	67	616
Ideological intensity		
Low	45	1,140
Moderate	59	560
High	63	468

Source: 1986 National Election Study.

Note: Partisanship is measured by a party identification scale: pure independents and apoliticals are classified as low in partisanship; independent leaners and weak identifiers are classified as moderate in partisanship; strong identifiers are classified as high in partisanship. Ideological intensity is measured by the position on a liberal-conservative scale: low = 4; moderate = 3 or 5; high = 1, 2, 6, or 7; respondents unable to place themselves on the liberal-conservative scale were classified as low in ideological intensity.

TABLE 2.3. Reported Turnout in 1986 by Electoral Competition

	Percentage Reporting Voting	N
House election		
Contested	54	1,642
Uncontested	48	532
Gubernatorial election		
Yes	54	1,727
No	47	447
Senate election		
Competitive	54	737
Noncompetitive	54	659
None	49	778

Source: 1986 National Election Study.
Note: States with competitive Senate races were Alabama, California, Colorado, Florida, Georgia, Louisiana, Missouri, North Carolina, Washington, and Wisconsin; states with noncompetitive Senate races were Arizona, Connecticut, Illinois, Indiana, Iowa, Kansas, Maryland, New York, Ohio, and Pennsylvania.

intensity of the campaign in a state or district, the more motivated citizens may be to vote.[5]

Table 2.3 shows the relationships between the types of campaigns to which citizens were exposed and their rate of turnout in 1986. Respondents living in House districts with contested races turned out at a slightly higher rate than those living in districts with uncontested races. Similarly, respondents living in states with gubernatorial elections in 1986 turned out at a slightly higher rate than those living in states without such contests. Finally, respondents living in states with Senate elections in 1986 turned out at a slightly higher rate than those living in states without Senate races. However, respondents living in states with competitive Senate races reported voting at the same rate as those living in states with noncompetitive Senate races. These results suggest that campaigning has a modest but noticeable impact on voter turnout.

Thus far we have separately examined the effects of demographic characteristics, political attitudes, and campaign intensity on voter turnout in 1986. In order to accurately estimate the impact of each of our independent variables on voter turnout, however, we must analyze their effects simultaneously. The technique that we use for this purpose is multiple regression analysis. This

---

5. Samuel C. Patterson and Gregory A. Caldeira, "Getting Out the Vote: Participation in Gubernatorial Elections," *American Political Science Review* 77 (1983): 686.

TABLE 2.4. Determinants of Voter Turnout in 1986

Independent Variable	b	SE	p
Age	.027	.003	.001
Age squared	−.00019	.00003	.001
Region (South)	−.084	.025	.001
Sex (female)	.003	.020	NS
Race (black)	.015	.029	NS
Education	.069	.006	.001
Partisanship	.134	.016	.001
Ideological intensity	.035	.012	.01
House race contested	.002	.024	NS
Gubernatorial contest	.035	.025	NS
Senate contest	−.011	.026	NS
Senate competition	.053	.026	.05
Constant		−.687	
R^2		.21	
N		2090	

Source: 1986 National Election Study.

Note: Entries shown are unstandardized regression coefficients with accompanying standard errors. Statistical significance is based on one-tailed *t*-tests. NS = not significant.

technique allows us to estimate the impact of each of our independent variables on voter turnout while controlling for all of the remaining variables. Thus, we arrive at an estimate of the unique contribution of each independent variable to citizens' decisions about whether or not to vote.

The results of the multiple regression analysis are presented in table 2.4. Since our dependent variable is whether or not a respondent reported voting (coded as 1 if the respondent voted and 0 if he or she did not), the coefficients shown in table 2.4 represent the estimated increase or decrease in an average respondent's probability of voting caused by an increase of one unit in a given independent variable.[6]

The results of the multiple regression analysis are generally consistent with the bivariate relationships described previously. Education and age had very strong, positive effects on turnout. The negative coefficient for the squared age variable indicates that the positive effect of age gradually diminishes and becomes negative beyond the age of 70. In addition, turnout among southerners was about 8 percentage points lower than would have been expected based on the other variables in the regression equation. After con-

---

6. Because our dependent variable, voter turnout, is dichotomous, we conducted a logistic regression analysis with the same set of independent variables used in the ordinary least squares regression analysis. Because the relative effects of the independent variables were almost identical in the two analyses, we have reported only the OLS coefficients, which are more readily interpretable, in the text. The results of the logit analysis are available from the authors.

trolling for the other variables in the regression equation, however, race had virtually no impact on turnout. Blacks were just as likely to vote as whites with similar social characteristics.

Both partisanship and ideological intensity had significant positive effects on turnout, although the impact of partisanship was by far the stronger of the two. According to our results, strong partisans turned out at a rate almost 27 percentage points higher than pure independents with all other variables held constant; strong liberals and conservatives turned out at a rate just 7 percentage points higher than ideological moderates and indifferents after controlling for all other variables.

After controlling for the other independent variables in the regression equation, neither a contested House race nor a gubernatorial race significantly increased the likelihood of voting. Neither did living in a state with a Senate race. However, living in a state with a *competitive* Senate race had a modest but significant impact, increasing the probability of voting by an estimated 5.3 percentage points.

These results are consistent with aggregate statistics on turnout in states with Senate elections in 1986. According to figures compiled by *Congressional Quarterly Weekly Report*, in fifteen states with competitive Senate races, average turnout declined by 0.4 percentage points between 1982 and 1986; in seventeen states with noncompetitive Senate races, average turnout declined by 6.2 percent during the same period. Turnout in the states with competitive Senate races averaged 41.4 percent of eligible voters compared with 36.9 percent in states with noncompetitive Senate races.[7] Thus, both aggregate turnout statistics and our analysis of the 1986 National Election Study data support the conclusion that states with competitive Senate races had a slightly higher turnout than would otherwise have been expected.

Our findings regarding the determinants of turnout in 1986 indicate that voters in midterm elections tend to be older and better educated than nonvoters. They are also more likely to identify strongly with a political party. However, the intensity of the Senate campaign in a state appears to have only a marginal influence on voter turnout. If Senate campaigns affect the outcomes of Senate elections, they must do so mainly by influencing voters' candidate preferences. Therefore, we will focus our attention in the remainder of this chapter on explaining these preferences.

Candidate Preference

One of the most important variables influencing candidate preference in congressional elections is party identification; therefore, one of the most im-

---

7. Congressional Quarterly, *Congressional Quarterly Weekly Report* 44 (November 8, 1986): 2805.

portant determinants of the competitiveness of any Senate or House election is the relative strength of the two major parties in the state or district. If the overwhelming majority of voters identify with one party, the opposing party can win only through massive defections among majority party supporters. Furthermore, the minority party in such a state or district may find it difficult to recruit well-qualified candidates, and campaign contributors may be reluctant to give money to a candidate who is perceived as having little or no chance of winning.

The average state contains a much larger and more diverse population than the average House district. Therefore, while many House districts are overwhelmingly Democratic or Republican, very few states, if any, can be considered safe for one party or the other.

One of the most important reasons House incumbents usually enjoy greater electoral security than Senate incumbents is that the distribution of party loyalties in the average House district is much more skewed toward the incumbent's party than the distribution of party loyalties in the average state. This difference is clearly evident in table 2.5, which displays the party loyalties of voters in the 1986 and 1988 Senate and House elections. House incumbents enjoyed an average advantage of 26 percentage points in 1986 and 23 percentage points in 1988. In addition to all of the difficulties that House challengers face in achieving voter recognition, the average challenger begins the campaign with a partisan base consisting of barely one-third of the electorate. Thus, in order to have any hope of winning, in addition to keeping his or her own party's base intact, the average House challenger must persuade a large minority of incumbent partisans to defect—a truly Herculean task.

According to the data in table 2.5, the task confronting Senate challengers is much less daunting. In 1986, the average Senate challenger actually had a 10 percentage point advantage in voter party loyalties; in 1988, the average incumbent had a relatively modest 5 percentage point advantage. In

TABLE 2.5. Party Identification of Voters in 1986 and 1988 Senate and House Elections (in percentages)

	1986 Elections		1988 Elections	
	Senate	House	Senate	House
Incumbent partisans	43	60	49	58
Independents	4	6	7	7
Challenger partisans	53	34	44	35
N	617	701	714	751

Source: 1986 and 1988 National Election Studies.

Note: Leaning independents are classified as partisans; based on voters in contested elections.

order to defeat an incumbent, the average Senate challenger in 1986 only had to keep his or her own party's base intact. Even in 1988, the average Senate challenger only needed a small minority of votes from incumbent partisans in order to be successful. These findings suggest that one of the most important reasons Senate elections are more competitive than House elections is that the division of the electorate between incumbent and challenger partisans is much less lopsided in the average state than in the average House district.

The data shown in table 2.5 also suggest that one of the reasons Senate incumbents fared poorly in 1986 was that many of these incumbents represented the minority party in their states. In the 1980 election, a number of Republican Senate candidates rode Ronald Reagan's coattails to upset victories in states with strong Democratic traditions. Jeremiah Denton in Alabama and Mack Mattingly in Georgia were the first Republicans elected to the Senate from their states since the end of Reconstruction. Six years later, without Ronald Reagan at the top of the ticket, several first-term Republican incumbents, including Denton and Mattingly, were unable to hold their seats. In fact, all of the GOP incumbents who lost in 1986 were freshmen. In the absence of a presidential contest, many voters in these states apparently reverted to their traditional partisan inclinations.

Despite its importance, partisanship alone does not completely explain the difference between the performance of incumbents in Senate and House elections or the difference between the performance of incumbents in the 1986 and 1988 Senate elections. It is not just the distribution of party loyalties in a state or district that determines the competitiveness of a Senate or House contest, but the ability of the candidates to attract support from their own party's voters and from the opposing party's voters. Thus, many House incumbents have been able to turn districts dominated by the opposing party into seemingly safe seats by inducing massive defections among challenger partisans.

Table 2.6 displays the rates of partisan loyalty and defection among incumbent and challenger partisans in the 1986 and 1988 Senate and House elections. In both elections, Senate and House incumbents received overwhelming support from their own partisans, with House members receiving only slightly greater support than Senators. House incumbents received an average of 95.5 percent support from incumbent partisans while Senate incumbents received an average of 89.0 percent support from incumbent partisans.

The most striking difference between the Senate and House elections, especially in 1986, involved the behavior of challenger partisans. In both 1986 and 1988, almost half of the House challenger partisans defected to the incumbent; in 1986, however, only 28 percent of the Senate challenger partisans defected to the incumbent. The high rate of success enjoyed by Senate

TABLE 2.6. Proportion Voting for Incumbents in 1986 and 1988 Elections by Party Identification

Election	Incumbent Partisans		Challenger Partisans	
	Percentage	N	Percentage	N
1986 Senate	87	268	28	326
1986 House	94	419	49	242
1988 Senate	91	346	39	316
1988 House	97	432	49	266

Source: 1986 and 1988 National Election Studies.
Note: Based on voters in contested elections; leaning independents are classified as partisans.

challengers in 1986 reflected not only the distribution of party loyalties in the electorate, but the success of those challengers in appealing to their copartisans. Conversely, the extraordinarily poor performance of challengers in the 1986 and 1988 House elections resulted from the inability of House challengers to appeal to even their copartisans.

One of the most important questions that must be addressed in order to explain why Senate elections are more competitive than House elections is why challenger partisans defect at a lower rate in Senate elections than in House elections. One possible answer to this question involves the relative visibility of incumbents and challengers in Senate and House elections.

Table 2.7 presents some evidence regarding the visibility of incumbents and challengers in the 1986 and 1988 Senate and House elections. In both years, respondents were asked, after the election, if they could remember the names of the candidates who ran for the Senate and House of Representatives. In both years, Senate incumbents enjoyed the highest name recall, followed by House incumbents, Senate challengers, and, finally, House challengers. Fewer than one out of six voters in either 1986 or 1988 could recall the name of the House challenger. In contrast, almost three out of five voters in 1986 and almost half of the voters in 1988 could recall the name of the Senate incumbent. The vulnerability of Senate incumbents in the 1986 elections clearly was not a result of low visibility.

The name recall question can give a misleading impression about the voters' familiarity with a candidate. Voters who are unable to recall a candidate's name can have meaningful opinions about that candidate. Another way of assessing the visibility of a candidate is to ask what proportion of the electorate were able to recognize the candidate's name and give an evaluation of the candidate on the feeling thermometer scale. The results displayed in table 2.7 show that overwhelming majorities of voters were able to recognize and evaluate Senate and House incumbents in 1986 and 1988. There was, however, a substantial gap between Senate and House challengers in both years. Almost three-fourths of the voters could recognize and rate Senate challengers, but no more than half of the voters could recognize and rate House challengers.

One final measure of voters' familiarity with House and Senate candidates is only available for 1986. That is the proportion of voters who were able to place the candidates on a seven-point, liberal-conservative scale. This measure, once again, showed a high level of voter familiarity with both House and Senate incumbents: 87 percent of the voters were able to place their Senate incumbent on this scale and 80 percent were able to place their House incumbent. Once again, however, voters were much more familiar with Senate challengers than with House challengers: 63 percent of the voters were able to place the Senate challenger on the scale, but only 30 percent were able to place the House challenger.

We can combine our three questions to create an index measuring voters' familiarity with Senate and House candidates. The data in table 2.7 show that, in both 1986 and 1988 (when only two of the questions were asked), voters

TABLE 2.7. Voter Familiarity with Senate and House Candidates in 1986 and 1988 (in percentages)

	1986		1988	
	Senate ($N = 642$)	House ($N = 751$)	Senate ($N = 791$)	House ($N = 842$)
Recall name of incumbent	59	39	49	42
Recall name of challenger	39	12	28	15
Evaluate incumbent	96	88	94	91
Evaluate challenger	74	42	72	50
Rate incumbent's ideology	87	80	NA	NA
Rate challenger's ideology	63	30	NA	NA
Incumbent familiarity score				
0	2	9	5	9
1	8	11	46	50
2	33	42	49	41
3	57	38		
Challenger familiarity score				
0	20	47	27	48
1	16	27	46	39
2	30	17	27	13
3	34	8		

Source: 1986 and 1988 National Election Studies.

Note: Based on voters in contested elections. NA = not available, question not included in 1988 election study.

were somewhat more familiar with Senate incumbents than with House incumbents and much more familiar with Senate challengers than with House challengers. In both years, almost half of all voters could not answer a single question about the House challenger. Only about one-fourth of voters displayed this level of ignorance about Senate challengers.

The results shown in table 2.7 may provide a clue about why Senate challengers are much more successful than House challengers in appealing to voters from their own party. It is possible that many challenger partisans defect to the incumbent in House elections simply because they know little or nothing about the challenger. Table 2.8 displays voters' familiarity with Senate and House challengers in 1986 according to their party identification. We expected voters to be more attentive to information about their own party's candidate than about the opposing party's candidate, so we expected challenger partisans to be somewhat more familiar with challengers than incumbent partisans. This was the case, but the difference between incumbent and challenger partisans was relatively small, especially in the House elections. More than two-fifths of the challenger partisans could not answer a single question about the challenger and only one-third of the challenger partisans could answer at least two questions about the challenger. Thus, even members of the challenger's party, who should have been motivated to learn something about their party's candidate, displayed an appalling lack of familiarity with the House challenger.

The consequences of voters' familiarity with Senate and House challengers are displayed in table 2.9. In both Senate and House elections, very few incumbent partisans defected, regardless of their familiarity with the challenger. However, familiarity with the challenger greatly increased the likelihood that challenger partisans would support their own party's candi-

TABLE 2.8. Voter Familiarity with Challengers in 1986 Senate and House Elections by Party Identification (in percentages)

Familiarity with Challenger	Senate Elections		House Elections	
	Incumbent Partisans ($N = 283$)	Challenger Partisans ($N = 329$)	Incumbent Partisans ($N = 446$)	Challenger Partisans ($N = 280$)
0	25	14	47	42
1	17	16	28	26
2	31	30	17	20
3	27	40	8	12

Source: 1986 National Election Study.
Note: Based on voters in contested elections; leaning independents are classified as partisans.

date. In the Senate elections, only 19 percent of challenger partisans who were familiar with the challenger defected compared with 50 percent of those who were unfamiliar with the challenger; similarly, in the House elections, only 25 percent of challenger partisans who were familiar with the challenger defected compared with 61 percent of those who were unfamiliar with the challenger.

The evidence presented thus far clearly demonstrates that the visibility of the challenger is one of the most important differences between Senate and House elections. Senate challengers were much more visible than House challengers, and this difference in visibility goes a long way toward explaining why challenger partisans were much less likely to defect in Senate elections than in House elections. However, the visibility of the challenger does not completely explain the difference between Senate and House elections. The data in table 2.9 show that voters were more likely to support House incumbents than Senate incumbents, even after controlling for their familiarity with the challenger. For example, 61 percent of challenger partisans who were unfamiliar with the House challenger voted for the incumbent compared with only 50 percent of challenger partisans who were unfamiliar with the Senate challenger. In order to explain this difference we must consider voters' evaluations of Senate and House incumbents.

Whenever an incumbent is running for reelection, the election becomes a referendum on the incumbent. Regardless of what kind of campaign the challenger runs, voters will base their decisions largely on how they evaluate the incumbent's record, because past performance is the best guide to future

TABLE 2.9. Proportion Voting for Incumbent by Familiarity with Challenger, 1986

	Familiarity with Challenger			
	Low		High	
Election	Percentage	N	Percentage	N
Senate				
All voters	73	204	45	385
Incumbent partisans	92	108	83	153
Challenger partisans	50	88	19	217
House				
All voters	84	485	60	187
Incumbent partisans	95	303	90	96
Challenger partisans	61	151	25	83

Source: 1986 National Election Study.
Note: Based on voters in contested elections. Low familiarity = 0–1; high familiarity = 2–3.

TABLE 2.10. Voters' Evaluations of Senate and House Candidates, 1986 and 1988

	1986				1988			
	Senate		House		Senate		House	
	Evaluation	N	Evaluation	N	Evaluation	N	Evaluation	N
Incumbent	57.1	649	66.2	690	61.4	749	65.5	764
Challenger	55.7	497	52.2	330	50.2	566	49.5	419

Source: 1986 and 1988 National Election Studies.

Note: The voters' evaluation is the average rating of the candidate on the feeling thermometer; based on voters in contested elections.

performance.[8] Therefore, unless there is widespread dissatisfaction with the incumbent's performance, a challenger generally has little or no chance of winning.

Table 2.10 displays the average evaluations of Senate and House incumbents and challengers on the feeling thermometer scale in 1986 and 1988. Of course, this table is based only on respondents who were able to recognize and rate the candidates. The most important finding that emerges from the data in table 2.10 is that Senate incumbents were evaluated much less favorably than House incumbents, especially in 1986. Not only were House incumbents much better known than their challengers in both 1986 and 1988, but even when voters were aware of the challenger, they evaluated the incumbent much more positively. In contrast, Senate incumbents in 1986 were evaluated only slightly more positively than their challengers.

Not surprisingly, evaluations of the incumbent were strongly related to voting decisions, as the data in table 2.11 demonstrate. In both Senate and House elections, the overwhelming majority of respondents who rated the incumbent above 60 degrees on the feeling thermometer voted for the incumbent. In contrast, only 22 percent of those who gave a negative or neutral rating to Senate incumbents in 1986 voted for the incumbent. However, the consequences of the low visibility of House challengers are clearly evident in the data shown in table 2.11. Even among respondents who gave the House incumbent a negative or neutral rating, 44 percent in 1986 and 55 percent in 1988 voted for the incumbent. In congressional elections, it appears to be true that "you can't beat somebody with nobody."

While a Senate or House election is largely a referendum on the performance of the incumbent, the challenger must provide dissatisfied voters with a viable alternative to the incumbent. Otherwise, many voters will choose a

---

8. See Morris P. Fiorina, *Retrospective Voting in American National Elections* (New Haven: Yale University Press, 1981).

known quantity, the incumbent, over an unknown one, the challenger. Beyond simply providing voters with an alternative to the incumbent, however, the challenger must also criticize the incumbent's performance. Between campaigns, it is relatively easy for incumbents to control the information that voters receive about their performance. This is especially true of House incumbents because the news media provide very little independent coverage of their actions. Almost all of the information that voters receive about House incumbents is provided by the incumbents themselves in the form of newsletters, press releases, and carefully controlled media events. Given the ability of both Senate and House incumbents to control the information that voters receive about their activities, increasing awareness of an incumbent should lead to more positive evaluations of the incumbent's performance.

Barring a scandal, the only time when voters are likely to be exposed to critical information about their own Senator or House member is during the campaign, and the major source of such critical information is the challenger. If this is the case, then increasing awareness of a challenger should lead to more negative evaluations of the incumbent's performance.

In order to test these hypotheses, we performed multiple regression analyses with evaluations of Senate and House incumbents in 1986 as our dependent variables. We used the feeling thermometer scale, which ranges from 0 (very cold) to 100 (very warm), to measure evaluations of Senate and House incumbents. Our independent variables were awareness of the incumbent and awareness of the challenger, both measured by a 0–3 scale based on name recognition, name recall, and ideological placement. (All of the respondents in this analysis scored at least 1 on the incumbent awareness scale by virtue of recognizing and rating the incumbent on the feeling thermometer.) We also included party identification and ideological identification in the

TABLE 2.11. Proportion Voting for Incumbent by Feeling Thermometer Evaluations, 1986 and 1988

Election	Feeling Thermometer Evaluation					
	0–50		51–60		61–100	
	Percentage	N	Percentage	N	Percentage	N
1986 Senate	22	241	57	97	85	258
1986 House	44	162	78	99	94	374
1988 Senate	38	252	71	112	88	323
1988 House	55	199	77	123	93	375

Source: 1986 and 1988 National Election Studies.
Note: Based on voters in contested elections.

regression analyses as control variables. The results of the regression analyses are presented in table 2.12.

The regression coefficients in table 2.12 tell us what effect a change of one unit in each of our independent variables would have on our dependent variable—the rating of the incumbent on the feeling thermometer scale—while holding constant all of the other variables in the analysis. For example, according to our results, an increase of one unit on the seven-point party identification scale would lead to an increase of about 3 degrees in the average rating given to a Senate incumbent and about 4 degrees in the average rating given to a House incumbent. This means that voters who identified strongly with the incumbent's party rated their House incumbent an average of about 24 degrees higher than voters who identified strongly with the challenger's party, just because of their party identification. (This is based on multiplying a difference of 6 units on the party identification scale by the estimated coefficient, 4.02.)

The results shown in table 2.12 indicate that, as expected, increasing awareness of both Senate and House incumbents led to more positive evaluations of these incumbents. With all of the other variables in the analysis held constant, voters who could recall the incumbent's name and place the incumbent on the liberal-conservative scale rated the House incumbent an average of about 11 degrees higher and the Senate incumbent an average of about 12 degrees higher than voters who could not recall the incumbent's name or place the incumbent on the liberal-conservative scale. The more voters knew about their Senator or House member, the better they liked him or her.

Increasing awareness of the challenger led to more negative evaluations of both Senate and House incumbents. According to the results shown in table 2.12, after controlling for their familiarity with the incumbent and their par-

TABLE 2.12. Determinants of Evaluations of Senate and House Incumbents, 1986

Independent Variable	Senate Incumbents		House Incumbents	
	b	SE	b	SE
Party identification	3.14	0.49	4.02	0.44
Ideology	2.95	0.80	1.42	0.71
Incumbent familiarity	6.15	1.81	5.43	1.48
Challenger familiarity	−4.28	1.03	−3.47	0.92
Constant	49.19		53.87	
R^2	.19		.20	

Source: 1986 National Election Study.
Note: The dependent variable is the rating of the incumbent on the feeling thermometer; based on voters in contested elections.

tisan and ideological predispositions, voters who had the highest level of awareness of the challenger rated the House incumbent an average of more than 10 degrees lower and the Senate incumbent an average of almost 13 degrees lower than voters who were completely unaware of the challenger. These results are consistent with the hypothesis that challengers are the major source of critical information about both Senate and House incumbents. One of the main reasons Senators received lower ratings than House members was that Senate challengers were much more visible than House challengers; voters were much more likely to be exposed to criticism of their Senator than of their House member.

The results shown in table 2.12 also indicate that ideology had a much stronger influence on evaluations of Senators than on evaluations of House members. According to these estimates, an extremely conservative voter would have rated a Republican Senator an average of almost 18 degrees higher and a Democratic Senator an average of almost 18 degrees lower than an extremely liberal voter; in contrast, an extremely conservative voter would have rated a Republican Representative an average of less than 9 degrees higher and a Democratic Representative an average of less than 9 degrees lower than an extremely liberal voter. These results support the hypothesis that Senate campaigns are generally more ideological than House campaigns.

The variables included in our regression analyses do not completely explain why incumbent House members were rated more positively than incumbent Senators in 1986. This can be determined by comparing the constants in the two equations. The constant in the House equation is almost 5 degrees higher than the constant in the Senate equation. This means that, after controlling for all of the variables in the regression equations, House incumbents were given somewhat more favorable ratings than Senate incumbents. This may reflect circumstances peculiar to 1986—we have mentioned that a disproportionate number of weak Senate incumbents were up for reelection that year. In 1988, Senate incumbents were rated almost as favorably as House incumbents and much more favorably than 1986 Senate incumbents.

A Comparison of Senate Voters in Large and Small States

Unlike House districts, states vary tremendously in population. Whereas a Senator from Wyoming represents fewer than 500,000 people, a Senator from California represents almost 30 million. It is therefore important to consider the possible effects of state size on Senate elections.

In some ways, it is clearly more difficult to represent a large state than a small state (we are using the terms large and small here to refer exclusively to differences in state population). A Senator from a small state such as

Wyoming or Delaware may have fewer constituents than an average House member. He or she can effectively utilize personal contact to cultivate constituency support. By making frequent trips back home, meeting with groups of citizens, and attending public events, it may be possible, over a six-year period, to meet a substantial proportion of the voters. A Senator from a large state such as California or Texas cannot possibly hope to meet more than a tiny fraction of his or her constituents during a six-year term. These Senators must, therefore, rely almost entirely on the mass media and bulk mailings to communicate with constituents. Furthermore, even though Senators' staff allowances are based on state population, voters in small states are probably also more likely to have personal contact with their Senators' staffs than voters in large states.

In addition to their ability to utilize personal contact with constituents, Senators from small states may have another advantage over their colleagues who represent large states. Small states are probably also more politically homogeneous than large states. Large states such as California, New York, and Florida have extremely diverse populations and economic interests. They have large urban, suburban, and rural populations that include many different ethnic, religious, and racial groups. In contrast, some small states, such as Wyoming, Idaho, and South Dakota, are dominated by a few major economic interests, with no large cities, and few members of racial or ethnic minority groups.

In general, we might expect it to be easier for a Senator to represent a small state with a relatively homogeneous population than a large state with an extremely diverse population. This may not always be the case, however. In a state dominated by a single economic interest, such as agriculture, a Senator who antagonizes that interest may have far more serious political problems than a Senator who antagonizes any single economic interest in a state with a diverse economic base. And if this seems like too remote a possibility to be worth mentioning, the reader should examine the case study of Senator James Abdnor's (R-South Dakota) unsuccessful reelection campaign in chapter 7.

There is, however, a more important reason Senators from small states may not enjoy greater electoral security than their colleagues from large states. Just as it is easier for an incumbent to cultivate a small constituency, it may be also be easier for the challenger to cultivate such a constituency. Like the incumbent, the challenger in a small state can effectively utilize personal contact to appeal to voters. And Senate challengers in small states often come from the House of Representatives, where they have already represented either the entire state or a large fraction thereof. So any advantage that small state incumbents enjoy due to higher visibility may be counterbalanced by the higher visibility of their challengers.

In order to examine the effects of state size on voters' awareness and evaluations of Senate candidates, we used data from the special 1988 Senate Election Study conducted by the University of Michigan Center for Political Studies. The relationships between state size and various measures of candidate familiarity, as well as candidate evaluations, are shown in table 2.13.

We divided states with Senate elections in 1988 into three groups—small states were those with between one and four House districts, medium states were those with between five and eleven House districts, and large states were those with twelve or more House districts. The data in table 2.13 show that voters in small states were somewhat more likely to recall the name of the incumbent Senator than voters in medium and large states, but no more likely to have an opinion about the incumbent or to place the incumbent on the seven-point liberal-conservative scale. Voters in small states were also more likely to recall the name of the Senate challenger than voters in large states. In addition, voters in small states were more likely to have an opinion about the challenger and to rate the challenger's ideological stance.

We combined these three variables—name recall, opinion holding, and ideological placement—into a single index measuring voters' overall familiarity with Senate incumbents and challengers. This candidate familiarity index was strongly related to voters' candidate preferences—when voters were more familiar with one of the candidates, they preferred that candidate over his or her less familiar opponent by an almost three-to-one ratio.

TABLE 2.13. **Voter Familiarity with Senate Candidates by State Population (in percentages)**

	Incumbents			Challengers		
	Small States	Medium States	Large States	Small States	Medium States	Large States
Recall name	33	17	14	24	21	14
Evaluate	95	95	93	85	68	65
Rate ideology	82	83	84	67	57	58
Overall familiarity						
Low	17	18	18	33	47	49
Moderate	52	66	69	47	41	43
High	31	16	13	20	12	8
Average evaluation[a]	61.6	64.9	59.8	51.7	48.5	48.0
N	560	362	283	559	361	281

Source: Special 1988 Senate Election Study.

Note: Small states have 1 to 4 House districts; medium-sized states have 5 to 11 House districts, large states have 12 or more House districts.

[a] Voters' average evaluations are measured on the 0–100 feeling thermometer scale.

46   Senate Elections

The results displayed in table 2.13 show, not surprisingly, that voters in all three types of states were much more familiar with incumbents than with challengers. However, both challengers and incumbents were better known to voters in small states. In terms of relative visibility, incumbents in large states actually had a slightly larger advantage over their challengers than incumbents in small states. Among voters in large states, 43 percent were more familiar with the incumbent while 8 percent were more familiar with the challenger; among voters in small states, 35 percent were more familiar with the incumbent while 9 percent were more familiar with the challenger.

If Senators from small states found it easier to represent their constituents than their colleagues from large states, this difference was not reflected in their overall evaluations. According to the data presented in table 2.13, incumbents from all three types of states were rated much more favorably than their challengers in 1988; however, small state Senators did not enjoy a larger advantage than their colleagues from large states. Incumbents in small states received an average evaluation of 62 degrees on the feeling thermometer scale compared with an average evaluation of 52 degrees for their challengers; incumbents in medium-sized states actually had a bigger advantage over their challengers—65 degrees to 49 degrees. Incumbents in large states had a slightly larger advantage in relative evaluations than their colleagues in small states—they received an average rating of 60 degrees compared with 48 degrees for their challengers.

Based on the data shown in table 2.13, it does not appear that small state incumbents had any electoral advantage in 1988 compared with large state incumbents. This conclusion is confirmed when we examine the actual candidate preferences of voters in small, medium, and large states. Sixty-five percent of the voters in small states cast their ballots for incumbents compared with 73 percent of voters in medium-sized states and 66 percent of voters in large states.

Our findings raise questions about the presumed advantage of small state incumbents in Senate elections. However, since these results are based on data from only one election year, we cannot rule out the possibility that incumbents from small states generally have such an advantage. We will examine the impact of state size on the aggregate outcomes of recent Senate elections in chapter 4.

Summary and Conclusions

Congressional elections are not conducted on a level playing field. Incumbents enjoy many advantages over challengers including greater visibility and an electorate that usually consists disproportionately of their copartisans. These advantages are much greater in House elections than in Senate elections, however. The electorate in an average House district is much more skewed in its party loyalties than the electorate in an average state. In addition, the average Senate challenger is much more visible than the average House challenger.

Our evidence demonstrates that the challenger plays a crucial role in the process of electoral accountability. A Senate or House election is largely a referendum on the performance of the incumbent, but unless voters are at least aware of the challenger, they will be reluctant to reject the incumbent even if they are less than delighted with his or her performance. In congressional elections, at least, voters appear to be risk averse, preferring a mediocre incumbent to an unknown challenger.

The role of the challenger goes beyond simply providing a viable alternative to the incumbent, however. Since the news media generally provide little objective coverage of the performance of Senators or House members, it is largely up to the challenger to provide voters with information critical of the incumbent's performance. The more voters know about the challenger, the more likely they are to question the way the incumbent has been doing his or her job.

The most important difference between Senate and House elections is the visibility of the challenger. Senate elections are more competitive than House elections mainly because voters in Senate elections are much less dependent on the incumbent for information. However, not all Senate challengers are successful in getting their message across to the voters. Senate campaigns vary enormously in their intensity. To understand why some Senate contests are much more competitive than others, we will turn our attention from national survey data to an analysis of aggregate election outcomes in chapter 4. Before analyzing the outcomes of Senate general elections, however, we will explore the first stage in the process of selecting U.S. Senators by analyzing Senate primary elections.

CHAPTER 3

Primary Elections

The first stage in the process of electing Senators is the selection of nominees by the major political parties. Throughout most of the country, Senate nominees are chosen in statewide primaries. These primary elections are the focus of chapter 3.

Party Nominating Systems

Progressive Reforms, Take Two: The Direct Primary

In chapter 1 we saw how the popular election of Senators, brought about by the Seventeenth Amendment, was one of the most prominent victories of the Progressive reform era. Perhaps even more notable was the movement during the Progressive era for direct primary elections.

During the early nineteenth century, party nominations for most state offices in the United States were controlled by caucuses made up of each party's members in the state legislature, sometimes supplemented by delegates elected from legislative districts that were represented by the opposing party. Similarly, presidential nominations were controlled by the members of each party's congressional caucus. During the 1820s, however, this system came under increasing criticism, especially by supporters of Andrew Jackson, as narrow and elitist. By 1832, the congressional caucus had been replaced by a national nominating convention made up of delegates from each state. Many of the state parties also changed their procedure for selecting candidates from the legislative caucus to a state party convention.[1]

The nominating convention, made up of delegates either elected directly by local party organizations or chosen at county conventions, remained the dominant method of selecting candidates for statewide office until the early twentieth century. By the 1890s, however, the convention system itself had come under attack for perpetuating the power of party bosses. After the end of Reconstruction, one-party domination became the prevalent political pattern in many states. With the Democratic party dominant in the South and the

---

1. V. O. Key, Jr., *Politics, Parties and Pressure Groups*, 5th ed. (New York: Crowell, 1964), 372.

Republican party dominant in much of the rest of the country, there was often little real competition in elections. The nomination of the dominant party was tantamount to election, and the nomination process was often controlled by a small group of party leaders.

Progressive reformers saw the direct primary as a tool to break the power of party leaders. Of course, the reformers were not motivated entirely by a disinterested concern for good government. Many, including Robert La Follette of Wisconsin, saw the direct primary as a means to achieve power for themselves. Mississippi adopted the first statewide direct primary in 1902, followed by Wisconsin in 1903. By 1916, Rhode Island, Connecticut, and New Mexico were the only states without some form of direct primary.[2]

Today, the direct primary is used in every state; New York was the last state to abandon a pure convention system in 1968. Even though primaries are used throughout the fifty states, there is considerable variation in the methods by which primaries are conducted. These variations have important consequences for the role played by party leaders and organizations in the nomination process. In some states, party leaders and organizations retain considerable influence in the selection of candidates; in others, the parties have become little more than passive spectators in the nomination process.

Mixed Convention and Primary Systems

In several states, party conventions still play an important role in the nomination process. Virginia law allows parties to select either a primary or a convention to nominate candidates for office. In recent years, both major parties have nominated candidates for statewide office by convention rather than using a primary election. Eight states (Connecticut, Colorado, Delaware, New Mexico, New York, North Dakota, Rhode Island, and Utah) provide for preprimary endorsements under state law, and in one state (Massachusetts) party rules governing endorsements have been accepted as legally binding by the state courts.[3] In three other states (Minnesota, Wisconsin, and Illinois), at least one party makes informal preprimary endorsements at its state convention.

The effects of preprimary endorsements on the nomination process vary considerably. In some states, a candidate must receive a minimum percentage of the votes at the party convention in order to obtain a place on the ballot. If only one candidate receives the required number of votes, then that candidate is nominated without a primary. In other states, a candidate who does not receive the required number of votes at the party convention may qualify for

---

2. Key, *Politics*, 375; Arthur A. Ekirch, Jr., *Progressivism in America* (New York: New Viewpoints, 1974), 114.

3. Malcom Jewell and David Olson, *American State Political Parties and Elections*, 3d ed. (Chicago: Dorsey, 1988), 95–97.

the primary ballot by obtaining a certain number of signatures on petitions. However, the often short time between the convention and the date set for obtaining the requisite signatures makes primary challenges to the official candidate difficult. Additionally, the candidate who receives the largest number of votes at the state convention may also receive the top position on the primary ballot.[4]

Types of Primaries

In most states, the primary election is the exclusive method of selecting candidates for public office. However, the rules governing the conduct of primary elections vary considerably from state to state. The most important differences among state primaries involve the requirements for voting in the primary. In states with closed primaries, a voter must be registered with a party in order to vote in that party's primary; in states with open primaries, party registration is not required and any registered voter may participate in a party's primary. As we shall see, these state primaries are thus subject to "raiding" by members of the opposition party.

Twenty-five states currently require voters to be registered with a party in order to vote in that party's primary election. However, eight of these states allow voters to enroll or change their registration on the day of the primary. In addition, two states require party registration but allow voters registered as independents to participate in either party's primary. In the states that require party registration before a voter can participate in a primary, the cutoff date for changing one's registration varies from less than two months to almost a full year before the date of the primary.[5]

Twenty-two states currently utilize an open primary to nominate candidates for state offices. Voters are free to participate in either party's primary, although eleven of these states require voters to publicly choose the party whose primary they wish to vote in. In nine states, voters are able to choose a primary in the privacy of the voting booth. Two states, Washington and Alaska, utilize a system known as the "blanket primary," under which a voter can participate in both parties' primaries for different offices at the same time. Finally, Louisiana uses a nonpartisan primary in which the names of all Democratic and Republican candidates appear on the same ballot. If a candidate receives a majority of the vote in the primary election, that candidate is elected; if no candidate receives a majority, then a runoff is held between the two top vote-getters in the primary, regardless of party affiliation.

In addition to the distinction between open and closed primaries, another important characteristic of a state's primary system is the presence or absence

---

4. Jewell and Olson, *State Parties*, 96.
5. Jewell and Olson, *State Parties*, 89–91.

of a runoff requirement. Eleven states currently use a runoff primary. These include all of the states of the old Confederacy except Tennessee, along with the border state of Oklahoma. Until recently, the Democratic nomination was tantamount to election in all of these states. Under the runoff system, if no candidate receives a majority of the vote in the first primary, a runoff election is held between the two leading candidates.

The argument for the runoff primary is that a candidate who receives a minority of the vote in a multicandidate field should not automatically receive a party's nomination. In the runoff primary, a candidate must demonstrate his or her acceptability to a majority of primary voters. However, in recent years, the runoff primary has come under attack from civil rights groups who charge that the system hinders the nomination efforts of minority candidates who might win in a crowded field but would probably not win in a one-on-one runoff against a white candidate.

Seeking Office

Senate elections begin when potential candidates first begin to seek their party's nomination. What factors lead those with political ambition to seek a seat in the Senate? The traditional approach, as in Joseph Schlesinger's *Ambition and Politics*,[6] is to examine the career patterns of those who have sought such seats. Schlesinger finds that unsuccessful major party candidates for the Senate had as their penultimate political position administrative office (21.6 percent), followed by law enforcement, such as a district attorney (17.8 percent), Congress or statewide elective office (14.3 percent each), and local elective office (6.1 percent). No prior office accounted for 11.4 percent. Among successful Senate candidates, 26.7 percent came penultimately from Congress, 22.2 percent from statewide elective office, 14.4 percent from administrative office, 12.7 percent from law enforcement, 8.9 percent from state legislatures, and 4.7 percent from local elective office. No prior office accounted for 8.2 percent. This study no doubt overstates dramatically the previous experience of the typical Senate office seeker, for it excludes those who sought but did not win their party's nomination.

A different approach to studying ambition is taken by David Rohde.[7] Rather than examine only those who sought a Senate seat, Rohde compares those who do so from those who do not in a highly relevant population, members of the House of Representatives. Rohde argues that House members

---

6. Joseph Schlesinger, *Ambition and Politics: Political Careers in the United States* (Chicago: Rand McNally, 1966).

7. David Rohde, "Risk-Bearing and Progressive Ambition: The Case of Members of the United States House of Representatives," *American Journal of Political Science* 23 (1979): 1–26.

will seek higher office when the benefits are higher and the risks are lower. Members of Congress typically must forfeit their House seat to run for Senate, so they should not run without a reasonable chance of winning. Consistent with this theory, Rohde finds that members of Congress are more likely to run for the Senate when they will not be opposed by an incumbent and when their state is not dominated by the opposition party. Members of Congress from small states are more likely to run than members of Congress from large states, for the former will be known by a larger proportion of the voters in the state and, thus, should have a better chance of winning. Senior members of Congress, who have advanced through the seniority system, will have more to lose and thus are less likely to seek the Senate than more junior members. Finally, risk takers, those who first sought their House seats against an incumbent or an entrenched opposition party, are more likely to run for the Senate than those who first ran for the House under more favorable circumstances. Rohde's findings were largely corroborated in a more sophisticated analysis by Paul Brace, who additionally found that members of Congress hurt by redistricting, and thus facing riskier prospects for their own seats, were more likely to run for the Senate.[8]

A third approach to the same question is taken by David Canon and associates,[9] who examine the overall candidate quality of the primary pool. For instance, a primary with a governor and two members of Congress running has a higher overall candidate quality rating than one with two state legislators and a political amateur. One *might* expect that the challenger pool on both sides will be stronger when an incumbent is retiring, for there should be a better chance of winning an open seat election. Canon, Alvarez, and Sellers's more sophisticated reasoning notes that if all potential candidates felt that way, then the overall probability of winning a Senate seat (i.e., the probability of winning a primary $\times$ the probability of winning the general election) might be lower for open seats, for the probability of winning the primary will be significantly lower.[10] Additionally, the authors find that in opposing-party Senate primaries, those in which the winner faces an incumbent, composite candidate quality increases when state-level income decreases, when state parties are weak (and thus unable to limit competition), and when there is a large pool of high-quality (statewide officeholders and members of Congress) potential challengers. The incumbent's expectation of

---

8. Paul Brace, "Progressive Ambition in the House: A Probabilistic Approach," *Journal of Politics* 46 (1984): 556–71.

9. David T. Canon, R. Michael Alvarez, and Patrick J. Sellers, "Contesting Senate Primary Elections: 1972–1988," paper presented at the annual meeting of the Midwest Political Science Association, 1990, Chicago.

10. See Jeffrey S. Banks and D. Rod Kiewiet, "Explaining Patterns of Competition in Congressional Elections," *American Journal of Political Science* 33 (1989): 997–1015.

winning in the Fall (as measured by *Congressional Quarterly*) had only a slight effect on the quality of the opposition candidate pool. In open seat primaries, composite candidate quality increases, again, when state-level income decreases, when there is a large pool of high-quality potential challengers, and when the party has a minimal role in endorsing candidates.

Challenging Incumbents

The responsiveness of the Senate to national and local political winds is maintained through the election process. Senators poorly representing their constituents' desires, or not in line with national trends (as we demonstrate in chap. 4) are more likely to suffer electoral defeat. Primary elections can also keep senators responsive to the desires of their partisan constituents. Though primary elections in recent years have more closely resembled House elections than anything else—low-quality challengers running poorly funded campaigns against entrenched incumbents—successful challenges against luminaries such as William Fulbright, Clifford Case, and Jacob Javits remind us that senators oblivious to the sentiments of constituents can be replaced, regardless of their institutional status. Moreover, as we demonstrate in chapter 4, unsuccessful challenges to incumbents can split the senator's party, making election in November less likely.

From a challenger's point of view, the most difficult path to the U.S. Senate is the path through an incumbent Senator of one's own party. One must first defeat what is likely to be the better known, better funded, and better organized Senator, and then hope that one has not so divided the party and exhausted one's revenues that the general election is lost.

As we saw in chapter 1, incumbent primary losses, whether for elected or appointed incumbents, are rare. Table 3.1 presents the average number of primary losses per year, by decade. During the 1930s and 1940s, approximately three incumbents per election year were defeated. From 1954 through 1964, not one incumbent was defeated in a primary election. The worst recent year for incumbents was 1980, when four Senators failed to receive their party's nomination. Since 1980, though, every incumbent seeking renomination received it until Alan Dixon's (D-Illinois) loss in March, 1992.

Between 1974 and 1990, 234 incumbents have sought renomination from their party (see table 3.2). In 124 races, incumbents received a free ride, that is, no credible candidate challenged them.[11] In 80 races, there was a single challenger, 24 incumbents faced two challengers, 5 faced three challengers, and 1, moderate Republican Bob Packwood of Oregon, faced four.

---

11. We define a credible candidate as one who receives over 5 percent of the vote in the primary.

TABLE 3.1. Primary Losses Per Year

Decade	Losses per Year
1910–19	2.0
1920–29	3.0
1930–39	2.4
1940–49	3.6
1950–59	1.2
1960–69	1.2
1970–79	0.6
1980–89	0.8

TABLE 3.2. Incumbent Challengers, 1974–90

Challengers	Number of Races	Percentage of Races
0	124	53.0
1	80	34.2
2	24	10.3
3	5	2.1
4	1	0.4
Total	234	100.0

Much like House races, Senate primaries are largely uncompetitive, whether we examine race outcomes or victory margins.[12] Out of the 110 incumbent races (including three runoffs), challengers won only 6 (see table 3.3). Challengers finished close, that is, they lost by 10 percentage points or less, in only 5 more. In 8 more races, they lost by less than 20 percentage points. In 68 of the 110 races, incumbents won by 50 percentage points or more. The average victory margin for incumbents was 56.1 percent.

What factors affect the ability of challengers to wage successful campaigns against incumbents? We will examine variables such as campaign spending, the quality of the opposition, and the effect of highly publicized political controversies. Of particular interest to the notion of responsiveness is the extent to which Senators who do not faithfully represent the views of their partisan constituents suffer electoral consequences for their behavior. We take two complementary approaches to these questions. First, we closely examine the six races since 1974 in which incumbents were denied their party's nomination. Following the case studies, we conduct a more systematic analysis

---

12. See David Mayhew, "Congressional Elections: The Case of the Vanishing Marginals," *Polity* 6 (1974): 295–317.

TABLE 3.3. Incumbent Victory Margins in Contested Races, 1974–90

Margin[a]	Number of Races	Percentage of Races
−30–0	6	5.5
0–9	5	4.5
10–19	8	7.3
20–29	2	1.8
30–39	5	4.5
40–49	6	5.5
50–59	11	10.0
60–69	22	20.0
70–79	32	29.1
80–89	13	11.8
Total	110	100.0

[a]The victory margin is in percentage points.

of factors that affect margins of victory or defeat in the 98 contested incumbent races through from 1974 through 1988, and then apply those results to the 1990 races. We begin with the six races between 1974 and 1990 in which elected incumbents suffered primary defeats: J. William Fulbright (D-Arkansas), who was defeated by Dale Bumpers in 1974; Clifford Case (R-New Jersey), who was defeated by Jeffrey Bell in 1978; Donald Stewart (D-Alabama), who was defeated by Jim Folsom in 1980; Mike Gravel (D-Arkansas), who was defeated by Clark Gruening in 1980; Richard Stone (D-Florida), who was defeated by Bill Gunter in 1980; and Jacob Javits (R-New York), who was defeated by Alfonse D'Amato in 1980.[13]

Fulbright vs. Bumpers

The first race we examine is the 1974 Arkansas race between incumbent Senator J. William Fulbright and his challenger, incumbent Governor Dale Bumpers. Fulbright was born on April 9, 1905, in Summer, Missouri. After attending Oxford University as a Rhodes Scholar, he earned a law degree from George Washington University. Fulbright served in the Justice Department before returning to academic life, where he was a law professor and then president of the University of Arkansas. Elected to the House of Representa-

---

13. We thus exclude the primary defeats of Howard Metzenbaum (D-Ohio) by John Glenn in 1974, Maryon P. Allen (D-Alabama) by Donald Stewart in 1978, and Paul Hatfield (D-Montana) by Max Baucus in 1978. The three incumbents were gubernatorial appointees who had not been elected to an incomplete or full term at the time of the primary.

tives in 1942, Fulbright sought and won election to the Senate just two years later.[14]

In the Senate, Fulbright emphasized foreign relations, perhaps to the neglect of constituent concerns. He sponsored the international fellowship program that bears his name. In the 1950s, Fulbright was attacked by Senator Joseph McCarthy (R-Wisconsin) as "Senator Halfbright" for the Senator's early challenge to the Wisconsin demagogue. In 1962, Fulbright called for normalized relations with China, the Soviet Union, and even Cuba. As chairman of the Senate Foreign Relations Committee, Fulbright used the committee as a forum to attack President Johnson's Vietnam policies, hardly a popular stand in conservative Arkansas.

Fulbright's record on civil rights was more mixed. As a Senate candidate in 1944 he declared, "I am not for Negro participation in our primary elections, and I do not approve of social equality."[15] Following the *Brown v. Board of Education* desegregation case,[16] Fulbright supported the Southern Manifesto, which called for massive resistance to the decision. He also voted against the Civil Rights Act of 1964 and the Voting Rights Act of 1965. By 1968, though, Fulbright was running against segregation and easily defeated the reactionary James Johnson with 70 percent of the black vote.[17] He further solidified support among black voters by being one of four Southern Senators to vote against the 1971 Supreme Court nomination of G. Harrold Carswell, a formerly avowed white supremacist.

Outside of his early opposition to civil rights, Fulbright was consistently more liberal than one would expect an Arkansas Democrat to be. As a Southern Democrat from a state that gave George McGovern only 31 percent of the vote in 1972, we would expect Fulbright to support the liberal position about 35 percent of the time in roll call votes, as measured by the Americans for Democratic Action (ADA).[18] As shown in figure 3.1, Fulbright was far more liberal than his constituents. From 1969 through 1973, Fulbright's ADA scores ranged from a low of 50 to a high of 85. Yet there were exceptions to Fulbright's general liberalism: election years. Like other Senators, Fulbright sought to bring his voting behavior in line with his constituents as election

---

14. Michael Barone, Grant Ujifusa, and Douglas Matthews, *Almanac of American Politics* (Boston: Gambit, 1974); "James William Fulbright," *Arkansas Gazette*, March 12, 1974.
15. Lou Cannon, "Fulbright Fighting to Stay in Senate," *Washington Post*, May 26, 1974.
16. Brown v. Board of Education, 346 U.S. 483 (1954).
17. Barone, Ujifusa, and Matthews, *Almanac* (1974).
18. The result is the prediction of ADA scores from a regression equation that includes partisanship, region, and state support for George McGovern in 1972 as independent variables. See Jeffrey A. Segal, Charles M. Cameron, and Albert D. Cover, "A Spatial Model of Roll Call Voting: Senators, Constituents, Presidents, and Interest Groups in Supreme Court Confirmations," *American Journal of Political Science* 36 (1992): 96–121.

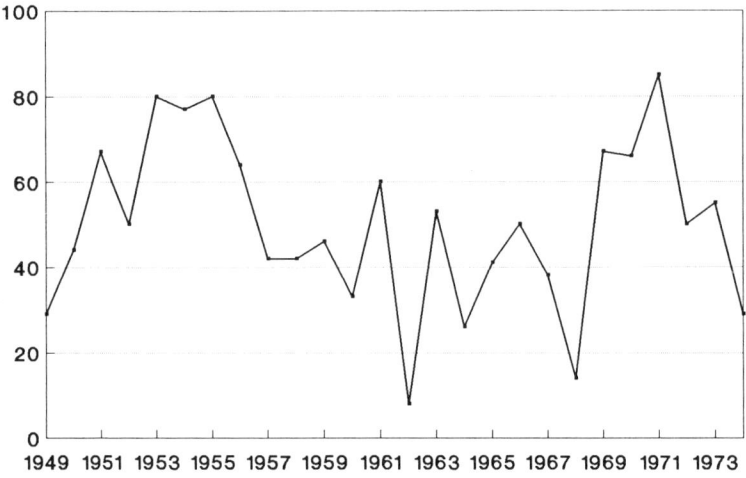

Fig. 3.1. Fulbright's ADA ranking, 1949–74

years approached.[19] Fulbright's ADA ratings dropped from 60 in 1961 to 8 in 1962, an election year, and back up to 53 in 1963. From 1967 to 1969, Fulbright's scores went from 38 (preelection) to 14 (election) to 67 (postelection). In 1973, Fulbright's score was 55; in 1974, when he faced reelection, it was down to 29.

Dale Bumpers, twenty years younger than Fulbright, was born on August 12, 1925, in Charleston, Arkansas. He received a law degree from Northwestern University in 1951, after which he returned to Charleston and was elected Charleston City Attorney, where he served through 1969.[20] In 1969, Bumpers was elected Governor of Arkansas, defeating former governor and arch-segregationist Orval Faubus in the Democratic primary runoff and incumbent Winthrop Rockefeller in the general election. Bumpers, like Rockefeller and unlike Faubus, was an outspoken opponent of segregation. "One of the most popular governors in the state's history," Bumpers supported consumer legislation, reformed state government, and supported a tax in-

---

19. See, e.g., Gerald Wright and Michael Berkman, "Candidates and Policy in United States Senate Elections," *American Political Science Review* 80 (1986): 567–88; Catherine R. Shapiro, David W. Brady, Richard Brody, and John A. Ferejohn, "Linking Constituency Opinion and Senate Voting Scores: A Hybrid Explanation," *Legislative Studies Quarterly* 15 (1990): 599–622.

20. Michael Barone, Grant Ujifusa, and Douglas Matthews, *Almanac of American Politics* (New York: E. P. Dutton (1976); "Dale Leon Bumpers," *Arkansas Gazette*, March 12, 1974.

crease that protected the state's solvency and produced large budget surpluses.[21] Bumpers was easily reelected in 1971.

Bumpers announced his candidacy for the May 28 primary on March 11, 1974, against the wishes of many prominent state Democrats. In declaring his candidacy, he made no attacks on Fulbright. "I am not running against Senator Fulbright but for the United States Senate. . . . I have agreed more than disagreed with Fulbright."[22] On the hottest issue of the day, Watergate, Bumpers announced his reluctance to call for Nixon's resignation until after the House Judiciary Committee had heard all of the evidence.

The leading paper in the state, the *Arkansas Gazette*, blasted Bumpers, who admitted interest in presidential politics, for running a campaign that had no reason for being other than political ambition. Bumpers "is asking the people to turn out a veteran incumbent senator, one of the most honored men ever reared in Arkansas, without even making a case against him!" Bumpers "has 30 years of Fulbright's record to examine, and surely he must object to *something* Fulbright has done."[23] Fulbright accused Bumpers of using the Senate as a stepping stone to the presidency.[24]

As the incumbent, Fulbright had a huge lead in fund-raising. Through the end of April, the senator led the governor in money raised, $428,000 to $151,000, and in money spent, $337,000 to $103,000. Almost one-third of those who gave money to Fulbright represented out-of-state interests, including oilmen, bankers, and "big name 'doves' from the East Coast foreign policy establishment."[25] Bumpers, for his part, had limited contributions to $1,000 and would not accept contributions from out-of-state people he did not know personally.[26] This, apparently, was a "precaution against a heavy influx of money from wealthy Jewish Democrats" who were furious about Fulbright's lack of support for Israel.[27] Fearing an anti-Semitic backlash,

---

21. Bill Terry, "Governor Bumpers Seeks Fulbright's Seat," *Washington Post*, March 12, 1974.

22. Terry, "Governor Bumpers"; Ernest Dumas, "Bumpers to Seek Seat of Fulbright; Cites State Service," *Arkansas Gazette*, March 12, 1974.

23. "An Issueless Campaign," *Arkansas Gazette*, March 14, 1974; Clayton Fritchey, "Fulbright vs. Bumpers: The Arkansas Dilemma," *Washington Post*, May 4, 1974.

24. Carol Griffee, "Senator Voices Regret, Predicts Tough Campaign," *Arkansas Gazette*, March 12, 1974; Terry, "Governor Bumpers."

25. "Fulbright Leads in Fund Campaign," *New York Times*, May 18, 1974; Dan Morgan, "Fulbright Knots Pursestrings on Foe," *Washington Post*, May 17, 1974; "Oil Men Compose Largest Segment on Fulbright List," *Arkansas Gazette*, March 21, 1974.

26. Dumas, "Bumpers to Seek."

27. Dan Morgan, "Fulbright Knots." Rumors that Jews from outside Arkansas were offering Bumpers large sums of money to run against Fulbright surfaced before Bumpers had even announced his candidacy; see Roy Reed, "Fulbright Facing a Strong Contest," *New York Times*, February 4, 1974.

an Arkansas Democrat explained "I could raise a fortune for Bumpers in five stops . . . but that is the one thing that could keep him from getting elected."[28] By the middle of May, Fulbright increased his spending lead to $648,000 to just under $200,000 for Bumpers.

Despite Fulbright's advantages, Bumpers quickly became the favorite in the race. At the time of his announced candidacy, 91 percent of the electorate gave Bumpers a favorable job rating, which may be the highest level of support for an elected official since George Gallup began polling.[29] Even Fulbright acknowledged that Bumpers "has a very attractive personality and one of the most engaging smiles and manners of anyone I know. . . . When you hear his speeches, they're downright inspirational."[30] Fulbright's own commercials ended with this disclaimer: "When you vote on May 28, don't ask yourself who you like better. Ask who will do the better job."[31] Bumpers's warm, personal style stood in contrast to the frequently condescending and ill-tempered Fulbright.[32] On the day Bumpers announced, one poll had him leading Fulbright by a 60 to 27 margin.[33] Later polls showed the lead holding at 60 to 40.[34]

Bumpers's platform capitalized on popular discontent with Washington and all it stood for during the closing weeks of the Nixon administration. Fulbright attempted to portray himself as one of the Nixon administration's enemies, but his close ties to Henry Kissinger and the policy of détente belied such contentions. Fulbright also assailed Bumpers's refusal to debate, but such attacks were blunted as the Bumpers campaign reminded the press of Fulbright's refusal to debate Republican Senate candidate Charles Bernard in 1968.

Two days before the primary, Bumpers agreed to debate Fulbright on the ABC news program "Issues and Answers." The debate sparked few policy disagreements between the candidates, as they agreed, for the most part, on the issues of the day. Their one policy dispute came when Fulbright called for military and foreign aid cuts and a tax cut, while Bumpers argued that a tax cut would fuel inflation. Bumpers continued to have little of what George Bush later referred to as "that vision thing," while Fulbright reacted to questions with petulance, indignance, and condescension.[35]

28. Morgan, "Fulbright Knots."
29. Lou Cannon, "Fulbright Fighting to Stay in Senate," *Washington Post*, May 26, 1974.
30. Cannon, "Fulbright Fighting."
31. Cannon, "Fulbright Fighting."
32. Cannon, "Fulbright Fighting."
33. Roy Reed, "Fulbright in Peril in 6th Senate Bid," *New York Times*, April 3, 1974; Bill Terry, "Fulbright Beaten in Arkansas," *Washington Post*, May 29, 1974.
34. Terry, "Fulbright Beaten."
35. Bob Kuttner, "Fulbright, Bumpers Meet; Styles Clash," *Washington Post*, May 27, 1974; Bill Lewis, "Both Expect A Victory In Election," *Arkansas Gazette*, May 27, 1974.

On the Friday before the primary, Bernard Gaer filed a suit against Bumpers, charging that Bumpers promised, in 1970, to have a federal indictment against Gaer dismissed in return for contributions to Bumper's gubernatorial campaign. Bumpers, who, as governor, had no authority to quash federal indictments, called the allegations "outrageous."[36]

The last-minute allegations, though played on page one by the *Arkansas Gazette*, had little effect on the vote. Bumpers won the election in a landslide, winning 65 percent of the vote. Fulbright lost all but 4 of Arkansas's 75 counties and did not even carry his home town of Fayetteville.[37] Bumpers likewise defeated Republican nominee John Harris Jones with 65 percent of the vote in the November election.

Bell vs. Case

Fulbright was the only incumbent defeated by a primary election in 1974 and none was defeated in 1976. In 1978, though, four-term Senator Clifford Case (R-New Jersey) was denied his party nomination by a Reagan-style conservative, Jeffrey Bell. Clifford Case, New Jersey's senior Senator, was born on April 16, 1904, in Franklin Park, New Jersey. He received his B.A. from Rutgers in 1925 and a law degree from Columbia in 1928. Case served in the New Jersey General Assembly in 1943–44 and was elected to the U.S. House of Representatives in 1945, where he served until 1953.[38] In 1954, Case won election to the Senate by a narrow, 0.2 percent margin.

Case, like Lowell Weicker (R-Connecticut), Charles Mathias (R-Maryland), Mark Hatfield (R-Oregon), Charles Percy (R-Illinois), and Jacob Javits (R-New York), represented the once-powerful liberal wing of the Republican party. As the senior Republican on the Senate Foreign Relations Committee, he helped lead the fight to end the war in Vietnam and won the battle for greater financial disclosure of Senators' personal and campaign finances.[39] His voting record, as measured by the ADA and shown in figure 3.2, made him one of the most liberal members of the Senate, Democrat or Republican. From 1965 through 1969, Case's ADA support scores never dropped below 94. In 1972, facing a moderate primary challenge from a strong conservative, Case's support score dropped to 80. In 1978, facing a much stronger challenge from Bell, Case's score dropped to 65.

Jeffrey Bell was born on December 13, 1943, in Washington, D.C.

---

36. Peggy Robertson, "Suit Alleges Bumpers Offered to Quash Federal Indictment," *Arkansas Gazette*, May 26, 1974.
37. Bill Lewis, "Bumpers Shatters Fulbright," *Arkansas Gazette*, May 29, 1974.
38. Michael Barone, Grant Ujifusa, and Douglas Matthews, *Almanac of American Politics* (New York: E. P. Dutton, 1978), 517.
39. Barone, Ujifusa, and Matthews, *Almanac* (1978), 517.

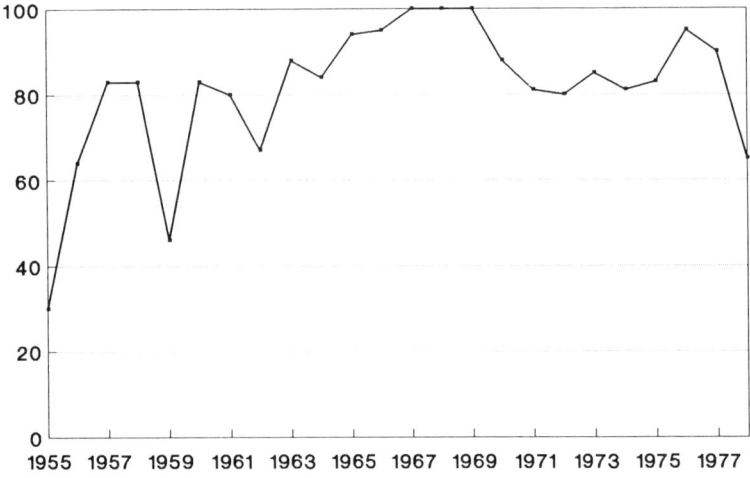

Fig. 3.2. Case's ADA ranking, 1955–78

Though only thirty-four at the time of the 1978 campaign against Case, Bell had a long history of conservative activism. At Columbia University in the early 1960s, Bell founded a conservative magazine called *Foundation*. Following college, Bell worked for two years at William F. Buckley's *National Review*, the most prominent conservative periodical in the country. During that time, Bell also served as a member of the Goldwater Youth. Bell served in Vietnam and returned to the United States to work as a speech writer and researcher for Richard Nixon's 1968 presidential race. After Nixon's victory, Bell turned down a speech writing job at the White House to become director of the American Conservative Union (ACU). In 1973, Bell temporarily left politics to become a fellow at Harvard's Kennedy Institute, but a year later he joined the staff of Ronald Reagan.[40] In 1976, Bell worked on Reagan's unsuccessful attempt to wrest the Republican presidential nomination from Gerald Ford. It was Bell who formulated Reagan's then-ridiculed plan to slash $90 billion from the federal budget. Of course, a variant of the plan was a centerpiece of Reagan's successful 1980 presidential race.

Following the 1976 campaign, Bell moved to New Jersey, where he had once lived, for the express purpose of challenging Case. Bell started the campaign early, announcing his candidacy in May, 1977, thirteen months before the Republican primary. He sought and received the support of many big-name conservatives, including former Senator James Buckley (Conservative-New York), former Treasury Secretary William Simon, and Congressmen Robert Bauman (R-Maryland), John Ashbrook (R-Ohio), and Jack Kemp (R-New

---

40. Joseph F. Sullivan, "From Sports Fan to Politician," *New York Times*, June 12, 1978.

York).[41] The one conservative whose active support Bell did not get was Ronald Reagan. Reagan, who had split the Republican party with his 1976 presidential quest, was the early frontrunner for 1980 and was preaching Republican unity. Reagan could win the Republican nomination without moderate support, but not the general election. Thus, he quietly turned down pleas to help his former idea man and speech writer.

Despite Reagan's official neutrality in the race, Bell had certain prominent advantages in his campaign against Case. Incumbents typically have much higher name recognition than incumbents. But while Bell was not well known, neither was Case. In a poll taken by the Eagleton Institute of Rutgers University in January and February of 1978, only 34 percent of New Jersey residents could name Case, who had served in the Senate for twenty-four years, as the Republican senator.[42] Republicans who had heard of Case were not necessarily fond of his liberal voting record. Six years earlier, an unknown conservative challenger, James Walter Ralph, with little money and no organization won 30 percent of the vote in a primary challenge to Case. Compared to Case's 1972 challenger, Bell, though a newcomer to New Jersey politics, had a national reputation, support from numerous conservative organizations, and moderate success at direct-mail fund-raising. Though Bell did not raise age as an issue, Case was seventy-four years old, "and looks it."[43]

Perhaps the biggest advantage that Bell had over Case was Bell's advocacy of what would later be called Reaganomics. Bell learned from 1976 that, while calling for massive cuts in federal *spending* does not excite many people, calling for massive cuts in federal *taxes* does. Bell enthusiastically endorsed the proposed Kemp-Roth 30 percent across-the-board tax cut, which was later passed following Reagan's 1980 election. Like Jack Kemp (R-New York), William Roth (R-Delaware), and, later, Ronald Reagan, Bell argued that a cut in taxes would so stimulate the economy that tax revenues would actually increase.[44] In the year that California voters passed the tax-slashing Proposition 13, Kemp-Roth stirred many who were bitter with federal marginal tax rates as high as 70 percent.

Case announced his bid for a fifth term on April 19. He did so with most of the state's county Republican leaders at his side and with the unanimous support of the Republican members of the State Assembly.[45] Political analysts

---

41. Rowland Evans and Robert Novak, "Reagan the Party Man," *Washington Post*, May 10, 1978.
42. "Only 34% in a Poll Know Who Case Is," *New York Times*, March 2, 1978.
43. T. R. Reid, "A Scholar-Athlete Pivots Into Politics," *Washington Post*, May 22, 1978.
44. This is the plan that George Bush labeled "voodoo economics" while running against Reagan for the Republican nomination in 1980.
45. Joseph Sullivan, "Case Announces Bid for 5th Term; Faces Opposition in June Primary," *New York Times*, April 20, 1978; "G.O.P. Legislators Back Case," *New York Times*, April 28, 1978.

considered Case, who won in 1972 with 70 percent of the vote in the primary and 64 percent of the vote in the general election, a heavy favorite to win renomination.[46] The fifteen-person New Jersey congressional delegation unanimously predicted that Case would win the Republican primary. Only one Congressman would go so far as to say the race would be close.[47] Indeed, an Associated Press/WNBC-TV poll released May 18 showed Republicans supporting Case by a seemingly insurmountable 50 to 14 margin.[48] An Eagleton Poll taken between May 7 and 16 showed that Republicans thought Case would be a better Senator by a 43 to 8 margin. Further, while only 18 percent of the electorate could name Case as a Republican candidate, only 3 percent could name Bell.[49] A week before the election, the *New York Times* thought Bell "too new on the scene to dislodge a 24-year veteran."[50]

Given his support from party leaders and in the polls, Case predicted an easy victory one week before the election.[51] So confident was Case that he spent more time in Washington than in New Jersey and he chose not to air any television commercials. He had raised only $152,000.[52] Bell, who by the end of May had raised $400,000, began running his commercials in the last week of the race. Bell played to the hearts of conservatives, calling for enactment of the Kemp-Roth tax cuts (which Case labeled "inflationary"), a blockade of Cuba, and an end to détente.[53]

In a stunning upset, Bell defeated Case by a 3,500-vote margin out of 230,000 cast. How had Bell won when only weeks before the election he was hopelessly behind? The most influential factor on the minds of voters as they left the voting booth was Bell's tax plans. Half of Bell's supporters mentioned this as a reason for supporting him, while one-fourth mentioned Case's age or his liberal voting record.[54]

Bell also benefited from an extremely low turnout that kept many moderate Republicans away from the polls. Over 1.5 million New Jerseyites

---

46. William Safire, "Republican Proxy War," *New York Times*, April 10, 1978; Reid, "Scholar-Athlete"; Sullivan, "Case Announces."

47. Edward C. Burks, "Jerseyans in House See Bradley Victory," *New York Times*, May 7, 1978.

48. Joseph F. Sullivan, "Bradley Leads Democratic Field," *New York Times*, May 19, 1978.

49. "Primary Question: Candidates' Name," *New York Times*, May 20, 1978.

50. "The Race Against Senator Case," *New York Times*, June 1, 1978.

51. Joseph Sullivan, "Case, Looking to Election, Expects the Usual Results," *New York Times*, June 1, 1978.

52. Joseph F. Sullivan, "2 Senate Races Heat Primaries," *New York Times*, June 4, 1978.

53. Joseph F. Sullivan, "Bell Finds Some Support on a Walk in Suburbs," *New York Times*, June 2, 1978.

54. T. R. Reid, "Bell's Victory: Tax Cut Idea Very Popular," *Washington Post*, June 8, 1978.

voted Republican in the 1980 election, in which Reagan won 52 percent of the vote, but only 230,000 voted in the 1978 primary election. The Case organization, overly confident of victory, made virtually no attempt to get out the vote.

Third, Bell benefited from the early stages of the emerging conservative trend that would give Reagan a landslide victory just two years later. The same day that Bell defeated Case, outspoken conservative Roger Jepsen easily defeated moderate Maurice Van Nostrand, who had the support of the incumbent governor, in Iowa's Senate primary, and voters in California passed the tax-slashing Proposition 13 by an overwhelming margin.[55]

Fourth, Case refused to adapt to the political realities of running campaigns in the contemporary United States: he made half-hearted attempts at fund-raising; he refused to run television commercials; he spent much of his time in Washington; and he ran only one poll, from an unknown organization. Bell, on the other hand, raised money from conservatives around the country and targeted Republicans likely to oppose Case through direct-mail campaigns. According to Republican leader Thomas Kean, who became governor of New Jersey in 1982, the operation of telephone banks in just two of the more populous counties would have been enough to ensure victory for Case. Several county chairmen stated that television commercials during the last week of the campaign also would have been sufficient. "He had to show people he was out there," said Bergen County Chairman Anthony Statile. According to state Republican Chairman David Norcross, who called voters on Case's behalf on election day, "People would say 'I'm mowing the lawn today—there's no problem.' "[56]

On the Democratic side, political neophyte Bill Bradley, former All-American basketball player at Princeton, All-Star forward for the New York Knicks, and Rhodes scholar, handily defeated former state treasurer Richard Leone. Bradley, with the help of celebrities Jack Nicholson, Dustin Hoffman, Paul Simon, and Patti Smith, defeated Bell in the November election by an easy, 12 percent margin. The Reagan revolution was still two years from fruition.

Javits vs. D'Amato

The Javits-D'Amato race of 1980 bears startling similarities to the Case-Bell race of 1978. Both Javits and Case had served four terms in the Senate and both Senators' main interests lay in the field of foreign affairs. When Bell

---

55. Adam Clymer, "Conservatives Win in Key Primary Races," *New York Times*, June 7, 1978.
56. Joseph F. Sullivan, "G.O.P. Leaders Lay Case's Defeat to His Failure to Change Tactics," *New York Times*, June 11, 1978.

defeated Case, Javits became the ranking Republican on the Senate Foreign Relations Committee. Javits, like Case, was a liberal Republican who was not popular with the conservative wing of his party. In fact, Javits ran for the Senate on both the Republican and Liberal party lines twice before.[57] Finally, neither were young men at the time of their last campaign: Case was seventy-four; Javits was seventy-six.

Javits was born May 18, 1904, in New York City, barely one month after Case. Like Case, Javits received his law degree from Columbia. Though liberal from the start, Javits entered politics as a Republican, largely because the corrupt Tammany Hall political machine of his youth was controlled by Democrats.[58] Javits served in the House of Representatives from 1947 to 1955. He left the House to run for state Attorney General against Franklin D. Roosevelt, Jr., whom he defeated, and Javits defeated New York City Mayor Robert Wagner by 7 percent in a tough race for U.S. Senate in 1956.

Javits quickly became one of the leaders of the liberal Republican bloc in the Senate. His ADA rankings, shown in figure 3.3, ranged between 55 and 100. In 1964 and 1965, Javits led Republican support for the civil rights and voting rights acts. According to civil rights attorney Joseph Rauh, the legislation "could never have passed without him."[59] In 1964, Javits angered many Republicans by his refusal to endorse Barry Goldwater for president. Javits's opposition to the undeclared war in Vietnam led him to sponsor the 1973 War Powers Act, which limits the right of U.S. presidents to send troops into battle without the approval of Congress. In one of Javits's lesser known acts, he broke a 142-year-old tradition by hiring a female page in 1971.[60] A poll of Senate staffers by Ralph Nader's Congress Watch rated Javits the brightest senator and the second most influential.[61]

Alphonse D'Amato was born in Brooklyn on August 1, 1937. He attended Syracuse University, where he received his J.D. in 1961. D'Amato's career began with the Nassau County Republicans on Long Island, one of the nation's last remaining political machines. In 1977, D'Amato was elected presiding supervisor of Hempstead Township and appeared to be a likely candidate some day for county executive. But D'Amato was more ambitious

---

57. The New York political landscape includes three influential minor parties—the Liberal party, the Conservative party, and the Right-to-Life party—that benefit from a state law that allows cross-endorsements. Thus, liberal Democrats fond of Javits found it easier to vote for him on the Liberal line than on the Republican line.

58. Jacob Javits, personal interview with authors, July, 1983.

59. Helen Dewar and Lee Lescaze, "Javits, Confounding Political Obit Writers, to Seek Fifth Term," *Washington Post*, February 26, 1980.

60. Bob Dole, *Historical Almanac of the United States Senate* (Washington, D.C.: U.S. Government Printing Office, 1989), 283.

61. Michael Barone, Grant Ujifusa, and Douglas Matthews, *Almanac of American Politics* (New York: E. P. Dutton, 1980), 575.

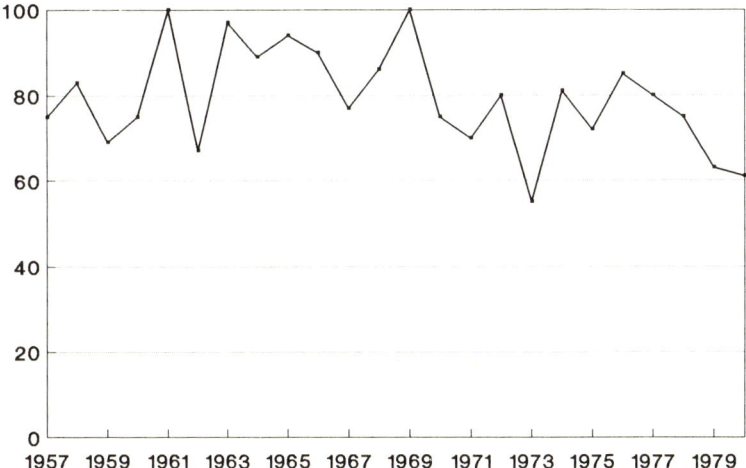

Fig. 3.3. Javits's ADA ranking, 1957–80

than that. On January 7, 1980, against the advice, but with the eventual backing, of Nassau County Republican political boss Joseph Margiotta, D'Amato announced his candidacy for the Senate seat held by Jacob Javits. The *New York Times* gave D'Amato so little chance of defeating Javits that they ran the article covering his announcement on page B6.[62]

Meanwhile, Javits had not yet revealed whether he would seek a fifth term. On February 18, an "exclusive" report on ABC by Barbara Walters stated that Javits would not run.[63] While the New York papers were quoting experts saying that Javits would not run, the Senator announced that he would on February 25. The international crises (i.e., the hostage takeover in Iran and the Soviet invasion of Afghanistan) was "the whole reason I'm standing here this morning instead of bidding you all a fond farewell."[64] Like Fulbright before him, Javits was running for statewide office on an international platform.

Despite the advantages Javits could bring to a campaign against an unknown township supervisor, D'Amato had assets of his own. First, Javits was not overly popular in the Republican party. Viewed as "aloof and abrasive,"[65] Javits had not cultivated party support. Asked Nassau County Republican

---

62. "D'Amato Seeking G.O.P. Nomination for Javits Seat," *New York Times*, January 8, 1980.
63. "Javits Reportedly Won't Run," *Washington Post*, February 19, 1980.
64. Dewar and Lescaze, "Javits."
65. Dewar and Lescaze, "Javits."

leader Joe Margiotta, "What has he ever done for the party? If one of my people had tried to challenge (Governor) Malcolm Wilson or (state Attorney General) Louis Lefkkowitz, I would have stopped it because they have campaigned for our candidates in Nassau and helped the party in fund-raising. Javits has no friends in the party."[66]

Second, Javits was far more liberal than most Republicans in New York. Like Jeffrey Bell, Al D'Amato offered a stark alternative to the incumbent he was challenging. Javits supported the Equal Rights Amendment; D'Amato opposed it. Javits supported a woman's right to choose to have an abortion; D'Amato supported a constitutional amendment barring abortion. Javits opposed the Republican party's call for the appointment of pro life judges; D'Amato supported it. Javits told reporters that he deplored the 1980 national Republican platform; D'Amato heartily endorsed it.[67]

Third, New York's Conservative party, the third largest party in the state and the party that had elected James Buckley to the Senate in 1970, endorsed D'Amato for the Senate. Doing so signaled to Republicans (1) that D'Amato would be a strong candidate if he won the Republican nomination by virtue of his dual endorsements, and (2) Javits, if he won, would be weakened in the November race by D'Amato's presence on the Conservative line. Alternatively, Javits's endorsement by the Liberal Party would help D'Amato in November—if D'Amato won the Republican line—because Javits would siphon liberal voters away from the Democratic nominee. So to the extent that voters concerned themselves with electability, Javits's position on the Liberal line was not necessarily harmful to D'Amato. D'Amato also won endorsement from the Right-to-Life party.

Fourth, and perhaps most important, Javits was aged and in ill health. We now know Javits was in the early stages of the progressive motor neuron disease amyotrophic lateral sclerosis (ALS), also known as Lou Gehrig's disease. The disease does not affect cognitive functioning, but it progressively attacks muscle functions and is eventually fatal. Though the severity of Javits's problems was not known at the time, D'Amato launched a vicious series of attacks. One commercial ended, "And now, at age 76 and in failing health, he wants six more years."[68] The camera then showed an old, crumpled picture of Javits, one that the Senator claimed was doctored to make him look ill. D'Amato's reply: "Actually in life, he looks worse than the picture."[69]

---

66. Frank Lynn, "D'Amato Could Last in Race for Senate," *New York Times*, January 13, 1980.

67. Frank Lynn, "Javits Deplores G.O.P. Policies; Foe Backs Them," *New York Times*, July 15, 1980.

68. Maurice Carroll, "D'Amato's TV Commercial Makes a Point of Javits's Health and Age," *New York Times*, August 8, 1980.

69. Joyce Wadler, "N.Y. Senate Primary: That's Entertainment," *Washington Post*, September 3, 1980.

"You take a look at the guy, and you tell me if he'll last six more years," D'Amato ghoulishly told one reporter.[70]

The Javits campaign called the spots "vulgar and crude," but evidently they were reaching enough people that Javits had to respond. "I know my age," says Javits in one commercial, "I know my health. I would not run if I could not serve."[71] Javits also brought in such Republican luminaries as Gerald Ford and Barry Goldwater for endorsements. Declared Goldwater, "I disagree with Jack Javits on just about everything, but I want him back in the United States Senate."[72] Through the middle of August, Javits had also raised more money than D'Amato, $829,000 to $600,000, but this was a much smaller advantage than usual for incumbents.[73]

D'Amato and Javits debated each other twice before the September 9 primary. In the first debate, on August 29, Javits called D'Amato "temperamentally unfit" for office. D'Amato's campaign, charged Javits, had focused with "crudeness and vulgarity" on the senator's illness. D'Amato defended his campaign and accused Javits of being "a liberal who was out of the Republican mainstream."[74] At the second debate, on September 3, Javits refused to promise his support for presidential candidate Ronald Reagan if Javits lost the Republican primary. "If the Republican nomination is denied to me, I do not know what I will do politically."[75] D'Amato promised his unequivocal and active support, regardless of the primary results.

A *New York Times* poll taken between August 23 and August 28 showed Javits leading, but D'Amato within striking distance. Among all Republicans, Javits held a 47 to 35 lead, with 18 percent undecided. About 52 percent of the Republicans (and 48 percent of the Democrats) approved of Javits's job performance. Among all voters, his approval rating was higher among Jews (63 percent) than Protestants (47 percent) or Catholics (41 percent), higher among senior citizens (52 percent) than those under 29 (34 percent), and higher among liberals (50 percent) than conservatives (44 percent).[76]

Among Republicans considered most likely to vote, Javits's lead was a more narrow 45 to 38.[77] Picking those most likely to vote in a primary is

---

70. Robin Herman, "A Persistent D'Amato Focuses On Javits's Record and Health," *New York Times*, August 23, 1980.

71. Maurice Carroll, "Javits, in Ads, Concedes His Illness and Age Are Issues in the Primary," *New York Times*, August 16, 1980.

72. Carroll, "Javits."

73. Maurice Carroll, "Two Candidates Report Spending Over $1 Million," *New York Times*, August 29, 1980.

74. Maurice Carroll, "Javits and D'Amato Debate, And the Air Is Full of Anger," *New York Times*, August 30, 1980.

75. "Excerpts from Candidates' Discussion," *New York Times*, September 2, 1980.

76. Maurice Carroll, "D'Amato's Showing In A Poll Indicates Strong Challenge," *New York Times*, September 3, 1980.

77. Carroll, "D'Amato's Showing."

fraught with difficulty, particularly in a state that had only one previous Republican Senate primary in its history; thus, the survey results could hardly be comforting to Javits. In fact, the Javits campaign was concerned that, in a low-turnout primary, a combination of highly motivated conservatives and the organizational efforts of the Nassau County Republican machine could provide enough votes for a D'Amato victory.[78] Three days before the campaign ended, a letter signed by D'Amato surfaced demonstrating D'Amato's involvement in a Nassau County kickback scandal, in which town and county employees were required to return 1 percent of their salary to the Republican party in order to receive promotions.[79] D'Amato had previously denied knowledge of the kickbacks under oath.[80]

The controversy, plus last minute visits on Javits's behalf by nine of his Senate colleagues,[81] proved insufficient to affect the outcome of the campaign. D'Amato won with 56 percent of the vote, largely as a result of sweeping his home base of Long Island, which contain the state's two largest Republican counties, by an almost 3 to 1 margin.[82] D'Amato's attacks on Javits had proven effective: one-third of the Republican voters cited Javits's age and health as a reason for voting against him.[83]

Much to the delight of D'Amato, Javits remained in the race for the general election on the Liberal line, thus siphoning votes from Democratic nominee, Congresswoman Elizabeth Holtzman. Javits won enough votes to allow D'Amato to squeeze past Holtzman by less than 2 percent of the vote.

The first three races in which incumbents were defeated featured nationally known, long-term senators, all of whom were, at the time of their defeat, their party's senior member on the Foreign Relations Committee. As the next three examples show, a great Senate career is not a prerequisite for losing a primary election.

Stewart vs. Folsom

The first low profile primary we examine is the 1980 Alabama race between incumbent Donald Stewart and challenger Jim Folsom. In 1980, Alabama had entered a new era. Through 1978, Alabama had not elected a Republican to

---

78. Maurice Carroll, "Javits Campaign Aides Call a Low Turnout Chief Fear," *New York Times*, September 1, 1980.
79. Joyce Purnick, "Letter in Nassau Kickback Case an Issue in D'Amato Campaign," *New York Times*, September 6, 1980.
80. "For the Senate From New York," *New York Times*, October 29, 1986.
81. Nancy Kassebaum of Kansas, William Cohen of Maine, Rudy Boschwitz of Minnesota, H. John Heinz 3d of Pennsylvania, Ted Stevens of Alaska, Robert Stafford of Vermont, John C. Danforth of Missouri, John Chaffee of Rhode Island, and Alan Simpson of Wyoming.
82. "County Listing of G.O.P. Vote," *New York Times*, September 10, 1980.
83. Joyce Wadler, "A Surprise Defeat," *Washington Post*, September 10, 1980.

the U.S. Senate since Reconstruction, but 1978 was the last year of Democratic electoral hegemony. George Wallace, who had run Alabama for all but a year and a half from 1962 through 1978, either directly or through his wife, retired from public office. Five-term Senator John Sparkman, a one-time populist who veered sharply to the right when civil rights hit the national agenda, also retired in 1978. The state's junior senator, James Allen, died suddenly of a heart attack in June of the same year.[84] Finally, through implementation of the Voting Rights Act of 1965, African-Americans were increasingly influential in state and local politics. The most dramatic case was Selma, where only 2.3 percent of eligible blacks were registered to vote in 1965. By 1972, this figure rose to 67 percent and blacks captured five of the ten city council seats.[85]

When James Allen died, Governor Wallace followed Southern tradition by naming Allen's widow, newswoman Maryon Allen, to the interim appointment to take his place. State Senator Donald Stewart then challenged Maryon Allen in the 1978 special election to complete James Allen's term.

Donald Stewart was born on February 8, 1940, in Munford, Alabama. He received his B.S. and J.D. from the University of Alabama in 1965 and 1972, respectively. Stewart was elected to the state House of Representatives in 1971 and to the state Senate in 1975. Stewart earned a reputation as a populist by using his seat to attack the Alabama Power Company. In 1978, Stewart sought election to the U.S. Senate seat vacated by Sparkman. Running third in the polls, Stewart dropped out of the race to challenge Maryon Allen for the remainder of her late husband's term. Stewart openly courted labor and black support, exemplifying the new generation of Southern politicians then represented by Jimmy Carter and Dale Bumpers.[86]

Maryon Allen, for her part, refused to campaign, preferring instead to spend most of her time in Washington. She caused a stir in socially conservative Alabama when she told a *Washington Post* reporter that, while in a nightgown, she invited two window washers outside her hotel room in for some coffee.[87] Allen refused to debate Stewart, at one point telling reporters that she had to miss a debate because she would be "washing my clothes (at) home" that night.[88] Allen received a plurality in the primary but not enough to avoid a runoff. Stewart won the runoff by a surprisingly easy 58 to 42 margin

---

84. See Tom Scarrit, "State's Grand Tradition of U.S. Senators: Is it Starting Anew or is Change Ahead?" *Birmingham News*, August 3, 1980.

85. Henry Abraham, *Freedom and the Court*, 4th ed. (New York: Oxford University Press, 1982), 361.

86. Bill Peterson, "Alabama Senate 'Sleeper' Catches Political Experts Dozing," *Washington Post*, October 3, 1978.

87. Sally Quinn, "Maryon Allen—The Southerngirl in the Senate," *Washington Post*, July 30, 1978.

88. Peterson, "Alabama Senate."

and then defeated Republican James Martin in the general election by a 56 to 44 margin.

Because Stewart only won the remaining two years of James Allen's term, he faced reelection just two years later. Stewart's main rival for the Democratic party nomination was state Public Service Commissioner Jim Folsom, Jr. The thirty-one-year-old Folsom was literally born to politics. His father, James "Big Jim" Folsom, served as Alabama's governor from 1947 to 1950 and from 1955 to 1958; Jim Jr. was born in the governor's mansion.[89] Folsom, Sr., was one of the few Southern politicians of his day who did not support segregation.[90] Prevented by state law from serving consecutive terms, he was not defeated until segregationist George Wallace beat him in 1962.

Jim Jr., was born on May 14, 1949. He graduated from Jackson State University and attended the Birmingham School of Law. Jim Folsom, Jr., despite his family background, had little political experience at the time of the race. Folsom worked in public relations before winning a seat on the state public utilities commission. In 1976, Folsom unsuccessfully challenged Congressman Tom Bevill for the Fifth District Democratic party congressional nomination.[91]

In the 1980 campaign, Folsom, a moderate, attacked Stewart, whose ADA rankings in two Senate years were 42 and 61, as too liberal for Alabama. According to Folsom, Stewart was a liberal puppet of the "great Washington power structure,"[92] and he was "beholden to out-of-state interests."[93] Folsom also took advantage of his family name. According to a Stewart aide, "Everywhere we went people would point to the road in front of their house and say 'Big Jim paved that road.' It had a significant impact."[94]

Stewart, for his part, used the advantages of incumbency to outspend Folsom $500,000 to about $75,000. Stewart, somewhat incredibly for a two-year senator, campaigned on the seniority he had accrued in the Senate. "Within four years, I could be in the upper fifty," Stewart told the *Birmingham News*.[95] For what it is worth in Alabama, Stewart had the support of orga-

---

89. Al Fox, "Born into Politics, Folsom Says Winning is Game's Name," *Birmingham News*, August 5, 1980.

90. Michael Barone and Grant Ujifusa, *Almanac of American Politics* (Washington D.C.: Barone and Company, 1982), 1.

91. Fox, "Born into Politics."

92. "Alabama Sen. Stewart Loses in Primary to Jim Folsom Jr.," *Washington Post*, September 24, 1980.

93. "Senator Stewart Loses in Alabama to Son of Popular Former Governor," *New York Times*, September 25, 1980.

94. "Senator Stewart Loses."

95. Tom Scarrit, "Stewart Works, Campaigns Hard to Return to Senate," *Birmingham News*, August 8, 1980.

nized labor and the state's black political organization, the Alabama Democratic Office.

Problems began to mount for Stewart in the summer when syndicated columnist Jack Anderson reported that the FBI was conducting an investigation of possible illegal campaign contributions to Stewart's 1980 campaign.[96] In his article, Anderson made the following allegations.

—Stewart accepted an illegal $22,000 corporate donation from a currently imprisoned con man, James Dennis.

—On the same day that Stewart allegedly returned the money to Dennis, Stewart loaned his own campaign $22,000. Anderson alleged (without any evidence) that Stewart might have paid Dennis by check and then received the money back from Dennis in cash. Stewart's statement that the money was a loan from a local bank was not corroborated by reports filed with the Federal Elections Commission (FEC).

—An eyewitness claimed to have seen Stewart accept $1,000 in cash from Dennis in 1978.

—Stewart had not returned another $1,500 in illegal contributions from Dennis because the FEC had not told him to do so.

On August 28, U.S. Attorney J. R. Brooks said that there had been no finding that Dennis made cash contributions to Stewart, but the government had not yet cleared Stewart.[97]

Folsom, attacking Stewart's ideology and integrity, received only 35 percent of the vote in the September 2 primary, but Stewart, with 49 percent of the vote, was 9,600 votes short of the 50 percent he needed to avoid a runoff. Stewart won easily in the heavily black counties throughout the state, but did not do as well in white, conservative counties.[98] Stewart blamed his failure to win a majority on the crowded field, but it is hard to imagine that the controversy did not cost Stewart the one additional percent of the vote he needed to avoid a runoff.[99]

Finally, on September 12, the Justice Department announced that it had cleared Stewart of all charges that he had violated federal laws on campaign financing. A letter to Stewart from Assistant Attorney General Philip Hey-

---

96. Jack Anderson, "Sen. Stewart's Answers Raise Questions," *Washington Post*, July 25, 1980.

97. Andrew Kilpatrick and Tom Scarrit, "U.S. Attorney: No Sign Stewart Got Dennis Cash," *Birmingham News*, August 29, 1980.

98. Al Fox, "Runoff Likely for Stewart as Smith, Denton Roll to Wins," *Birmingham News*, September 3, 1980.

99. Fox, "Runoff Likely."

mann said it "found no evidence to support the charges."[100] Stewart celebrated his vindication at a Montgomery fund-raiser featuring Senate Majority Leader Robert Byrd playing the fiddle.[101] Nevertheless, Jack Anderson continued to insist that Stewart was guilty.[102]

The remaining controversy in the campaign centered around Alabama's open primary system. Under that system, voters choose which party's primary to vote in on election day. On the day of the first race, Republicans presumably voted in the Republican primary and Democrats in the Democratic primary. In the Republican primary, Jeremiah Denton won a majority and, thus, faced no runoff. According to state Attorney General Charles Graddick, no state law prohibited those who voted in the Republican primary from voting in the Democratic runoff.[103] Because Folsom was the more conservative candidate, this undoubtedly helped him.[104]

Folsom won the September 24 runoff by a narrow 51 to 49 margin, or about 7,000 votes out of 400,000 cast. Folsom carried two-thirds of the counties in Alabama and even did reasonably well among black voters.[105] Stewart at first refused to concede, but finally acknowledged defeat on September 26.[106] Folsom lost in November to Jeremiah Denton, the highly religious former prisoner of war who blinked T-O-R-T-U-R-E in Morse code while being filmed by his North Vietnamese jailers. Denton was the first Republican to win a Senate seat from Alabama since Reconstruction.

Gravel vs. Gruening

The 1980 Gravel-Gruening battle was the second time in twelve years that Mike Gravel fought a Gruening for Alaska's Democratic party nomination for the Senate. In 1968, Gravel, who served as Speaker in the Alaska House of Representatives, defeated incumbent Ernest Gruening in the primary. Gruening, one of the leaders of Alaska's statehood drive, was, with E. L. Bartlett, Alaska's first Senator. He was also one of two Senators to have voted against

---

100. "Campaign Notes," *Washington Post*, September 13, 1980; "Senator Cleared of Charges," *New York Times*, September 13, 1980; Tom Scarrit, "Justice Dismisses Stewart Probe, Finds No Election Law Violation," *Birmingham News*, September 13, 1980.

101. Ralph Holmes, David Kepple, and Tom Scarrit, "Sen. Byrd Fiddles While Stewart Burns Runoff Foe," *Birmingham News*, September 16, 1980.

102. Jack Anderson, "Stewart Financial Questions Persist," *Washington Post*, September 19, 1980.

103. "Graddick Says Crossover Voting OK Next Tuesday," *Birmingham News*, September 18, 1980.

104. Unless there were some rather sophisticated Republicans who thought that Denton would have an easier race against the liberal Stewart than against the moderate Folsom.

105. "Senator Stewart Loses."

106. "Campaign Notes," *Washington Post*, September 27, 1980.

the Gulf of Tonkin Resolution, which led to our increased military involvement in the Vietnam War. In the 1980 race, thirty-seven-year-old Clark Gruening, a member of Alaska's legislature and Ernest's grandson, avenged his grandfather's loss by defeating Gravel for the same seat.

Mike Gravel was born on May 13, 1930, in Springfield, Massachusetts. Following a three-year hitch in the army, Gravel received his B.S. from Columbia University in 1956. In 1962, Gravel was elected to the Alaska House of Representatives, where he was elected Speaker in 1965. In 1966, Gravel unsuccessfully challenged incumbent Senator Ralph Rivers for the Democratic nomination for Alaska's sole House seat. Rivers, in turn, then lost to Republican Howard Pollock. In 1968, Gravel defeated incumbent Ernest Gruening by less than 2,000 votes in the Democratic primary, and then, with Gruening running as an independent, won the Senate seat in a three-way race.

Gravel was a maverick, if not an eccentric, in the Senate. When the Pentagon papers were temporarily banned, he attempted to read portions into the *Congressional Record*. When his effort was defeated by a timely objection, he broke down and cried. In 1972, Gravel nominated himself for vice president at the Democratic convention.[107] Ideologically, Gravel was a moderate (see fig. 3.4). His ADA scores ranged from 81 in 1971 to 39 in 1980. His two lowest rankings coincided with his two reelection bids, 43 in 1974 and the 39 in 1980.

Government regulation, particularly from Washington, is anathema in Alaska, where the Libertarian party is a real force in state politics. Alaskans are particularly concerned when regulations cost jobs, such as efforts to prevent the Alaska pipeline and the Carter administration's plan to withdraw millions of acres of land from all development.[108] Gravel earned tremendous goodwill among Alaska's voters in 1973 when he pushed legislation through the Senate that exempted the oil pipeline from the Environmental Impact Act. The next year he handily won his party's primary and easily defeated Republican candidate and John Bircher, C. R. Lewis, 58 to 42 in the general election.

The 1980 Gravel-Gruening race centered around the Carter administration's land bill. Most Alaskans and both Senators opposed the measure; the only question was how best to fight it. Back in 1978, the Carter administration temporarily protected 80 million acres of land pending a resolution of the matter by Congress. The House followed this by protecting even more land than the Carter administration. Alaska's senior Senator, Republican minority whip Ted Stevens, engineered a compromise that protected less than the 80 million acres the Carter administration wanted and freed up much more land for development. Environmentalists thought Stevens had won far too much.

---

107. Barone and Ujifusa, *Almanac* (1982), 19.
108. Barone and Ujifusa, *Almanac* (1982), 19.

76 Senate Elections

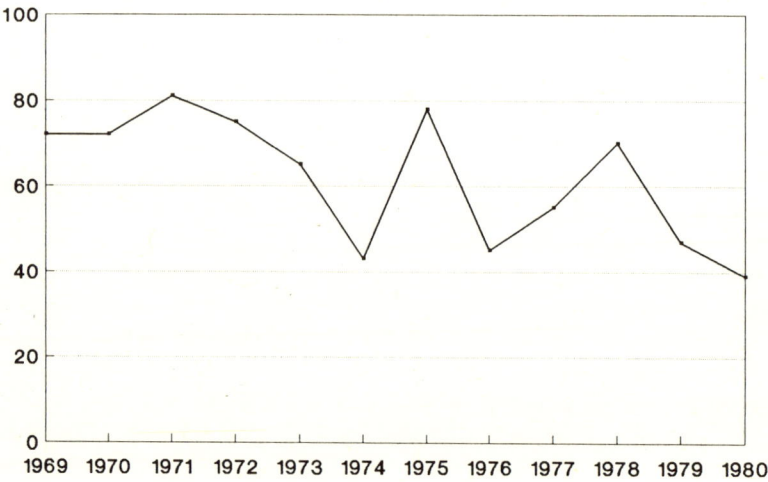

Fig. 3.4. Gravel's ADA ranking, 1969–80

But Gravel opposed the compromise and single-handedly defeated the bill by filibustering until the end of the session.[109]

Gravel's victory was short lived, for Interior Secretary Cecil Andrus reacted by unilaterally protecting 102 million acres through various administrative procedures. This administrative freeze on development was permanent, though it could be altered by Congress.[110]

The 1978 scenario repeated itself in 1980, just weeks before the primary. The House passed a bill that protected 159 million acres from development. Stevens again sought a compromise, while Gravel again attempted to filibuster. This time the filibuster was defeated by a sixty-three to twenty-five vote.[111] The Senate passed the bill the next day, seventy-eight to fourteen.[112] Gravel's campaign, which was based on his seniority and influence in Washington, was badly damaged.[113] Gravel started the campaign trailing Gruening by about nine points, but was six to nine points ahead while he was fighting the bill. After the filibuster was defeated and the bill passed, Gravel lost

---

109. Barone and Ujifusa, *Almanac* (1982), 19.
110. Barone and Ujifusa, *Almanac* (1982), 19.
111. Betty Mills, "Senate Shuts Off D2 Debate," *Anchorage Times*, August 18, 1980.
112. "Senate Passes Bill," *Anchorage Times*, August 19, 1980.
113. Ellis Conklin, "Insiders Say Gravel's on the Run," *Anchorage Times*, August 20, 1980; Wallace Turner, "Polls Indicate Gravel Is in Trouble in Alaska's Senate Primary Today," *New York Times*, August 25, 1980.

somewhere between nine and eighteen points.[114] Two weeks later, polls still showed a six-point Gruening lead.[115]

Further damaging Gravel's campaign was an unprecedented endorsement of Gruening in the Democratic primary by the Republican, Stevens. Though Stevens said he would support the Republican nominee no matter who won the Democratic primary, he also told voters "I know I could work better with (Gruening) than I could with Mike."[116] While an attack from an opposition party senator would not ordinarily hurt a senator in his own primary, two factors worked against Gravel here. First, Stevens was enormously popular: he was elected in 1972 and 1978 with over 75 percent of the vote; he was also no doubt still receiving sympathy for the 1978 plane crash that injured him and killed his wife. Second, under Alaska's open primary, voters are handed a ballot with both party's races printed on them; they then choose whichever party's race they want, and Gruening openly appealed for crossover support.[117] With little opposition to businessman Frank Murkowski in the Republican primary, crossover voting could be crucial to the race.

Additionally, Gravel was under attack from the Friends of Alaska Committee, an independent campaign organization headed by Barney Gottstein, a former Gravel supporter who broke with the Senator over his support for arms sales to Egypt. The group ran countless radio advertisements poking fun at Gravel's vice presidential bid, his plan to build a domed city on Mt. McKinley, and his killing of the 1978 compromise land bill.[118] Though the committee was run independently of Gruening's campaign, Gottstein was also Gruening's chief fund-raiser. Gravel went to court to get an injunction against further airing of the commercials, but U.S. District Court Judge James Fitzgerald turned him down.[119]

The final twist to the campaign came following Gravel's lost filibuster. With only one week left in the race, Gravel seemed a probable loser. In a last-ditch effort to save his faltering campaign, Gravel accused Gruening of accepting money from a special interest group: Jews. According to Gravel, Gruening broke a pledge not to accept money from special interests by soliciting donations from out-of-state Jewish individuals.[120] "There's no question

---

114. Helen Dewar, "Gravel's Stand Against a Land Bill Could Help Him," *Washington Post*, August 3, 1980; Turner, "Polls Indicate."

115. Bill Kosen, "Senate Race Narrows to 6 Points," *Anchorage Times*, August 24, 1980.

116. Wallace Turner, "Animosity Marks Alaska Senate Race," *New York Times*, June 19, 1980.

117. Helen Dewar, "Maverick Gravel is Defeated," *Washington Post*, August 28, 1980.

118. Conklin, "Insiders."

119. Ellis Conklin, "Angry Gravel Seeks Court Order to Halt Radio Ads," *Anchorage Times*, August 15, 1980.

120. Ellis Conklin, "Gravel vs. Gruening," *Anchorage Times*, August 22, 1980.

[the money] is from a special interest group that seeks to influence the foreign policy of the U.S.," declared Gravel.[121] Gravel himself had raised $540,000, of which $230,000 came from special-interest PACs. Gruening accepted no PAC contributions. About one-fourth of Gruening's $230,000 in individual contributions came from out of state. In Gruening's own words, "Undoubtedly some Jewish individuals contributed; so did Protestants."[122]

Gruening won the August 26 primary by a 55 to 44 percent margin in voting that contained a heavy crossover element.[123] Nineteen thousand Alaskans voted in the 1978 Democratic primary and 27,000 voted in the 1984 Democratic primary. Yet, 71,000 voted in the 1980 Democratic primary. This cannot be explained simply by a 1980 turnout increase, for, on the Republican side, turnout was down in 1980. Thirty-nine thousand Alaskans voted in the 1974 Republican primary, 65,000 Alaskans voted in the 1984 Republican primary when Stevens ran unopposed, while only 25,000 voted in the three-person 1980 primary.

While Republicans may have given Gruening the Democratic nomination for Senator, they were not about to give him the election. Republican nominee Murkowski defeated Gruening by a 54 to 46 percent margin in the November election.

Stone vs. Gunter

The final primary during the 1974–90 period in which a Senate incumbent was defeated was the 1980 race between Florida's Democratic incumbent Richard Stone and former Congressman Bill Gunter, who was then state insurance commissioner. The Stone-Gunter primary was a rematch of the 1974 race, when Gunter finished first in an eleven-person race but lost in the runoff to Stone.

Richard Stone, like so many Floridians, is a transplanted Yankee. Stone was born on September 22, 1928, in New York City. He received his B.A. from Harvard in 1949 and his LL.B. from Columbia in 1954. Stone began his political career in 1966, when he served as Miami city attorney. That same year he was elected to the Florida Senate, where he served until 1970. In 1970, Stone was elected to statewide office as Florida's secretary of state. He served there until 1974, when he sought election to the U.S. Senate.

Bill Gunter was born in Florida, on July 16, 1934. He received a B.S.A. from the University of Florida in 1956. Gunter worked in the insurance

---

121. John Greely, "Gravel Raps Rival on Jewish Donors," *Washington Post*, August 26, 1980.

122. Greely, "Gravel."

123. Wallace Turner, "Gravel Loses a Bitter Fight in Senate Primary in Alaska," *New York Times*, August 28, 1980.

business before his election to the Florida Senate in 1966. He served in the state Senate until 1972, when he was elected to a newly created Congressional district that included a substantial portion of Gunter's state district. This was hardly coincidence: Gunter served on the state Senate Reapportionment and Redistricting Committee that created the district.[124]

The authors of *The Almanac of American Politics* considered Gunter a potential opponent to Republican Senator Edward Gurney in 1974.[125] Gurney was then best known as President Nixon's staunchest defender on the Senate Watergate Committee. In 1974, the association of Gurney and Nixon grew even closer as Gurney was indicted for taking bribes from developers in return for help dealing with the FHA. Gurney chose not to run for reelection.

The two leading candidates in the 1974 Democratic primary were Gunter and Stone. Gunter was the favorite, but Stone successfully downplayed his New York/Miami/Jewish/Harvard image by playing a harmonica and spoons on campaign trips in North Florida. Stone's 20 percent of the vote in the primary was 300 votes more than third-place finisher Richard Pettigrew's, and put Stone into the runoff with first-place finisher Gunter. Stone's big issue in the runoff was a vote by Gunter for a bill to compensate owners of deceased diseased chickens. Stone argued that this was not the government's job and won the runoff by a narrow 51 to 49 margin.[126] In the Republican primary, millionaire drug store owner Jack Eckerd defeated state public utilities commissioner Paula Hawkins. The November race also included the candidacy of John Grady, who ran on George Wallace's American Independent party ticket and received 16 percent of the vote. Stone defeated Eckerd by a narrow 1.6 percent margin.

From 1975 through 1980, Stone served as a moderate-to-conservative Southern Democrat. Though his ADA ratings hit 50 in 1976, he was otherwise consistently in the 20s and 30s (see fig. 3.5). He voted for the neutron bomb, for deregulation of natural gas, and against funding medically necessary abortions, but voted for the Panama Canal treaty, for public funding of congressional campaigns, and against an early version of the Kemp-Roth tax cuts.[127] Stone served on the Agriculture and Foreign Relations committees.

Stone's service in the Senate left him vulnerable to challenge on several counts. First, Stone infuriated organized labor by reneging on a promise to vote for cloture on the 1978 labor law reform. According to two witnesses, Stone promised to vote for cloture, but gave no promise on the bill itself. When cloture came to a vote, Stone voted no. He later accused one of the

---

124. Barone, Ujifusa, and Matthews, *Almanac* (1974), 197.
125. Barone, Ujifusa, and Matthews, *Almanac* (1974), 197.
126. Barone, Ujifusa, and Matthews, *Almanac* (1976), 161–62.
127. Barone, Ujifusa, and Matthews, *Almanac* (1980), 174.

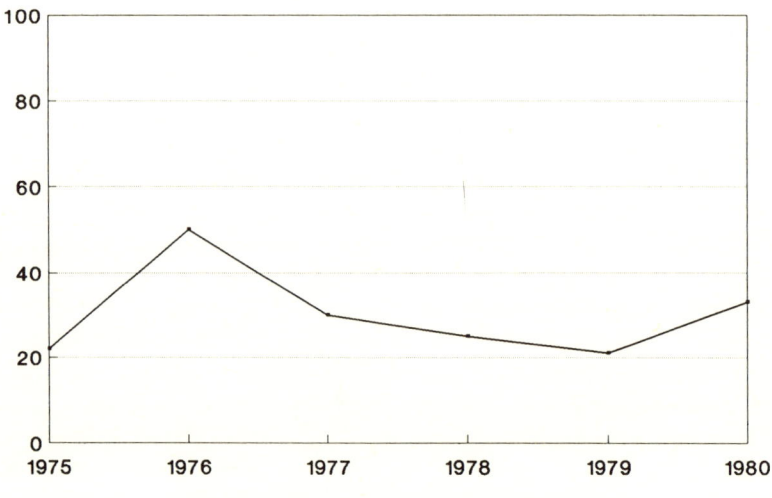

Fig. 3.5. Stone's ADA ranking, 1975–80

witnesses to his promise of lying.[128] As a result, the AFL-CIO actively campaigned against Stone.

Stone also changed his mind on several highly emotional issues. In 1974, Stone campaigned against the proposed Panama Canal Treaty; he voted for it in 1978. In 1980, Stone voted in committee for substantial cuts in food stamps for families with school-age children, then switched and opposed the cuts. He originally opposed prayer in schools but then voted for it in 1979; later still he called his vote a mistake.[129] Stone voted for and against the B-1 bomber, and for and against higher pay for the military.[130]

Stone was seen as so weak that six Democrats entered the race for their party's nomination. The most prominent challenger was Bill Gunter, who was then Florida's treasurer and insurance commissioner. Also challenging Stone was Florida state Senator Kenneth (Buddy) MacKay, former Florida House Speaker Richard Pettigrew, gasoline retailer Jim Miller, retired Air Force officer John Coffey, and a twice-convicted felon, restaurant owner Don MacKenzie of Miami Beach.

However weak Stone appeared to his fellow Democrats, he was the incumbent and thus had fund-raising opportunities unavailable to his opponents. By the middle of August, Stone had raised about $1.4 million, more than all of his opponents combined. Construction industries supportive of his antilabor stands gave $75,000; restaurants appreciative of his support for

---

128. Robert Ryan, "Stone Learns to Avoid Promises," *Miami Herald*, August 25, 1980.
129. Ryan, "Stone Learns."
130. Robert Shaw, "Sizing Up the Senate Races," *Miami Herald*, October 5, 1980.

subminimum wages for their employees gave $33,000; utility companies grateful for his support of nuclear power added $30,000. In contrast, Gunter had raised about $500,000, 20 percent of which came from the insurance industry he regulated. Buddy MacKay had raised about $350,000, but was wealthy enough to kick in $400,000 of his own money. Pettigrew, the AFL-CIO endorsed candidate, had raised only $115,000. The remaining candidates had raised less than $10,000.[131]

Of the four leading contestants, Stone, Gunter, MacKay, and Pettigrew, only Pettigrew ran to the left of center. Pettigrew opposed efforts to balance the budget, as the country was in a recession. Stone, Gunter, and MacKay supported a balanced budget regardless of economic conditions. Pettigrew also supported wage and price controls on the nation's 1,000 largest corporations, and ultimately wanted to break them up. Stone took the most extreme position on federal spending, supporting a constitutional amendment to limit spending to a fixed percentage of the Gross National Product. All favored higher defense spending, with Pettigrew proposing a 6 percent increase, Stone a 5 percent increase, and Gunter and MacKay some unspecified amount. Pettigrew alone opposed the B-1 bomber. Pettigrew supported Stone's vote for the Panama Canal treaty, while Gunter and MacKay railed against it.[132]

Stone's run as a conservative was enhanced by the support of former Congressman Robert Sikes and several former backers of George Wallace.[133] Despite Sikes's uncontested promilitary credentials, Gunter tried to paint Stone as weak on defense during the primary's only televised debate.[134]

One week before the primary, a *St. Petersburg Times* poll showed Stone leading his rivals with 29 percent, followed by Gunter with 24 percent and MacKay at 18 percent. Among those most likely to vote, MacKay was almost even with Gunter, though both still trailed Stone. Twenty percent of the voters remained undecided.[135]

The results of the primary were consistent with the polls. Stone led with 32 percent—not enough to avoid a runoff—followed by Gunter with 30 percent and MacKay at 25 percent. The 1980 runoff would be the same as the 1974 runoff: Stone versus Gunter.

---

131. Robert Shaw, Jr., "Special Interests Open Wallets to Help Stone Keep Senate Seat," *Miami Herald*, August 24, 1980.

132. Robert Shaw, "Pettigrew is Sticking with his Fiscal Principles," *Miami Herald*, August 28, 1980; Barbara O'Reilley, "How Stone, Rivals Stand on the Issues," *Miami Herald*, August 29, 1980; William Amlong and Stephen Doig, "Senate Hopefuls Agree—But Still Fuss," *Miami Herald*, September 7, 1980.

133. Fay S. Joyce, "Stone is Favorite In Fla. Race but Runoff is Likely," *Washington Post*, September 9, 1980.

134. William Amlong, "'Mister' Stone Backs his Record in Debate," *Miami Herald*, August 29, 1980.

135. Joyce, "Stone Favorite."

The runoff quickly turned ugly as the candidates leveled charges and countercharges at each other. A Gunter television commercial accused Stone of voting against efforts "to get the cocaine cowboys off the streets of Miami," based on a Stone vote against foreign aid to Columbia.[136] Stone scheduled an advertisement, later withdrawn, asserting that insurance rates had doubled or tripled under Gunter. In fact, some rates had gone down, while others were up no more than 25 percent. Stone accused Gunter of covering up $200,000 in anonymous campaign contributions even though Gunter had publicly distributed lists of all contributors and was in compliance with FEC regulations. To the extent that the candidates discussed substantive issues, it was largely Gunter attacking Stone's vote on the Panama Canal, Gunter's attempts to repatriate criminal Cuban refugees, and Stone's return to the diseased chickens issue.[137] According to Robert Shaw of the *Miami Herald*, the only thing the candidates had in common was that each thought the other to be "vicious, sleazy, unprincipled, callow and basically unfit to be a U.S. Senator."[138]

With Stone's other opponents out of the race, Gunter raised an additional $400,000 through the middle of September, while Stone had only raised another $200,000. An independent poll showed the two men essentially tied: 44 percent for Gunter and 43 percent for Stone. It appeared that the race would largely depend on turnout. Stone was favored in the panhandle, where Sikes campaigned with Stone for the conservative vote, and heavily favored in South Florida, where he made explicit appeals for the Jewish vote. According to one supporter, "He'll get well over 60 percent in Broward. The question is: 60 percent of what?"[139]

A day before the runoff, Florida papers published stories linking Stone to a grand jury investigation of a government sale of peanut oil. The *Dallas Morning News*, which originally broke the story, later reported that Stone was not a subject of the investigation, and the Justice Department said that Stone was cleared of any involvement. Unfortunately for Stone, there was hardly time for such news to help.[140]

Gunter won the runoff by a 52 to 48 percent margin. Stone won by 2 to 1 in South Florida's Dade and Broward counties, home of Miami and Fort Lauderdale, and 3 to 2 in Palm Beach, but lost everywhere else.[141] Stone even

---

136. Shaw, "Senate Races."
137. "Both Contenders Losing Points in Bitter Florida Runoff," *New York Times*, October 6, 1980.
138. Shaw, "Senate Races."
139. Shaw, "Senate Races."
140. "Campaign Notes," *Washington Post*, October 7, 1980; "Challenger Gunter Defeats Sen. Stone in Florida Democratic Primary Runoff," *Washington Post*, October 8, 1980; Robert Shaw, "For Sen. Stone, No News is Good News," *Miami Herald*, October 6, 1980.
141. Robert Shaw and Stephen Doig, "Gunter Unseats Sen. Stone Despite South Florida Vote," *Miami Herald*, October 8, 1980.

lost the panhandle, which, according to Stone's campaign manager, William Rubin, was largely due to Stone's support for the Panama Canal treaty.[142] Stone agreed.[143]

Gunter, like Jeff Bell, Jim Folsom, and Clark Gruening, defeated his party's incumbent for the Senate nomination but was unable to win the November election. Gunter lost to former state public service commissioner Paula Hawkins, whose 1986 bid for reelection is chronicled in chapter 7.

Defeating Incumbents

We stated at the beginning of this section that the most difficult path to a Senate seat is by challenging an incumbent for his or her party's nomination. Between 1974 and 1990, 147 people have done so in 110 races. Only six won their party's nomination and only two, Governor Dale Bumpers of Arkansas and Hempstead Township Supervisor Alphonse D'Amato of New York, won the November election. Bumpers won largely due to a personal popularity unmatched in modern times, and D'Amato held on in a tight November race only because the defeated incumbent, Jacob Javits, remained on the Liberal party ticket.

The overwhelming rate at which incumbents receive their party's nomination makes systematic analyses of the factors involved when they lose difficult, but our case studies point in the following directions.

In four of the six races, Arkansas, New Jersey, New York, and Alabama, the defeated incumbents were significantly more liberal than their party constituents. The incumbent's liberalism was one of the major issues in all of these races except Arkansas. Case's voting record was the major reason Bell was able to defeat him, and it is unlikely that D'Amato could have beaten, or indeed would have challenged, Javits on the health issue alone. Stewart was close enough to avoiding a runoff in Alabama that his moderate voting record in conservative Alabama is one of two factors that probably prevented him from winning. In Arkansas, Bumpers never challenged Fulbright's record, and did not offer himself as a more conservative alternative to the senior senator. It would be speculative, at best, to claim that support for Bumpers was due to voter disenchantment with the positions of Fulbright with little consideration of his opponent.[144] Finally, though ideology per se was not an

---

142. Judith Miller, "Senator Beaten in Florida Race for Nomination," *New York Times*, October 8, 1980.

143. Fay Joyce, "South Florida Vote Didn't Pull Stone Through," *Washington Post*, October 9, 1980.

144. But see V. O. Key, *The Responsible Electorate* (New York: Vintage, 1966), 61; Morris Fiorina, *Retrospective Voting in American National Elections* (New Haven: Yale University Press, 1981).

issue in Florida, one particular issue was: Stone's vote for the Panama Canal treaty. Thus, in five of the six races, voters rejected incumbents who, in one way or another, were not broadly (four cases) or narrowly (one case) representing the preferences of their party constituents. This pattern holds for defeated incumbent Alan Dixon (D-Illinois) as well, who was significantly more conservative than one would expect an Illinois Democrat to be. The Illinois primary winner, Carol Mosely Braun, particularly focused attention on Dixon's vote in support of conservative Supreme Court nominee Clarence Thomas.

In four of the races, the incumbent was weakened by a significant controversy in one form or another. In the New York race it was the deteriorating health of Senator Javits. In Alabama and Florida, there were real and alleged investigations into the financial affairs of the incumbent. In the Alabama case, Stewart might have easily won without a runoff had he been cleared prior to the first-round voting. In Florida, Stone was attacked and then cleared in the last two days of the campaign, and there is simply not enough information available to determine whether the charges affected the runoff. In Alaska, the controversy surrounding Gravel centered around his refusal to compromise on the Alaska land bill, resulting in a far worse bill than otherwise could have been achieved. Though neither Bumpers nor Bell raised age as an issue, voters in both states were no doubt aware that the incumbents were sixty-nine and seventy-four years old.

Finally, money has not been a necessary condition for defeating incumbents in primaries. Only Jeffrey Bell outspent his competitor, who, certain of victory, refused to campaign actively. In New York and Florida, the challengers raised reasonable amounts of money, but the challengers in Arkansas (Bumpers), Alabama (Folsom), and Alaska (Gruening) were badly outspent, with Bumpers and Gruening actually aiding their opponents' fund-raising advantages by strictly limiting the contributions they would accept. Though Folsom, Bumpers, and Gruening were outspent, all had name-recognition advantages that made money less important to them than it is for typical challengers: Folsom's father was governor, Bumpers himself was governor, and Gruening's grandfather was senator. No primary challenger defeated an incumbent without a well-known name or money to make it known.[145]

Vote Shares and Victory Margins

To the extent that the factors discussed previously affect primary elections, they should have an influence across the population of cases, not just those in

---

145. In the 1992 Illinois race, Braun, a Cook County office holder, neither spent a large amount of money nor had tremendous name recognition outside of Chicago. She did benefit, though, from the $4 million a third candidate, Albert Hofeld, spent attacking Dixon.

which the incumbent won. While these factors are usually not sufficient to change the result of the primary, they should be strong enough to significantly affect the vote margin of the incumbent. As we show in chapter 4, a divisive primary can have catastrophic effects on incumbents even when they win: those who win primaries by anything less than a sixty-eight-point landslide can be expected to be hurt in November; those who win a close primary will lose, on average, over seven points in the November race. Thus, it is crucial to incumbents not just to win primaries, but to win by overwhelming margins. Using the ninety-eight races in which credible candidates challenged incumbents between 1974 and 1988 as our sample, we examine the effect of challenger quality, incumbent ideology, well-publicized controversies, and campaign expenditures on election margins. We then apply these results to the 1990 primaries.

Candidate Quality

Through the 1988 primaries, the average victory margin in primary elections is fifty-four points in favor of the incumbent. One reason for the poor showing by primary challengers of incumbents is that the overwhelming majority lack sufficient political experience to launch a serious campaign. In House races, political scientists have usually considered anyone who has held any elected office as a "high-quality" challenger.[146] But just as being a House member has been insufficient experience in running for president, merely holding some elected office is usually insufficient experience to unseat a senator of one's own party. We therefore narrow the criteria for "high-quality" candidates in these races to governors and members of Congress. In only ten of the ninety-eight races did incumbents face a high-quality challenger. High-quality candidates finished first in two of their ten races (20 percent) while low-quality challengers finished first in only four of eighty-eight races (4.5 percent) ($p = .051$, $\gamma = .68$). More important in terms of the competitiveness of such races, high-quality challengers lost by an average of 12.6 points (with a standard deviation of 22.8), while low-quality challengers lost by an astonishing average of 59.0 points (with a standard deviation of 24.6). The difference between the two means is significant at $p < .001$.

Incumbent Ideology

One factor that can aid a primary challenger is a lack of responsiveness of an incumbent to his or her partisan constituents. For example, Republican chal-

---

146. Gary Jacobson, "Strategic Politicians and the Dynamics of U.S. House Elections, 1946–1986," *American Political Science Review* 83 (1989): 773–94.

lengers might fare better if a credible case can be made that the incumbent is too liberal. The same might be true for primary challengers to Southern Democrats. Alternatively, challengers to Northern Democrats might increase their support if the incumbent they face is too conservative for his or her partisan constituents.

To test whether incumbents are punished in primaries for flouting the ideological desires of their partisan constituents, we compared how liberally Senators voted, as measured by the support scores given by the Americans for Democratic Action (ADA), with how liberally we predict them to vote given the ideology of their constituents, their party, and, for Southern Democrats, their region.[147] Next, we divided Senators into three groups, those who were more liberal than their constituents, those who were about where their constituents were, and those who were more conservative. We then compared primary results of those who were *super partisans* (Democrats who are more liberal than their constituents; Republicans and Southern Democrats who are more conservative than their constituents), *partisans* (Democrats and Republicans who vote within twenty points of where one would expect), and *insufficient partisans* (liberal Republicans and Southern Democrats and conservative Northern Democrats).

In terms of both election outcomes and victory margins, the super partisans fared at least as well as the partisans, and both did significantly better than insufficient partisans. For election outcomes, the super partisans won all twelve of their races (100 percent), the partisans won sixty-six of their sixty-eight races (97 percent), and the insufficient partisans won fourteen of their eighteen races (78 percent) ($p < .01$, $\gamma = .85$). The average victory margins were 59.6 percent for the super partisans (SD = 24.1), 57.5 percent for the partisans (SD = 25.7) and 38.3 percent for the insufficient partisans (SD = 34.6). The significance of the findings during the period studied are clear. For primary elections, one could not be too liberal a Northern Democrat or too conservative a Southern Democrat or Republican. Yet, as conservative white Southerners leave the Democratic party, leaving the party more liberal, the situation for Southern Democratic Senators should change.

Political Controversies

Attacks by challengers on incumbents need not be limited to the overall voting record of the incumbent. Scandals, health questions, and well-publicized

---

147. The expected ADA scores are the predictions from a regression equation with actual ADA scores as the dependent variable and state-level ideology (as measured by state support for McGovern in 1972 and Mondale in 1984) and partisanship (with Northern and Southern Democrats counting separately) as the independent variables (see Segal, Cameron, and Cover, "Spatial Model".)

political controversies can reduce support for incumbents. Although no members of the Senate were convicted of a crime during the period covered by this chapter, several Senators were subjects of investigations based on allegations of official or personal misconduct. Others were involved in incidents that raised questions about their honesty, personal judgment, or competence. Others still were subject to questions about their health or physical vigor.

Of the ninety-eight incumbents facing primary challenges from 1974 through 1988, fourteen were involved in controversies of this type.[148] Incumbents involved in significant controversies won ten out of fourteen races (71 percent) while those uninvolved in such controversies won eighty-two of eighty-four races (98 percent) ($p < .001$, $\gamma = .89$). In terms of victory margins, those involved in controversies won by an average of 26.5 percent (SD = 32.2), while those uninvolved won by 58.9 percent (SD = 24.6). The difference in means is significant at $p < .001$.

Campaign Expenditures

Finally, we might expect campaign spending to affect the electoral consequences of challengers and incumbents. Modern senate races are dominated by television advertising, even in such rural states as South Dakota (see chap. 7). Challengers will typically have little chance of getting their message across if they do not have the ability to spend large amounts of money.

We are limited in our consideration of the impact of campaign expenditures by both practical and theoretical concerns. Practical concerns involve the availability of data. The Federal Elections Commission does not have records on preprimary campaign expenditures until 1978. Thus, we must exclude the 1974 and 1976 races from our analysis. This leaves us with seventy-two incumbent races to consider instead of our original ninety-eight.

The theoretical concerns involve our ability to assess the effect of campaign expenditures from campaign spending data. The problem is that incumbents who expect a tight race will spend as much as possible, while

---

148. The fourteen included as being involved in a significant controversy of one form or another are taken from Alan Abramowitz, "Explaining Senate Election Outcomes," *American Political Science Review* 82 (1988): 385–404, where the Senators overlap. Where they do not, we add Jacob Javits (1980), whose failing health became the critical issue in his primary race against D'Amato; Mike Gravel (1980), whose refusal to compromise on the Alaskan land bill led to a much worse bill for Alaskans than otherwise could have been achieved; Donald Stewart (1980), whose campaign finances were being investigated by the Justice Department throughout his primary campaign; Richard Stone (1980), who was linked to a grand jury investigation of a peanut oil scandal just one day before his runoff; and David Durenberger (1988), whose personal financial dealings were just beginning to come under public scrutiny. Finally, we subtract from the Abramowitz list James Abdnor (1986), whose gaffes concerning farm policy occurred after the primary.

incumbents who expect an easy victory might save their money for the general election or might simply not put much effort into raising money. Thus, incumbents in close races will be expected to spend a lot of money, while incumbents in easy races might not be expected to spend much money at all. The result of this is that we might seriously underestimate the effect of campaign expenditures.

With these concerns in mind we examine the data. In the fifty primaries we examine since 1978, incumbents overwhelmed their competitors in preprimary expenditures. Incumbents spent an average of $922,000; their *combined* opponents spent an average of only $164,000. In the average race, incumbents accounted for 87.8 percent of all expenditures. Thus, in the average race, challengers have virtually no ability to attack the incumbent's record. We present the distribution of expenditures in table 3.4. In fifty-one of the seventy-two races, incumbents accounted for 90 percent or more of the total spent. In other words, in these races they outspent the combined totals of their opponents by better than nine to one. In ten of the remaining twenty-three races, incumbents spent 70 percent to 89 percent of the preprimary total.

Alternatively, there were five races where incumbents were outspent. In 1978, Edward Brooke (R-Massachusetts) was barely outspent by his opponent, Avi Nelson. Brooke won the primary by a slender 6.6 percent margin, only to lose in November. Mark Hatfield (R-Oregon) was also outspent by his opponents in 1978, but it took three of them to do so. Hatfield spent $65,000, Bert Hawkins spent $64,000, Richard Schneppie spent $4,000, and Robert Maxwell reported no expenditures. Despite Hawkins's spending, Hatfield won by a 48 percent margin. Three Senators were outspent in 1982: Howard Cannon (D-Nevada), Robert Stafford (R-Vermont), and Daniel Moynihan (D-New York). Cannon won a narrow 50 to 46 victory despite being badly

TABLE 3.4. Proportion of Preprimary Expenditures by Incumbents, 1978–88

Percentage of Total Expenditures	Number of Races	Percentage of Races
0	1	1.4
30–39	1	1.4
40–49	3	4.2
50–59	2	2.8
60–69	3	4.2
70–79	4	5.6
80–89	6	8.3
90–100	51	70.8

Note: Neither William Proxmire (D-Wisconsin) nor his opponent recorded any expenditures in their 1982 primary.

outspent by Congressman James Santini. Like Brooke, Cannon then lost his November race. Stafford was slightly outspent by challenger Stewart Ledbetter, who lost in a three-person race by a respectable 11.5 percent. Finally, Daniel Patrick Moynihan reported no primary expenditures in his race against Melvin Klenetsky, a follower of currently imprisoned U.S. Labor party leader Lyndon LaRouche. Moynihan defeated Klenetsky by a 70 percent margin.

Despite the Moynihan race, the correlation between incumbent expenditure share and incumbent vote margin is $r = .61$. If the Moynihan race is excluded, the correlation jumps to $r = .75$. Thus, in the cases we examine, there appears to be a strong relationship between campaign expenditures and vote margins.

If primary campaign expenditures are crucial to primary vote margins, we might ask what affects the ability of challengers to spend large amounts of money? Obviously, challengers who are millionaires will be able to spend large amounts of their own money. Additionally, high-quality candidates, previously defined as governors or members of Congress, should be able to raise and spend large amounts of money. In fact, the quality of the challenger is an excellent predictor of challenger expenditures. High-quality challengers spent an average of $1,138,000 in primary campaigns; low-quality challengers spent only $77,000 on average. In races with high-quality challengers, 60 percent of the expenditures were by incumbents; in races with low-quality challengers, 90 percent of expenditures were by incumbents. Virtually no relationship exists between the existence of a political controversy and the challenger's ability to raise funds.

A Multivariate Analysis

We conclude this chapter with an examination of the independent effect that each of our variables has on the vote margin through multiple regression analysis. We present two analyses: one for the entire data set (1974–88), thus excluding campaign finance, and one for the 1978–88 data set, with campaign finance. The results are presented in tables 3.5 and 3.6.

For 1974 through 1988 (table 3.5), three variables appear to be extremely important in predicting the incumbent's vote margin: the existence of a controversy, the incumbent's voting record, and the quality of the challenger. A high-quality challenger will decrease the incumbent's vote margin by almost 34 points, controlling for other factors. An insufficient partisan, that is, a conservative Northern Democrat, a liberal Southern Democrat, or a liberal Republican, will lose more than 11 points compared to a senator who faithfully represents his or her partisan constituents. (Note though that there is no penalty, and perhaps some bonus, for super partisans. Democrats who are too liberal for their districts, and Republicans and Southern Democrats who are too conservative, do not appear to suffer electoral consequences in primaries. As shown in chapter 4, though, such ideologues will suffer electoral consequences in the November elections. Additionally, the number of challengers, included as a control variable, does not affect the incumbent's victory margin.) Finally, the existence of a controversy appears to cost incumbent Senators more than twenty-two points.

If we examine only the 1978–88 races and add campaign spending to the model (table 3.6), a slightly different picture appears. Challenger quality and the existence of a political controversy remain important; they cost incumbents twenty-one and seventeen points respectively. Challenger quality additionally has a crucial indirect effect on electoral margin because of the strong effect it has on the incumbent's spending ratio ($r = .42$). Ignoring the preferences of one's partisan constituents appears less important in this model. The results suggest that insufficient partisans will lose, on average, almost six points after controlling for other factors, but the results are not statistically

TABLE 3.5. Regression Analysis of Vote Margin, 1974–88

Variable	b	SE	β	p
Quality	−33.98	5.98	−.47	.001
Controversy	−22.72	6.73	−.28	.001
Super partisan	6.99	7.04	.08	NS
Insufficient partisan	−11.46	6.09	−.16	.03
Number of challengers	−1.45	3.61	−.03	NS
Constant	98.82	8.38	—	.001

Notes: $N = 98$; Adjusted $R^2 = .38$. b = unstandardized regression coefficient; SE = standard error; β = standardized regression coefficient; significance levels are based on one-tailed t-tests; NS = not significant at $p < .05$.

TABLE 3.6. Regression Analysis of Vote Margin, 1978–88

Variable	b	SE	β	p
Quality	−20.74	9.98	−.21	.02
Controversy	−17.25	7.17	−.23	NS
Super partisan	−0.04	7.40	−.00	NS
Insufficient partisan	−5.86	6.72	−.08	NS
Expenditure ratio	0.64	0.13	.48	.001
Number of challengers	0.80	3.59	.02	NS
Constant	23.61	19.44	—	NS

Notes: $N = 72$; Adjusted $R^2 = .45$. b = unstandardized regression coefficient; SE = standard error; β = standardized regression coefficient; significance levels are based on one-tailed t-tests; NS = not significant at $p < .05$.

significant. However, challengers of insufficient partisans are not better able to raise money than are other challengers ($r = .08$), so the decline in effect shown in the second model is due to the exclusion of the 1974 and 1976 cases. Clearly, more work is needed before firm conclusions can be reached on the effects of ideology in Senate primaries. Finally, there is an enormous effect of campaign spending after controlling for other factors. Every 10 percent increase in the incumbent's spending ratio increases his or her victory margin by almost 6.5 percent. The difference in electoral margin between an incumbent who spends half of the money in a campaign and one who spends 90 percent is over 25 percent. As judged by the standardized β, .48, money has a much greater effect on outcomes than any other single factor.

The 1990 Primaries

In 1990, seventeen of twenty-nine incumbents (59 percent) were unchallenged for their party's nomination, not much different than other recent elections. Nine candidates had one opponent, while three incumbents faced two challengers.

In 1990 not only did no challengers win, none came close. One Senator won by forty percentage points, a second by fifty-nine points and a third sixty-two points, and all others won by seventy points or more. The average margin of victory was seventy points, substantially above the average margin in all 1974–88 races.

The 1990 primary elections saw what may be the worst candidate quality pool ever. First, not a single governor or member of Congress challenged an incumbent. Further, the low-quality candidates were not just low in experience, they were abysmal. Only one had ever won elected office, Public Service Commissioner John Driscoll of Montana. Other challengers included a dental hygienist (Oklahoma), a school teacher (Alaska), an unemployed worker (New Jersey), and a handful of business executives.

Of the twelve 1990 Senators facing primary challenges, ten were within twenty points of their predicted ADA scores for their partisan constituents. One Senator, Howell Heflin (D-Alabama), can be labeled a super partisan, for his ADA score was substantially more conservative than predicted for a Southern Democrat, and only one senator, Mark Hatfield (R-Oregon) can be labeled an insufficient partisan, as attested by his 1989 ADA score of 80. Thus, Hatfield alone was potentially vulnerable to a partisan challenge on ideological grounds.

In 1990, spending by challengers was minuscule. None of the challengers spent more than $7,000. Incumbent preprimary spending, much of it no doubt aimed at influencing November voters, ranged from a low of $182,000 (Kansas) to a high of $4,232,000 (Minnesota), and averaged $1.49

million. In no race did challengers spend as much as 1 percent of what the incumbent spent.

Primary challengers were financially handicapped, in part, because they lacked experience. High-quality challengers through 1988 spent an average of $1,138,000 in primary campaigns; low-quality challengers spent only $77,000 on average. In races with high-quality challengers, 60 percent of the expenditures were by incumbents; in races with low-quality challengers, 90 percent of the expenditures were by incumbents. Thus, the primary challengers in 1990 compare poorly even to other low-quality candidates. In sum, the 1990 primaries resembled House elections: a group of amateur politicians without any money challenge incumbents with totally defensible voting records. The results of such elections should surprise no one.

Summary and Conclusion

This chapter examined the process by which Senate candidates are nominated and the factors affecting such nominations. After reviewing state procedures for selecting nominees, we closely examined the six primaries since 1974 in which elected incumbents lost their party's Senate nomination through a primary defeat: William Fulbright (D-Arkansas) in 1974, Clifford Case (R-New Jersey) in 1978, Jacob Javits (R-New York), Richard Stone (D-Florida), Donald Stewart (D-Alabama), and Mike Gravel (D-Arkansas). A number of factors unite significant subsets of these cases. First, Fulbright, Case, Javits, and Stewart were all significantly more liberal than we would expect, given their partisan constituents. Second, Javits, Stone, Stewart, and Gravel were all involved in a significant controversy during the campaign: Javits's health was rapidly failing; Stone and Stewart were reported to be under investigation for financial improprieties; and Gravel harmed Alaska's vital interests by refusing to compromise on a crucial land bill.

Even when incumbents win, they can be hurt by a primary challenge (see chap. 4). Because of the effect that primary challenges can have in general elections, we systematically examined several factors that have influenced primary victory margins since 1974. The evidence suggests that incumbents will fare less well in primaries when they do not represent the ideological tendencies of their party constituents, when they are involved in scandals or significant controversies, when their opponents are governors or members of Congress, and when their opponents are well funded. A multivariate analysis generally confirmed these findings, but cast some question on the extent to which ideology can harm candidates.

CHAPTER 4

Explaining Senate Election Outcomes

A congressional election is both a national contest for control of the Senate and House of Representatives and a collection of 468 or so separate state and local races. In this chapter, we will first explain the outcomes of Senate elections at the national level—how many seats each party gains or loses. We will then explain the outcomes of the individual races in each state—the proportion of the vote each candidate receives. We have seen that voters' decisions in Senate elections are based primarily on their evaluations of the individual candidates. At the national level, however, the strengths and weaknesses of the candidates in each state tend to cancel each other out.[1] The national outcome depends primarily on voters' evaluations of national political conditions. But how do national political conditions affect the outcomes of Senate elections?

Students of U.S. politics have long recognized the existence of certain regular patterns in the national outcomes of elections for the House of Representatives. The party winning the White House almost invariably gains seats in the House. Even more predictably, the party holding the White House can expect to lose seats in the midterm election. The size of a party's gain or loss in the House of Representatives depends on the state of the economy,[2] the popularity of the incumbent president,[3] and the number of House members who rode into office on the winning presidential candidate's coattails in the

---

1. This may not be entirely true. When national conditions clearly favor one party, that party may recruit stronger candidates than the opposing party, and the candidates of the favored party may also raise more money than their opponents. For a discussion of the influence of strategic decision making by candidates and contributors on congressional elections, see Gary C. Jacobson and Samuel Kernell, *Strategy and Choice in Congressional Elections*, 2d ed. (New Haven: Yale University Press, 1983). However, the effects of national issues on congressional elections appear to be due mainly to their direct influence on voting decisions rather than their indirect influence through the decisions on candidates and contributors; see Alan I. Abramowitz, "National Issues, Strategic Politicians, and Voting Behavior in the 1980 and 1982 Elections," *American Journal of Political Science* 28 (1984): 710–21.

2. Gerald H. Kramer, "Short-Term Fluctuations in U.S. Voting Behavior, 1896–1964," *American Political Science Review* 65 (1971): 131–43.

3. Edward R. Tufte, "Determinants of the Outcomes of Midterm Congressional Elections," *American Political Science Review* 69 (1975): 812–26.

preceding election.[4] The worse the economy's performance, the lower the president's popularity, and the longer the president's coattails two years earlier, the more seats the president's party can expect to lose in a midterm election. Thus, in 1964, thanks to Lyndon Johnson's landslide victory over Barry Goldwater, Democrats gained thirty-seven seats in the House of Representatives. Two years later, with no presidential race on the ballot and the president's popularity waning, the Democrats lost forty-eight House seats. Similarly, in 1980, Republicans gained thirty-three House seats as Ronald Reagan recaptured the White House. Two years later, many Democrats and Independents who had voted for Reagan and his GOP ticket mates in 1980 reverted to their normal voting habits. As a result, the Republicans lost twenty-six seats in the House.

Senate elections have not displayed as regular a pattern of party gains and losses as House elections. Since 1920, when the first popularly elected Senate class faced reelection, the party winning the White House has gained seats in the Senate in only eleven of seventeen presidential election years; during the same period, the party holding the presidency has lost seats in twelve of sixteen midterm elections. With greater visibility of Senate candidates, far fewer seats at stake in each election, and a completely different set of seats at stake every two years, Senate elections appear to be much less predictable than House elections. At least, political scientists have assumed that Senate elections are much less predictable than House elections.

Explaining the National Outcome

In House elections, the number of seats the president's party can expect to lose in a midterm election depends largely on how many seats it won two years earlier. Other things being equal, the more seats a party must defend, the more seats it can expect to lose. We expect the same thing to be true in Senate elections. The difference between Senate and House elections is that only one-third of the Senate's seats are at stake each election year, and the president's party must defend the seats that it won *six* years earlier. The more seats the president's party must defend of the thirty-three or thirty-four Senate seats at stake in a given year, the more seats it can expect to lose.

In addition to the number of seats each party must defend in a given election year, national issues also influence the outcomes of congressional elections. Voters are doing more in House and Senate contests than just choosing a representative for their own district or state. They are also passing judgment on the performance of the incumbent president. Despite the separa-

---

4. James E. Campbell, "Explaining Presidential Losses in Midterm Congressional Elections," *Journal of Politics* 47 (1985): 1140–57.

tion of powers between the executive and legislative branches of government, there is an element of party accountability in congressional elections: congressional candidates of the president's party are held accountable for his performance. Furthermore, evaluations of presidential performance may have a stronger influence on voters' decisions in Senate than in House elections. Because a typical state has a much larger population than a typical House district, Senators probably cannot rely on casework and constituency service activities to insulate themselves from the effects of national issues. The Senate's unique constitutional responsibilities, greater media coverage of Senate races, and direct presidential involvement in Senate campaigns should increase the salience of national issues in Senate elections. Thus, the greater the popularity of the incumbent president, the more Senate seats his party should win.

A number of previous studies have found that, along with presidential popularity, economic conditions have a significant influence on the outcomes of House elections: the stronger the performance of the economy, the more seats the president's party can expect to win.[5] However, this research has not explained what connects the state of the economy with voters' choices in congressional elections. A recent study of House elections suggested that short-term evaluations of political parties may link the state of the economy with the results of congressional elections.[6] Economic conditions influence voters' evaluations of the relative competence of the two major parties in dealing with such economic problems as inflation and unemployment; favorable economic conditions lead to positive evaluations of the president's party, while unfavorable conditions lead to negative evaluations of the president's party. These evaluations, in turn, influence voters' candidate preferences in House elections. We expect to find the same relationship in Senate elections: the stronger the economy, the more positive voters' evaluations of the relative competence of the president's party will be, and the more seats the president's party will win.

According to our reasoning, the influence of economic conditions on Senate elections is indirect—favorable or unfavorable economic trends should affect the outcomes of Senate elections only if they affect voters' evaluations of the relative competence of the two major parties or their evaluations of the president's job performance. The state of the economy should have no direct influence on the results of Senate elections.

One of the most regular patterns of U.S. electoral politics is the tendency of the president's party to lose seats in the House of Representatives in

---

5. See Kramer, "Short-Term Fluctuations"; Tufte, "Determinants."
6. Alan I. Abramowitz, Albert D. Cover, and Helmut Norpoth, "The President's Party in Midterm Elections: Going From Bad to Worse," *American Journal of Political Science* 30 (1986): 562–76.

midterm elections. This pattern is based partially on the fact that the president's party usually has won more than its normal share of seats in the preceding presidential election. In addition, however, the party controlling the White House may lose support in midterm elections because of negative voting: when the president himself is not on the ballot, voters who are dissatisfied with his performance may take out their discontent on candidates representing the president's party. Thus, in midterm elections, negative evaluations of the incumbent president may have a stronger impact on voting decisions than positive evaluations.[7] This phenomenon may help to explain why the president's party usually loses Senate seats in midterm elections, even though the same seats were not at stake in the preceding presidential election year. Since 1936, the president's party has lost seats in ten of thirteen midterm elections, with an average loss of 4.7 seats. With all other factors held constant, we expect the party controlling the White House to win fewer Senate seats in midterm elections than in presidential election years, due to negative voting.

The diagram shown in figure 4.1 summarizes our hypotheses about the factors that influence the national outcomes of Senate elections. This diagram represents a causal model of Senate election outcomes. The arrows show which variables (or factors) are expected to influence which other variables: the direction of each arrow represents the direction of influence between two variables.

In order to estimate the effects of each of the variables in our model on the outcomes of Senate elections, we used multiple regression analysis. This technique allows us to estimate the impact of each of the independent variables in our model (the factors that are expected to influence the outcomes of Senate elections) on our dependent variable (Senate election outcomes), while controlling for the effects of all of the other independent variables.

The dependent variable to be explained by our model is the change in Senate seats controlled by the president's party (outcome). Our independent variables are the number of seats being defended by the president's party (initial seats), the president's approval rating in the Gallup Poll closest to the election (presidential popularity), the public's rating of the relative competence of the two major parties in handling the most important problem facing the nation (party competence), the change in real disposable income during the election year (economic conditions) and whether it was a midterm rather than a presidential election year (midterm).[8] Initial seats, presidential popu-

---

7. See Samuel Kernell, "Presidential Popularity and Negative Voting: An Alternative Explanation of the Midterm Congressional Decline of the President's Party," *American Political Science Review* 71 (1977): 44–66.

8. Information on presidential popularity and party competence were taken from the Gallup Poll closest to the date of the election.

Explaining Senate Election Outcomes 97

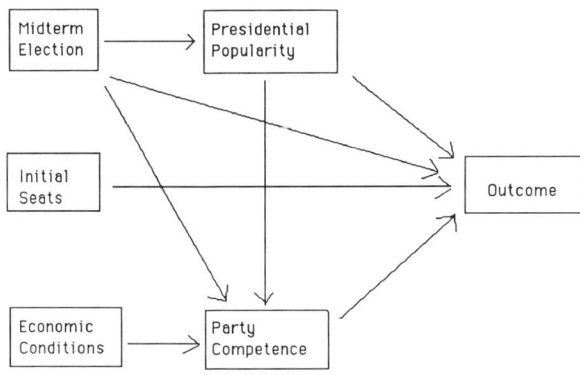

Fig. 4.1. A causal model of Senate election outcomes

larity, party competence, and midterm directly affect outcome; economic conditions indirectly affect outcome through presidential popularity and party competence.

We estimated the model with data on all Senate elections between 1946 and 1986, except for the 1950 and 1952 elections, for which party competence evaluations were not available. The results of the multiple regression analysis are presented in table 4.1. Each regression coefficient represents the estimated impact on the number of Senate seats won by the president's party of a change of one unit on each independent variable. For example, the coefficient for presidential popularity ($b = .123$) means that an increase of one unit (in this case, one percentage point) in presidential popularity would cause the president's party to win an additional .123 Senate seats (or approximately one-eighth of a seat). Thus, an increase of eight percentage points in the president's approval rating is worth one additional Senate seat to his party.

TABLE 4.1. Multiple Regression Analysis of National Senate Election Outcomes, 1946–86

Variable	b	SE	β	p
Initial seats	−.754	.178	−.672	.001
Presidential popularity	.123	.075	.283	.10
Party competence	.226	.101	.397	.025
Midterm	−2.57	1.54	−.240	.10
Constant	−5.97	5.16	—	—

Notes: $N = 19$; adjusted $R^2 = .65$. b = unstandardized regression coefficient; SE = standard error; $β$ = standardized regression coefficient; significance levels are based on one-tailed t-tests.

The results presented in table 4.1 generally confirm our expectations about the factors that influence the national outcomes of Senate elections. All of the estimated coefficients are either marginally or highly statistically significant (there is a very low probability that these results are due to chance) and in the expected direction. The average margin of error in predicting the outcomes of the nineteen elections included in the study is about two seats.[9]

The single most powerful predictor of the national outcome of a Senate election is the number of seats being defended by the president's party. For every additional seat that the president's party must defend in a given election year, it can expect to lose an additional three-quarters of a seat ($b = -.754$). Thus, the outcome of a Senate election depends largely on the outcome of the Senate election that took place six years earlier.

The estimated coefficient for the midterm election variable indicates that the president's party can expect to win an average of 2.6 fewer seats in a midterm year than in a presidential election year, with all other factors held constant. This result is consistent with Kernell's negative voting hypothesis.

Party competence evaluations had a strong influence on the outcomes of Senate elections. Every one percentage point increase in the competence of the president's party leads to an increase of .226 Senate seats. Thus, the president's party can expect to win an additional Senate seat for each increase of 4.4 percentage points in the public's evaluation of his party's relative competence. Thus, the direct influence of party competence evaluations on Senate election outcomes was substantially stronger than the direct influence of presidential popularity. Furthermore, when a measure of economic conditions (the percentage change in real disposable income during the election year) was added to the regression analysis, it had almost no additional impact on the outcomes of Senate elections. This result is consistent with our expectation that economic conditions only affect Senate elections indirectly—through their influence on party competence evaluations.

The state of the economy did have a strong impact on party competence evaluations and, therefore, an indirect impact on Senate election outcomes. We performed an additional regression analysis with party competence as the dependent variable and three independent variables: midterm, presidential popularity, and economic conditions (again measured by the change in real disposable income during the election year). The state of the economy had by far the strongest influence on party competence evaluations. Each 1.0 percent

---

9. This margin of error is inflated somewhat due to specific problems with our data for the 1948 election. Unfortunately, the only measure of party competence available for 1948 was from a Gallup Poll conducted in the spring, more than six months before the November election. The results of the poll showed a Republican advantage that probably evaporated by November. As a result, the model underpredicts the Democrats' gains in the 1948 Senate elections by about seven seats, by far the largest error for the entire series.

increase in real disposable income during an election year produced an estimated increase of 2.2 percentage points in the public's evaluation of the relative competence of the president's party. Combining this result with our estimate of the effect of party competence evaluations on Senate elections, the president's party can expect to win an additional Senate seat for each 2.0 percent rise in real disposable income during an election year.

One way of evaluating the model of Senate election outcomes is to determine how accurately it predicted the outcomes of future elections. We used our model to predict the outcomes of the 1986, 1988, and 1990 Senate elections. The 1986 Senate elections provide an especially interesting test for the model. In 1980, the Republican Party gained control of the Senate for the first time in over a quarter-century by winning twenty-two out of thirty-four contests for a net gain of twelve seats. In 1982 and 1984, the GOP was able to maintain its majority in the upper chamber, but in 1986 the Republicans had to defend the seats they won six years earlier. It would not be easy, and leaders of both parties saw the 1986 elections as the Democrats' best chance for regaining control of the Senate in many years. Almost nobody, however, expected what happened—a net loss of eight Republican seats that gave the Democrats a comfortable 55 to 45 seat majority for the final two years of the Reagan administration.[10]

In order to use the model to predict the outcome of the 1986 Senate elections, we first reestimated the regression equation using data for 1948 through 1984. We then used the 1986 data on Republican seats (22), presidential popularity (63 percent), and relative party competence (48 percent), along with the fact that 1986 was a midterm election year, to predict the net change in Republican Senate seats. The model yielded a predicted GOP loss of six seats (actually, 5.9 seats). Thus, our model underestimated actual Republican losses by only two seats—a very accurate prediction. Moreover, the model clearly predicted that the Republicans would lose control of the Senate, since a six seat loss would have given the Democrats a 53 to 47 seat majority.

We then used our model, estimated with data from Senate elections between 1946 and 1986, to predict the outcomes of the 1988 and 1990 Senate elections. In 1988, the Republicans had two major advantages in the Senate elections that they lacked in 1986—it was a presidential election year with a popular Republican incumbent in the White House, and only fifteen of the thirty-three Senate seats up for election were held by Republicans. Despite these advantages, and despite George Bush's decisive victory over Michael

---

10. One Democratic Senator, Edward Zorinsky of Nebraska, died of a heart attack during 1987. The Republican governor of Nebraska appointed a Republican to succeed Zorinsky until his term expired in January, 1989. This left the Democrats with a 54 to 46 seat majority in the Senate.

Dukakis in the presidential election, the GOP suffered a net loss of one seat in the Senate.

According to a Gallup Poll conducted in September, 1988, the Republicans enjoyed a clear advantage over the Democrats in party competence evaluations. Among respondents expressing a preference, 54 percent chose the GOP as the party best able to handle the nation's most important problem while 46 percent chose the Democrats. In early November, according to another Gallup Poll, 57 percent of Americans approved of Ronald Reagan's job performance.

Based on these results and the fact that only fifteen of the thirty-three Senate seats up for election were held by Republicans, our model predicted a net GOP gain of two seats in 1988. Thus, our model erred by a margin of three seats in favor of the Republicans—fairly close to our average margin of error of two seats. We regard this as a very good prediction considering the fact that the results of the 1988 election were not used in estimating the model.

Our model performed even better in 1990. The GOP was defending seventeen of the thirty-four seats at stake in the midterm election. According to a Gallup Poll conducted in October, Americans favored the Republicans over the Democrats by a 51 to 49 percent margin as the party best equipped to handle the nation's most important problem, and in early November, President Bush's approval rating stood at 58 percent. Based on these factors and the estimated coefficients from table 4.1, our model predicted a Republican loss of 3 Senate seats—very close to the actual result, which was a 1 seat loss for the GOP.

Explaining the Outcomes of Individual Races

Although the national outcome of a Senate election is very important to party leaders and to the president, most citizens are probably more concerned about the outcome of the contest in their own state. Senate campaigns generally receive much greater media coverage than House campaigns.[11] Therefore, voters are generally better informed about Senate candidates than they are about House candidates, especially nonincumbent candidates. When incumbent Senators seek reelection, they often attract prominent, well-financed challengers. A large proportion of Senate challengers in recent years had held a major elected office. Several other Senate candidates had achieved prominence outside politics, including three former astronauts, a former professional basketball player, two former Vietnam POWs, and the sixth husband of

---

11. Richard F. Fenno, *The United States Senate: A Bicameral Perspective* (Washington, D.C.: American Enterprise Institute, 1982), 9–12. See also Peter Clarke and Susan Evans, *Covering Campaigns: Journalism in Congressional Elections* (Stanford: Stanford University Press, 1983).

actress Elizabeth Taylor. These elected officials and celebrities not only enjoyed high public visibility, but they also usually spent large sums of money on their campaigns. A number of other Senate candidates in recent years have been multimillionaires who were willing to invest large sums of their personal wealth in their own campaigns. As a result, many Senate challengers have been able to use television advertising extensively in their campaigns.

Of course not all Senate challengers are prominent or wealthy.[12] However, the fact that many Senate challengers are well-known public officials, celebrities or millionaires may explain why Senate incumbents have much greater difficulty holding their seats than House incumbents: the visibility of the challenger is one of the most important differences between Senate and House elections.[13]

The visibility of Senate challengers and extensive media coverage of Senate campaigns may also increase voters' awareness of candidates' issue positions and ideologies. National and international issues appear to play a larger role in Senate campaigns than in House campaigns.[14] Presidential campaigning for Senate candidates and the involvement of ideological political action committees such as the National Conservative Political Action Committee (NCPAC) have probably increased the ideological content of Senate campaigns in recent years.

State Characteristics

The first set of factors that we will examine in this section involve the political characteristics of the state in which a Senate contest occurs. Three characteristics that should affect Senate elections are the partisan composition of the electorate, the ideological composition of the electorate, and the size of the state's population.

Although the proportion of U.S. voters who identify with the Democratic and Republican parties and the influence of party identification on voting decisions have both declined in recent years, party labels still provide an important cue for many voters. There are still substantial differences in partisan orientation among states, although these differences have diminished in recent years. The proportion of Democratic and Republican identifiers in a state should have a significant impact on the outcome of a Senate election. A

---

12. See Mark C. Westlye, "Competitiveness of Senate Seats and Voting Behavior in Senate Elections," *American Journal of Political Science* 27 (1983): 253–83.

13. Alan I. Abramowitz, "A Comparison of Voting for U.S. Senator and Representative," *American Political Science Review* 74 (1980): 635; see also Barbara Hinckley, "House Reelections and Senate Defeats: The Role of the Challenger," *British Journal of Political Science* 10 (1980): 441–60.

14. Fenno, *United States Senate*, 17–19.

Democratic candidate should have an advantage in Georgia or Alabama, while a Republican candidate should enjoy an advantage in Nebraska or Idaho.

In addition to partisanship, the ideological composition of the electorate may affect the outcomes of Senate elections. Voters generally perceive the Democratic party as more liberal than the Republican party and voters' ideological identifications, although not strongly related to attitudes on specific issues, have had significant effects on their candidate preferences in several recent presidential elections.[15] Given the salience of national issues in many recent Senate campaigns, ideological identifications may also affect voting for Senate candidates: the proportion of liberal identifiers in a state should have a positive impact on the vote for Democratic Senate candidates. States vary in their ideological orientations just as they vary in their partisan orientations. Thus, a Democratic candidate should have an advantage in a relatively liberal state such as Massachusetts, while a Republican candidate should have an advantage in a relatively conservative state such as Utah.

Population size may affect the outcomes of Senate elections in a somewhat different manner than either partisanship or ideology. The size of a state's population should affect not support for the parties, but support for the incumbent senator. The larger the population of a state, the more difficult it may be for a senator to cultivate the support of the voters.[16] As population size increases, so does political and economic diversity. In addition, the size of a state's population should be inversely related to personal contact with voters. As a state's population increases, the ability of an incumbent senator to cultivate support through personal contact with constituents should diminish fairly rapidly. Once a state's population reaches several million, personal contact with constituents becomes impractical and a senator probably must rely almost exclusively on the mass media to communicate with citizens.

Candidate Characteristics

The second set of factors that we will examine in this section involve the characteristics of the Senate candidates. When an incumbent is seeking re-election, the incumbent's past performance is usually the major focus of the campaign: the challenger criticizes the incumbent's record, while the incumbent defends that record. Several aspects of the incumbent's performance may

---

15. See John D. Holm and John P. Robinson, "Ideological Identification and the American Voter," *Public Opinion Quarterly* 42 (1978): 235–46; Teresa E. Levitin and Warren E. Miller, "Ideological Interpretations of Presidential Elections," *American Political Science Review* 73 (1979): 751–71.

16. See John R. Hibbing and Sara L. Brandes, "State Population and the Electoral Success of U.S. Senators," *American Journal of Political Science* 25 (1981): 808–19.

affect the outcome of a Senate election, including the incumbent's voting record, scandals or political controversies, health concerns, and serious intra-party opposition.

The key question concerning the incumbent's voting record is its congruence with the ideological preferences of the state's voters. The greater the distance between a Senator's ideology, as reflected by his or her voting record, and the ideology of the average voter, the greater should be the challenger's opportunity to win votes by taking a position closer to that of the average voter in the state.

In recent years there have been several senators whose voting records appeared to be inconsistent with the ideological orientation of the voters who elected them. James Buckley was elected to the Senate in 1970 from one of the most liberal states in the nation—New York. Buckley owed his election to the presence of two liberal candidates on the ballot—the Republican incumbent, Charles Goodell, and the Democratic challenger, Richard Ottinger. Buckley, who ran as the candidate of the Conservative party, won the election with 39 percent of the vote. Six years later, after compiling an almost unblemished conservative voting record, Buckley lost his Senate seat to Daniel Patrick Moynihan, a Democrat whose moderate brand of liberalism was much closer to the position of the average voter in New York.

George McGovern (D-South Dakota) is another example of a Senator whose ideology and voting record displayed a marked discrepancy with the views of his constituents. After winning election to the Senate in 1962, McGovern compiled a moderately liberal voting record while emphasizing his support for programs beneficial to South Dakota's farmers. However, after winning reelection to the Senate in 1968 against a very weak opponent, McGovern's voting record took a turn to the left with his disastrous 1972 presidential campaign. In 1974, McGovern was opposed by a former Vietnam POW who had never previously run for public office. In a strongly Democratic election year, McGovern won reelection with only 53 percent of the vote. Six years later, however, McGovern found himself running against a national Republican tide and a formidable Republican opponent—Congressman James Abdnor.

McGovern was one of six liberal Democratic senators targeted for defeat in 1980 by NCPAC. NCPAC ran its own advertising campaign in South Dakota emphasizing McGovern's liberal record and positions. McGovern suffered a crushing defeat, receiving only 38 percent of the vote against Abdnor, a conservative whose views appeared much closer to those of the average South Dakotan. Thanks to good luck and weak opposition, George McGovern managed to serve three terms in the Senate. In 1980, however, against a strong challenger, his luck ran out and his liberal record came back to haunt him.

Involvement in well-publicized scandals or political controversies should also reduce support for an incumbent officeholder.[17] Although no member of the Senate was indicted or convicted of a crime during the period covered by this study, several senators were the subjects of investigations based on allegations of official or personal misconduct. A larger number were involved in incidents that raised questions about their honesty, personal judgment, or competence. Media coverage of such incidents probably had a negative impact on the incumbents' reputations among their constituents.

One of the most widely publicized Senate scandals of the past two decades involved Senator Edward Brooke (R-Massachusetts). The first black to serve in the Senate since the end of Reconstruction, Brooke appeared almost invulnerable after easily winning reelection to a second term in 1972 with 65 percent of the vote. Brooke's liberal voting record stood him in good stead in normally Democratic Massachusetts. Following his reelection, however, Brooke became embroiled in a messy legal dispute over his divorce, including allegations that he had lied about his financial worth. Questions were also raised in the media about how Brooke's mother had received $72,000 in Medicaid payments. Although Brooke was never convicted or even indicted for any violation of the law, the negative publicity that he received because of these incidents contributed to a difficult primary contest against a conservative media personality. In the general election, Brooke was beaten by Democratic Congressman Paul Tsongas by a decisive 55 to 45 percent margin.

Brooke was not the only seemingly entrenched incumbent whose career was ended by scandal. Herman Talmadge (D-Georgia) was elected to the Senate in 1956 after serving two terms as governor of Georgia. A staunch conservative, Talmadge had won reelection with little or no opposition until 1980. However, in April, 1978, Talmadge was accused by a former aide of diverting official funds to personal use. Although he denied these charges, Talmadge was forced to admit that he had never withdrawn any cash from his personal checking account, but instead had relied on small contributions from constituents for spending money. Talmadge also admitted that he suffered from alcoholism. After a lengthy investigation, Talmadge was officially denounced by the Senate for financial misconduct. In the 1980 Democratic primary election, Talmadge was forced into a runoff by Lt. Governor Zell Miller. Talmadge easily won the runoff election with 59 percent of the vote but, to the surprise of most political observers, was narrowly defeated in the general election by Republican Mack Mattingly, a conservative businessman who had never held elected office. Mattingly thus became the first Republican to win a statewide election in Georgia since Reconstruction.

---

17. See John G. Peters and Susan Welch, "The Effects of Charges of Corruption on Voting Behavior in Congressional Elections," *American Political Science Review* 74 (1980): 697–708.

Along with scandals and political controversies, questions about a Senator's health or physical vigor may also have a negative impact on electoral support for the incumbent. The issue here is not age—Senators in their seventies or eighties have had no difficulty winning reelection if they appeared to be in reasonably good health and physical condition. In 1990, Strom Thurmond (R-South Carolina) easily won reelection to the Senate with 64 percent of the vote. The former governor and 1948 presidential candidate of the States' Rights party celebrated his eighty-eighth birthday less than one month after the election.

Warren Magnuson (D-Washington) was not as fortunate as Strom Thurmond. Although he was only seventy-five years old when he sought his seventh Senate term in 1980, Magnuson did not enjoy Thurmond's physical vitality. The incumbent could only walk slowly and experienced considerable difficulty with his hearing during the campaign. Despite outspending his Republican opponent by almost a two-to-one margin, Magnuson's long Senate career ended with a 54 to 46 percent loss to fifty-two-year-old Slade Gorton, Washington's attorney general.

One additional potential problem for an incumbent Senator is intraparty opposition. Serious opposition to an incumbent Senator in his or her own party's primary is unusual. However, when such opposition does develop, it can cause major political problems for the incumbent even if he or she wins the primary. Criticism of the incumbent's record by a credible intraparty challenger may lead to an erosion of public support that carries over into the general election.[18] In some cases, a difficult primary contest may exacerbate other political difficulties, such as a scandal. Both Edward Brooke (R-Massachusetts) and Herman Talmadge (D-Georgia) survived difficult and divisive primary contests only to lose in the general election. Even without a scandal or political controversy, however, a divisive primary campaign may create problems for an incumbent that carry over into the general election campaign. Thus, in 1976, Senator John Tunney (D-California) was challenged in the Democratic primary by antiwar activist Tom Hayden. Despite a radical image stemming from his activities at the 1968 Democratic National Convention and his marriage to actress Jane Fonda, Hayden received 40 percent of the Democratic primary vote. Hayden's attacks on Tunney's effectiveness and

---

18. See Patrick J. Kenney and Tom W. Rice, "The Effect of Primary Divisiveness in Gubernatorial and Senatorial Elections," *Journal of Politics* 46 (1984): 904–15. Kenney and Rice did not distinguish between incumbents' and challengers' primaries; however, we would not expect the closeness of the challenger's primary to have the same impact on the general election as the closeness of the incumbent's primary. A closely contested primary in the challenger's primary could reflect either the absence of a strong contender or a strong field of candidates attracted by the perceived vulnerability of the incumbent. Moreover, we would not expect intraparty divisions in the challenger's party to be as salient to the electorate as those involving an incumbent. When the challenger's margin of victory in the primary was included in the multiple regression analysis, it had a negligible impact on the outcome of the general election.

integrity may have contributed to Tunney's defeat in the general election at the hands of Republican S. I. Hayakawa.

Although a Senate campaign involving an incumbent usually revolves around the record of the incumbent, the ability of the challenger to effectively criticize the incumbent's record also depends on the resources and political skills of the challenger. Three characteristics of Senate challengers that should affect their ability to conduct an effective campaign are political experience, celebrity status, and campaign spending.

A candidate who has held elected office has several advantages over one who has never won an election. The experience of conducting at least one successful campaign should be an advantage in organizing a Senate campaign. Depending on the importance and visibility of the office, the candidate may begin the campaign with a high level of recognition among the electorate. Holding elected office probably also enhances a candidate's credibility among both the voters and members of the media. A candidate who holds an important elected office will probably receive more extensive and favorable coverage in the media and will be taken more seriously by the voters than a candidate who has never held elected office.

The larger the constituency that a candidate has represented and the greater the public exposure provided by the office, the greater the advantage that a previous office should provide. In both of these regards, the office of governor probably provides the most advantageous position from which to run for the Senate. A governor already represents an entire state and probably receives at least as much media coverage as an incumbent Senator. This should provide a sitting governor or even a former governor with an enormous boost in seeking a Senate seat, providing that most of this publicity has been favorable.

The 1986 Florida Senate election provides an excellent example of the potential advantages enjoyed by a governor running for the Senate. After two terms as governor, Robert Graham was able to claim credit for such popular policies as improving public education and enforcing the death penalty. He also maintained a high media profile by regularly taking time off from his official duties to work at blue-collar jobs. Although the Republican incumbent, Paula Hawkins, enjoyed high ratings in the polls, she could not match Graham's visibility. Graham was considered the frontrunner in the race from the moment he declared his candidacy and eventually won the Senate race by a decisive 55 to 45 percent margin.

Of course, not every governor who ran for the Senate enjoyed approval ratings as high as Bob Graham's. A candidate's record in office can be a liability as well as an asset. In 1982, Governor Jerry Brown of California announced his candidacy for the Senate seat being vacated by S. I. Hayakawa. As a two-term governor, Brown was much more familiar to California's voters than his Republican opponent, San Diego Mayor Pete Wilson. Unfortunately for Brown, however, this was one case in which familiarity did, indeed, breed contempt on the part of many voters. Dogged by controversy over his handling of the Medfly infestation of California's fruit orchards as well as his image as "Governor Moonbeam," Brown lost the Senate race by a decisive margin in a strongly Democratic election year.

A candidate who has achieved prominence through activities other than holding elected office should enjoy many of the same advantages as one who has held elected office. A famous athlete, entertainer, astronaut, or military hero will begin the campaign with greater public recognition and will probably receive more extensive and favorable media coverage than a candidate who is not a celebrity. Since 1972, two astronauts (John Glenn of Ohio and Harrison Schmitt of New Mexico), a former Vietnam POW (Jeremiah Denton of Alabama), a former professional basketball player (Bill Bradley of New Jersey), and the sixth husband of actress Elizabeth Taylor (John Warner of Virginia) have been elected to the Senate. None of these celebrities had previously held an elected office, although John Warner had served as secretary of the navy during the Nixon administration.

Of course, even candidates who are not celebrities and have never held elected office can achieve a high level of public visibility by spending large sums of money on their campaigns. This is relatively easy for candidates who are independently wealthy and are willing to finance their own campaigns. It is more difficult, but by no means impossible, for candidates who have to rely on PACs and individual contributors for campaign funds. By raising a large campaign war chest, a candidate can not only buy television advertisements to increase his or her visibility among the public, but also enhance his or her credibility among members of the news media. A good example of the effective use of money is provided by the campaign of Frank Lautenberg (D-New Jersey). A multimillionaire businessman, Lautenberg spent more than five million dollars of his own money on his 1982 campaign. After narrowly winning the Democratic nomination with 26 percent of the vote in a ten-candidate primary field, Lautenberg was a heavy underdog to the Republican candidate, Congresswoman Millicent Fenwick, best known as the model for the Doonesbury comic strip character Lacey Davenport. By outspending Fenwick by a better than two-to-one margin, however, Lautenberg was able to overcome his initial disadvantage in name recognition and win a 51 to 48 percent victory in the general election.

Even if there are weaknesses in an incumbent senator's record and a strong challenger emerges in the opposing party, the incumbent has one additional resource at his or her disposal: the ability to raise and spend large sums of money on his or her reelection campaign. An incumbent senator can usually outspend even a prominent and well-financed challenger. However, it is not clear how much good this does. Studies of campaign spending in House elections have generally found that spending by incumbents has little or no impact on their electoral fortunes—only the challenger's spending has a substantial impact on the outcome of a House election.[19] The explanation for this finding is that the incumbent is already well known by the time the campaign gets under way, but the campaign is the only opportunity for the challenger to get his or her message across to the electorate. Therefore, a high level of campaign spending is usually essential for a challenger to have a realistic chance of upsetting an incumbent Senator.[20]

National Political Conditions

We have already seen that national political conditions strongly influence the number of seats each party can expect to win in a Senate election. These national political conditions must, therefore, affect the vote for the candidates in each state. We will estimate the impact of presidential popularity, party competence evaluations, and the timing of an election (midterm vs. presidential election years) on the share of the vote received by candidates representing the president's party and the opposing party in each Senate race.

Open Seats

Almost one-fourth of all Senate contests in recent years have involved open seats—because of death, retirement, or a primary defeat, no incumbent was involved in these races. Without an incumbent's record to serve as the focus of the campaign, the outcome of an open seat contest may depend primarily on the electorate's judgment of the relative qualifications of the candidates. That judgment will probably be influenced by the candidates' actual qualifications (their relative political experience), and their ability to explain those qualifications to the voters during the campaign (the relative size of their campaign war chests). Other factors that influence races involving incumbents should also affect contests for open seats: the partisan and ideological composition of the electorate in the state and national political conditions.

---

19. See Stanton A. Glantz, Alan I. Abramowitz, and Michael P. Burkart, "Election Outcomes: Whose Money Matters?" *Journal of Politics* 38 (1976): 1033–38; see also Gary C. Jacobson, "The Effects of Campaign Spending in Congressional Elections," *American Political Science Review* 72 (1978): 469–91; Gary C. Jacobson, *Money in Congressional Elections* (New Haven: Yale University Press, 1980).

20. Campaign spending by both incumbent and nonincumbent candidates is probably subject to diminishing marginal returns—as a candidate spends more money and becomes better known, the impact of further spending should diminish. The amount of money necessary to wage an effective campaign will also vary depending on the population of the state. A detailed description of the techniques used to measure campaign spending is included in appendix A.

Overall Results

We used multiple regression analysis to analyze the results of all contested Senate races between 1974 and 1986. (Data on campaign spending are not available for elections before 1974.) During this period there were 226 contested Senate races, including 174 races involving incumbents and 52 contests for open seats. Ten Senate races in Alaska and Hawaii (eight of which involved incumbents) were dropped from the analysis because there was no data available on the partisan or ideological composition of the electorates in those states, leaving 166 races with incumbents and 50 open seat contests in the analysis.

Table 4.2 presents the results of the multiple regression analysis for all Senate races involving incumbents. The dependent variable in this analysis is the incumbent's percentage of the major-party vote. Therefore, each unstandardized regression coefficient in table 4.2 represents the expected change in the incumbent's percentage of the vote given an increase of one unit on each independent variable, with all of the other independent variables held constant. Because different independent variables are measured on different scales, the unstandardized regression coefficients cannot be used to compare the effects of different independent variables on the incumbent's vote. How-

TABLE 4.2. Multiple Regression Analysis of Incumbent Vote Percentage

Variable	b	SE	β	p
State partisanship	.146	.032	.233	.001
State ideology	.110	.038	.193	.005
State population	−.770	.413	−.081	.05
Ideological distance	−.084	.031	−.122	.005
Scandal	−7.28	2.41	−.130	.005
Controversy	−3.21	1.49	−.094	.025
Health problem	−8.40	2.99	−.117	.005
Primary contest	−7.29	1.80	−.382	.001
Primary margin	.107	.026	.393	.001
Challenger experience	−1.95	.487	−.197	.001
Celebrity challenger	−5.31	2.48	−.095	.025
Challenger spending	−3.59	.429	−.483	.001
Incumbent spending	1.33	.614	.113	.025
Presidential popularity	.107	.071	.096	.10
Party competence	.103	.053	.136	.05
Midterm	−2.01	.606	−.159	.001
Constant	69.6	2.15	—	—

Notes: $N = 166$; adjusted $R^2 = .73$. b = unstandardized regression coefficient; SE = standard error; β = standardized regression coefficient; significance levels are based on one-tailed t-tests.

ever, the standardized regression coefficients in table 4.2 can be used for this purpose. Standardized regression coefficients range in value from +1.0 (strong positive relationship) through zero (no relationship) to −1.0 (strong negative relationship). The higher the absolute value of the standardized coefficient, the greater the effect of that variable on the incumbent's percentage of the vote.

All of the estimated coefficients are statistically significant and in the expected direction except the coefficient for presidential popularity, which is in the expected direction but is not significant at the .05 level. (That is, there is a greater than 5 percent probability that the estimated effect of presidential popularity is due to chance.) The regression equation explains almost three-fourths of the variation in the incumbent's share of the vote and the "predictions" of incumbents' vote shares are quite accurate—the standard error of 4.9 percentage points comes close to the expected margin of error of a poll conducted immediately before an election.

Effects of State Characteristics

The most interesting results of the multiple regression analysis are the estimated effects of each of the independent variables on the incumbent's vote. Looking at the effects of state political characteristics, for example, we find by comparing the standardized coefficients that the ideological orientation of the electorate ($\beta = .193$) was almost as important as the partisan orientation of the electorate ($\beta = .233$). Although Democratic candidates enjoyed an advantage because Democratic identifiers outnumber Republican identifiers in most states, this advantage was largely offset by the fact that conservative identifiers outnumber liberal identifiers in all forty-eight states included in this analysis. Some of the most Democratic states, in terms of partisanship, are in the Deep South. But these states are also among the most conservative in the nation.

Based on the partisan and ideological make-up of the electorate, the best states for Republican candidates are Utah and Idaho, while the best states for Democratic candidates are Georgia and Louisiana. With all other factors held constant, a Democratic Senate candidate in Georgia or Louisiana could expect to receive about 3 percent more of the vote than a Democratic candidate in an average state while a Democratic Senate candidate in Utah or Idaho could expect to receive about 7 percent less of the vote than a candidate in an average state. While these are substantial differences, no state can be considered safe for either party in a Senate election.

As expected, support for the incumbent Senator decreased as state population increased ($\beta = -.081$). A Senator from a small state such as Delaware or Wyoming could expect to receive about 3 percent more of the vote than a Senator from California, with all other factors held constant.

Effects of Candidate Characteristics

According to our results, a Senator whose voting record was inconsistent with the ideological preferences of his or her constituents could expect to pay a substantial price in electoral support for this discrepancy. A very liberal Senator representing a very conservative state or a very conservative Senator representing a very liberal state could expect to receive almost 5 percent less of the vote than a Senator whose voting record matched the preferences of the electorate.

During the period examined here, there were several Senators whose voting records demonstrated a marked discrepancy with the ideological preferences of the voters in their states. It is probably no coincidence that most of these Senators lost reelection bids to challengers whose views were more in tune with the voters. George McGovern (D-South Dakota), Frank Church (D-Idaho), and James Buckley (C-New York) suffered the same fate as eighteenth-century English political philosopher Edmund Burke, who ran for Parliament on a pledge to vote for his conscience rather than his constituents' wishes and discovered, when he lost the election, that the voters preferred to be represented by a delegate rather than a trustee.

According to the results presented in table 4.2, Senators who were involved in scandals experienced a substantial loss of electoral support: an average drop of 7.3 percentage points with other factors held constant.[21] Four of the five Senators accused of involvement in illegal activities—Democrat Joseph Montoya of New Mexico (accused of using members of his Senate staff to manage business properties, leasing space in a commercial property to the Post Office, and blocking a tax audit), Republican Edward Brooke of Massachusetts (accused of lying about his financial worth in divorce proceedings), Democrat Herman Talmadge of Georgia (reprimanded by the Senate for financial improprieties), and Republican Roger Jepsen of Iowa (accused of membership in a "health spa" that was actually a brothel)—were defeated when they sought reelection. Controversies that raised questions about a Senator's honesty or competence were much more common than full-blown scandals and far less costly: the average decline in electoral support was only 3.2 percentage points. Nevertheless, seven of the fourteen senators involved in such political controversies were defeated. Four Senators with significant

---

21. A detailed description of each scandal, controversy, and health problem affecting an incumbent senator is included in appendix B.

physical ailments or health problems—Jacob Javits (R-New York), Peter Dominick (R-Colorado), Barry Goldwater (R-Arizona), and Warren Magnuson (D-Washington)—sought reelection between 1974 and 1986. Javits was defeated in a Republican primary, while Dominick and Magnuson lost in general elections. Only Goldwater was reelected (with 51 percent of the vote) and this issue produced an estimated average drop in electoral support of 8.4 percentage points.

Senators who had significant opposition in their own party's primary experienced a substantial loss of support in the general election. The estimated coefficients for the primary contest and primary margin variables indicate that, in order to avoid any negative impact from the primary, an incumbent had to overwhelm his or her closest challenger by a margin of at least 68 percentage points. An incumbent who barely survived a primary challenge could expect a decline in support of more than 7 percentage points in the general election—an impact similar to that of a major scandal. Of the twenty-one Senate incumbents who won primaries by margins of less than 50 percentage points, eleven were defeated in the general election. Based on these results, a divisive primary appears to constitute one of the most serious threats to the survival of an incumbent senator.

The challenger's characteristics also had a strong impact on the outcomes of Senate elections. Challengers who held elected office had a considerable advantage over those who did not. For example, a challenger who had been elected governor could expect to receive an additional 5.8 percent of the vote compared with a challenger who had never been elected to public office, with all other factors held constant.

The elected office held most often by Senate challengers was member of the House of Representatives. Between 1974 and 1986, thirty-six current or former members of the House sought a Senate seat by challenging an incumbent. Based on the estimated coefficient for the political experience index, membership in the House was worth 3.9 percent of the vote to a Senate challenger. Sixteen of the challengers who had served in the House, or 44 percent, were successful—a success rate about twice the average for all Senate challengers.

Celebrity challengers also enjoyed a decided advantage in Senate elections.[22] In fact, being a celebrity was worth almost as much—an additional 5.3 percent of the vote—as being the governor of a state. Three of the five celebrity challengers who ran for the Senate between 1974 and 1986 were successful—California Republican S. I. Hayakawa (a former president of San Francisco State University who became a media celebrity because of his

---

22. A description of the background of each challenger classified as a celebrity is included in appendix C.

confrontational tactics in dealing with student demonstrators), New Mexico Republican Harrison Schmitt (a former astronaut), and New York Democrat Daniel Patrick Moynihan (a former UN ambassador and presidential advisor). It appears from these results that public prominence is just as valuable to a Senate challenger as political experience.

Perhaps the most interesting results in table 4.2 involve the effects of campaign spending by incumbents and challengers. Although both coefficients are statistically significant, the estimated coefficient for challenger spending is almost three times as large as the estimated coefficient for incumbent spending. In fact, challenger spending was easily the most important single factor influencing the outcomes of Senate elections.

Because of the way campaign spending was measured (see appendix A for an explanation of this variable), it is difficult to directly interpret the coefficients for the incumbent and challenger spending variables. Based on our results, however, we can estimate that an average challenger increased his or her share of the vote by 9.7 percentage points as a result of his or her own campaign expenditures while an average incumbent increased his or her share of the vote by 4.9 percentage points as a result of his or her own campaign expenditures.[23] Combining these estimates, the net impact of campaign spending in an average Senate race was to increase the challenger's share of the vote by 4.8 percentage points, even though the average incumbent outspent the average challenger by a substantial margin.

Although challengers receive a much higher electoral return from their campaign expenditures than incumbents, the ability of an incumbent to raise an enormous campaign war chest was crucial in at least one well-publicized recent Senate contest. In 1984, Jesse Helms of North Carolina set an all-time spending record for a Senate campaign. Faced with a strong challenge from Governor James Hunt, Helms spent almost 17 million dollars on his reelection campaign. Based on our estimate of the effect of incumbent spending, Helms' campaign expenditures increased his share of the vote by about eight percentage points. Helms won the election with 52 percent of the vote. Hunt spent over 9 million dollars on his campaign to unseat Helms. If Helms had only matched Hunt's expenditures, he probably would have won the election with about 51 percent of the vote.

Effects of National Political Conditions

National political conditons had a strong influence on the outcomes of Senate elections between 1974 and 1986. Based on party competence evaluations and

---

23. These figures were obtained by multiplying the unstandardized regression coefficients for the challenger and incumbent spending variables by the average scores of challengers and incumbents on these variables.

presidential popularity, 1976 was the most favorable election year for Democratic candidates, while 1980 was the most favorable year for Republican candidates. A Democratic Senate candidate in 1976 would have received 4.9 percent more of the vote than a Democratic Senate candidate in 1980, with all other factors held constant.

Even after controlling for party competence evaluations and presidential popularity, Senate candidates representing the president's party received an average of 2.0 percent less of the vote in midterm election years than in presidential election years. In the four midterm elections between 1974 and 1986, only 71 percent of Senate incumbents from the president's party were reelected; in the same elections, 94 percent of the incumbents from the opposition party were reelected.

Why Incumbents Lose

A high rate of incumbent eviction has been one of the most interesting features of recent Senate elections and one that clearly distinguishes them from House elections. Between 1974 and 1986, there were 166 contested Senate races involving incumbents for which complete data were available; 129 of the incumbents (78 percent) were reelected while 37 (22 percent) were defeated. The average winning incumbent received 61.8 percent of the major party vote, while the average losing incumbent received 46.2 percent of the major party vote. We can use the results of our multiple regression analysis to estimate the relative contribution of each of our independent variables to the defeat of incumbent Senators.[24]

About 75 percent of the difference in support between winning and losing incumbents is explained by the variables included in the regression analysis. Of these variables, by far the most important factor contributing to the defeat of incumbent Senators was the challenger's campaign spending. This variable alone accounts for 30 percent of the difference in electoral support between winning and losing incumbents. Other candidate characteristics explain an additional 28 percent of the difference in support between winning and losing incumbents. The most important of these were divisive primaries involving the incumbent (7 percent), and the challenger's political experience (6 percent). State political characteristics (10 percent) and national political conditions (9 percent) were much less important factors in the defeat of incumbent senators than either candidate characteristics or campaign spending.

---

24. These results are based on an estimate of the contribution of each independent variable to the difference in support between winning and losing incumbents. This involved calculating the difference between the mean scores of winning and losing incumbents on each variable and multiplying this difference by the estimated regression coefficient for each variable.

Based on these results, it is clear that the main reason so many incumbent Senators lose is that they attract strong challengers who are able to spend large sums of money on their campaigns. This contrasts sharply with the situation in House elections—very few House challengers are able to raise enough money to wage an effective campaign against the incumbent. The electoral advantage of incumbency is much greater in the House than in the Senate because Senate challengers generally wage much stronger campaigns than House challengers.

Results for Open Seats

About one-fourth of all Senate contests between 1974 and 1986 did not involve an incumbent. The results of a multiple regression analysis of these races are presented in table 4.3. Because of the relatively small number of open seat contests included in this analysis, the coefficients should be interpreted cautiously. Although all of the estimated coefficients except presidential popularity are in the expected direction, only two are statistically significant and the seven independent variables together only explain about 55 percent of the variation in the outcomes of open seat contests. The typical error in predicting results from the open seat regression equation (7.4 percentage points) is substantially larger than the error from the incumbent support equation (4.9 percentage points).

The results presented in table 4.3 do indicate that the outcomes of Senate contests for open seats are overwhelmingly based on the backgrounds and financial resources of the candidates. The two independent variables that had by far the strongest effects on the results of these races were the relative political experience of the candidates and the relative campaign expenditures

TABLE 4.3. Multiple Regression Analysis of Open Seat Contests

Variable	b	SE	β	p
State partisanship	.105	.092	.126	NS
State ideology	.209	.149	.148	NS
Relative experience	3.09	0.771	.418	.001
Relative spending	4.51	1.27	.400	.001
Presidential popularity	−.253	.303	−.160	NS
Party competence	.329	.205	.315	.10
Midterm	−0.42	1.66	−.029	NS
Constant	48.10	3.22	—	—

Notes: $N = 50$; adjusted $R^2 = .55$. b = unstandardized regression coefficient; SE = standard error; $β$ = standardized regression coefficient; significance levels are based on one-tailed t-tests.

of the candidates. Such other factors as national political conditions and the partisan and ideological make-up of a state's electorate were much less important.

Predicting the 1988 and 1990 Senate Elections

We used the estimates obtained in our analyses of individual Senate contests between 1974 and 1986 to predict the outcomes of thirty-two of the thirty-three Senate races in 1988 and twenty-eight of the thirty-four Senate races in 1990. No predictions were made for the 1988 or 1990 Hawaiian Senate races or the 1990 Alaskan Senate race because data on party and ideological identification were not available for Hawaii or Alaska. In addition, no predictions were made for the 1990 Senate elections in Arkansas, Louisiana, Mississippi, and Virginia, in which incumbents had no major party opposition. Of the sixty contests for which predictions were made, fifty involved incumbents and ten involved open seats. The predictions, along with the actual results of these sixty contests, are presented in table 4.4.

On the whole our incumbent support and open seat models performed extremely well in 1988, correctly predicting the outcomes of twenty-nine of the thirty-two contests, including all seven open-seat contests. The average margin of error of our thirty-two predictions was 4.7 percentage points. This is close to the average margin of error of preelection polls in Senate contests. Based on our predictions for the thirty-two individual races, we would have expected no net change in party control of Senate seats, compared with an actual gain of one seat by the Democrats.

Although our incumbent support and open seat models generally performed well in 1988, there were a few contests for which the models yielded very inaccurate predictions, including three races in which the models erred by at least 10 percentage points. The incumbent support model failed to predict the defeats of Senators Lowell Weicker (R-Connecticut) or John Melcher (D-Montana) and incorrectly predicted the defeat of Senator Quentin Burdick (D-North Dakota).

In the North Dakota Senate race, our model predicted that Quentin Burdick would receive only 43 percent of the vote. However, the eighty-year-old incumbent was easily reelected, receiving 60 percent of the vote against his Republican opponent, State Senator Majority Leader Earl Strinden. Preelection reports had indicated that Senator Burdick's health was a serious concern among North Dakota voters. Apparently, the incumbent was able to allay much of this concern by waging a vigorous reelection campaign. In addition, the challenger's acerbic personality may have alienated many voters. Finally, although North Dakota is normally one of the most Republican states in the nation and Senator Burdick had compiled a very liberal voting record,

TABLE 4.4. Predictions of 1988 and 1990 Senate Election Results

State	Incumbent[a]	Actual Democratic Percentage	Predicted Democratic Percentage	Error
			1988 Predictions	
Arizona	D	58	63	+5
California	R	45	45	+0
Connecticut	R	51	47[b]	−4
Delaware	R	38	48	−10
Florida	N	50	48	−2
Indiana	R	32	36	+4
Maine	D	81	63	+18
Maryland	D	62	63	+1
Massachusetts	D	66	65	−1
Michigan	D	61	59	−2
Minnesota	R	42	48	+6
Missouri	R	32	39	+7
Montana	D	48	56[b]	+8
Mississippi	N	46	48	+2
Nebraska	N	58	57	−1
Nevada	R	52	51	−1
New Jersey	D	54	55	+1
New Mexico	D	63	58	−5
New York	D	68	66	−2
North Dakota	D	60	43[b]	−17
Ohio	D	57	50	−7
Pennsylvania	R	32	37	+5
Rhode Island	R	45	46	+1
Tennessee	D	65	61	−4
Texas	D	60	58	−2
Utah	R	32	39	+7
Vermont	N	30	40	+10
Virginia	N	71	70	−1
Washington	N	49	45	−4
West Virginia	D	65	66	+1
Wisconsin	N	52	53	+1
Wyoming	R	50	41	−9
			1990 Predictions	
Alabama	D	61	63	+2
Colorado	N	43	39	−4
Delaware	D	63	65	+2
Idaho	N	39	31	−8
Illinois	D	65	56	−9
Indiana	R	46	38	−8

(*continued*)

TABLE 4.4—*Continued*

State	Incumbent[a]	Actual Democratic Percentage	Predicted Democratic Percentage	Error
Iowa	D	54	54	+0
Kansas	R	26	29	+3
Kentucky	R	48	45	−3
Maine	R	39	37	−2
Massachusetts	D	57	63	+6
Michigan	D	58	57	−1
Minnesota	R	52	38[b]	−14
Montana	D	70	59	−11
Nebraska	D	59	56	−3
New Hampshire	N	33	37	+4
New Jersey	D	51	62	+11
New Mexico	R	27	34	+7
North Carolina	R	48	45	−3
Oklahoma	D	83	67	−16
Oregon	R	46	42	−4
Rhode Island	D	62	61	−1
South Carolina	R	34	31	−3
South Dakota	R	46	33	−13
Tennessee	D	70	68	−2
Texas	R	38	40	+2
West Virginia	D	69	70	+1
Wyoming	R	36	26	−10

Note: Predictions are based on estimates presented in tables 4.2 and 4.3 and data collected by authors.
[a]D = Democrat; R = Republican; N = none.
[b]Wrong winner predicted.

the Republican challenger was hurt by the depressed condition of the state's farm-based economy. Like South Dakota voters in 1986, many North Dakota voters apparently took out their dissatisfaction with the Reagan administration's farm policies by voting against the Republican Senate candidate in 1988.

Our incumbent support model also failed to predict the close call experienced by Senator Malcolm Wallop (R-Wyoming), who received barely 50 percent of the vote against his Democratic challenger, State Senator John Vinich. In addition to Vinich's strong campaign, Wallop's main problem was that he came across as an intellectual who was more concerned about national and international issues than about the problems of his constituents in Wyoming.

One incumbent who our model predicted would have a close call but did not was Howard Metzenbaum of Ohio. The liberal Democratic incumbent was expected to face a stiff challenge from Cleveland Mayor George Voinovich, and our model predicted an even split in the vote. Despite spending over

8 million dollars on his campaign, however, Voinovich received only 43 percent of the vote to Metzenbaum's 57 percent. The explanation, according to most observers of Ohio politics, was that Metzenbaum ran a much better campaign than Voinovich. While Voinovich's campaign floundered for a theme, Metzenbaum's television advertisements portrayed the incumbent as a fighter for the common man and emphasized his attention to local issues and problems. As a result, Senator Metzenbaum, despite having one of the most liberal voting records in the Senate, ran 13 percentage points ahead of Democratic presidential candidate Michael Dukakis.

Our models again performed well in predicting the results of the 1990 Senate elections. We correctly predicted the outcomes of twenty-seven out of twenty-eight contests, including all three open seat races. However, our model failed to predict the biggest upset of the 1990 Senate elections—the defeat of incumbent Rudy Boschwitz (R-Minnesota) at the hands of Paul Wellstone. Wellstone, a political science professor who had never held elected office, was the only challenger to defeat an incumbent senator in 1990. He won despite being outspent by a margin of 6.2 million dollars to 1.3 million dollars. But Wellstone garnered an enormous amount of free publicity by contrasting his low-budget "people's campaign" with Boschwitz's extravagant PAC-financed effort. In addition, Boschwitz may have alienated voters by running a television commercial questioning Wellstone's religious faith; both candidates are Jewish, but Boschwitz's advertisement implicitly criticized the fact that Wellstone, whose wife is Christian, is not raising his children in the Jewish faith—a peculiar campaign tactic in an overwhelmingly Protestant state.

Our model also failed to predict the extraordinarily close call experienced by New Jersey Senator Bill Bradley. Bradley was held to 51 percent of the vote by a little-known Republican challenger who spent less than one million dollars on her campaign. The explanation for this unexpectedly poor showing was apparently voter outrage at New Jersey's Democratic governor, James Florio, over recent tax increases. Even though Bradley had nothing to do with the tax hikes, a number of voters evidently took out their anger at Florio, who was not on the ballot, by voting for the Republican Senate candidate, Christine Todd Whitman.

These contests illustrate the difficulty of quantifying all of the factors that influence the outcomes of Senate elections. They demonstrate that Senate campaigns matter and that they sometimes produce unexpected results. Furthermore, although money is one of the most important factors in Senate campaigns, it is not everything. Even in an age of paid consultants and media-based campaigns, strategy, skill, hard work, and luck still count for something. The case studies of four Senate campaigns in chapters 6 and 7 provide much more evidence along these lines.

One feature of the 1988 and 1990 Senate elections deserves special attention—the high rate of reelection enjoyed by incumbents. Of the fifty-seven incumbents who ran for reelection, only four were defeated. The 93 percent success rate of Senate incumbents in these two elections was much higher than the 78 percent average of the previous two decades.

Whether the high reelection rate of Senate incumbents in 1988 and 1990 was a temporary aberration or the beginning of a trend remains to be seen. Based on our model of incumbent support, however, we can identify three factors that contributed to incumbent success in these elections. The most obvious was that there were relatively few well-financed challengers. Just as important, however, was the absence of any overriding national issues in these elections. Thus, neither Democratic nor Republican challengers benefited from a strong national tide. Finally, and this may represent a longer term trend, not one incumbent in these two elections had a difficult primary contest. We have seen that a close primary contest often leads to a significant erosion of support for the incumbent in the general election. Any decline in primary competition would, therefore, make incumbent senators less vulnerable in general elections as well.

Summary and Conclusions

Based on the evidence presented in this chapter, candidate characteristics clearly emerge as the strongest influence on the outcomes of individual Senate contests. In Senate races involving an incumbent, the incumbent's record and the challenger's qualifications and financial resources were the most important factors influencing the outcome; in contests for open seats, the relative experience and financial resources of the candidates were the most important determinants of the outcome.

The challenger's campaign expenditures are the most important variable affecting an incumbent senator's chance of being reelected. Although an incumbent faced with a well-financed challenger can usually respond by increasing his or her own campaign spending, the incumbent's spending has much less impact on the outcome of a Senate race than the challenger's spending.[25]

---

25. It has been suggested that the relationship between campaign spending and election outcomes may be spurious—expectations of potential contributors regarding the outcome of an election could affect the candidates' fund-raising, and the same factors that influenced these expectations could affect the outcome of the elections. If the factors influencing both elite expectations and election outcomes were not included in our models, then our estimates of the effects of campaign spending could be biased. In order to test for this possibility, we added a measure of elite expectations (the preelection forecast published about a month before the election by *Congressional Quarterly Weekly Report*) to the incumbent support and open seat regression equations. In each case, the proportion of variance in election outcomes explained by the regression model increased only slightly, indicating that elite expectations were not based on factors excluded from our models.

One of the most important trends in American electoral politics in recent years has been a shift from party-centered to candidate-centered campaigns. This trend has had at least two major consequences for Senate elections. First, two-party competition has spread to every state and region of the country. Second, money is now more important than ever before—especially for challengers and candidates for open seats. The weakening of party loyalties in the electorate means that candidates must increasingly rely on personal appeal to win votes. Incumbents can use the perquisites of office for this purpose; challengers have to spend money.

Although the candidates' records, qualifications, and financial resources are the most important factors influencing the results of individual Senate races, national political conditions also have a significant influence on election outcomes. The president's popularity, evaluations of the national parties, and negative voting in midterm elections strongly influence the results of individual races and largely determine the national outcome—the overall number of seats won by each party. The state of the economy indirectly affects the outcomes of Senate elections by influencing voters' evaluations of the parties. Thus, Senate elections are more than the sum of thirty-three or thirty-four separate local races; they are also referenda on the performance of the incumbent president and his party.

CHAPTER 5

Money in Senate Elections: Who Gives It and Who Gets It?

Running for the U.S. Senate has become a very expensive proposition. Between 1974 and 1990, total spending by Senate candidates more than doubled after controlling for inflation, and this does not include independent expenditures by individuals and PACs or coordinated expenditures by party committees on behalf of Senate candidates, which have increased even more rapidly than spending by the candidates.[1] In the 1990 Senate elections, the sixty-seven major party candidates reported spending a total of 173 million dollars, down slightly from the record 190 million dollars spent by Senate candidates in 1988. The average Senate candidate in 1990 spent just under 2.6 million dollars.[2]

In 1988, the most recent year for which information is available, state and national party committees spent almost 17 million dollars on behalf of Senate candidates, while independent expenditures by individuals and PACs supporting or opposing Senate candidates totaled over 4 million dollars. Altogether, more than 200 million dollars were spent on the 1988 Senate elections—an average of close to 6 million dollars per seat.[3]

The rising cost of Senate campaigns has made fund-raising an increasingly onerous task for Senate candidates. In recent years, a number of incum-

---

1. Under the current campaign finance laws, party committees are allowed to spend up to a fixed amount of money on behalf of a Senate candidate. The spending limit is based on the population of the state and expenditures may be coordinated with a candidate's campaign. Independent expenditures by individuals or PACs to support or oppose Senate candidates are not limited and may not be coordinated with a candidate's campaign.
2. These figures and all subsequent campaign spending figures are based on combined primary and general elections expenditures of major party candidates in the general election. They exclude spending by defeated primary candidates and minor party candidates.
3. Data on the 1990 election was taken from a preliminary report issued by the Federal Election Commission; no data were available on coordinated expenditures by party committees or independent spending in the 1990 Senate elections. All earlier data on campaign spending, except the expenditures by individual candidates, are taken from Norman Ornstein, Thomas Mann, and Michael Malbin, *Vital Statistics on Congress, 1989–1990* (Washington, D.C.: Congressional Quarterly Press, 1990), 67–112. Data on expenditures by individual candidates are taken from various editions of *The Almanac of American Politics*.

bents and would-be candidates have cited the time and effort required for fund-raising as reasons for retiring or deciding not to run for the Senate in the first place. Skyrocketing campaign costs have also led to increased demands for changes in the campaign finance laws to limit spending by Senate candidates.

Campaign Finance Laws and Senate Elections

The financing of Senate campaigns is governed by the Federal Election Campaign Act (FECA) of 1971. This law, for the first time, required House and Senate candidates to disclose their contributions and expenditures. In 1974, in the aftermath of the Watergate scandal, Congress enacted several major amendments strengthening the FECA, including limitations on individual contributions and total expenditures. However, the Supreme Court's 1976 decision in the case of *Buckley v. Valeo* overturned several provisions of the FECA and severely restricted Congress's ability to regulate campaign finance.

Under the provisions of the FECA, all House and Senate candidates who spend over $5,000 on their campaigns are required to file reports with the Federal Election Commission (FEC) detailing their expenditures and listing all individuals and groups contributing $100 or more. Individual contributions to a single candidate cannot exceed $1,000, while political action committees are limited to $5,000. Despite inflation, these ceilings have not been changed since 1974.[4]

One of the most important FECA amendments adopted by Congress in 1974 allowed corporations and trade associations to form political action committees. Since then, the number of PACs has grown from under 600 to over 4,000, and their contributions to House and Senate candidates have skyrocketed from less than $10 million in 1972 to almost $150 million in 1990. PACs now provide about one-third of all campaign funds in House elections and one-fourth of all campaign funds in Senate elections.

In *Buckley v. Valeo,* the Supreme Court threw out several provisions of the Federal Election Campaign Act, including limits on candidates' total expenditures, limits on the amount of money a candidate is allowed to spend on his or her own campaign, and limits on the amount of money an individual or PAC can independently spend to support or oppose a candidate. The Court held that these limitations on campaign spending violated the First Amendment's guarantee of freedom of speech. However, the Court upheld the provision of the FECA that set spending limits in presidential campaigns, which were tied to candidates' voluntary acceptance of federal campaign funds.[5]

---

4. Frank J. Sorauf, *Money in American Elections* (Glenview, Ill.: Scott, Foresman, 1988), 34–39.

5. Sorauf, *Money*, 40.

Since the *Buckley* decision there have been several unsuccessful attempts to legislate limits on congressional campaign expenditures. The most important of these was a bill introduced by Senator David Boren (D-Oklahoma) in 1987 that would have set voluntary spending ceilings for Senate campaigns and provided public financing for any candidate abiding by the spending ceiling whose opponent exceeded the ceiling. However, this bill was blocked by a Republican filibuster. A similar bill was introduced at the beginning of the 101st Congress in 1991.

If it had been enacted into law, the Boren bill would have had a significant impact on Senate campaign finance: in the 1988 election, fifteen of thirty-three Democratic candidates and seventeen of thirty-three Republican candidates exceeded the spending ceiling proposed in the bill for their state. Eleven of twelve Republican incumbents and seven of fifteen Democratic incumbents exceeded the spending ceiling, compared with two of fifteen Republican challengers and five of twelve Democratic challengers. Four of six Republican candidates and three of six Democratic candidates for open seats also exceeded the spending ceiling proposed in the Boren bill.

Republican opposition to limits on campaign spending has been based on the assumption that such limits would have a more adverse impact on GOP candidates than their Democratic opponents. In 1986, the average Republican Senate candidate spent over $3 million while the average Democratic candidate spent just over $2 million. However, this advantage was due, in part, to the fact that, as a result of the GOP's dramatic gains in the 1980 Senate elections, eighteen of the twenty-seven incumbents running for reelection in 1986 were Republicans. In the 1988 election, Republican Senate candidates were outspent by their Democratic opponents by an average of $2.9 million to $2.6 million. In 1988, Democratic incumbents enjoyed a larger spending advantage over their challengers than did Republican incumbents and Democratic candidates for open seats outspent their GOP opponents. Before we accept the conclusion that spending ceilings would benefit Democrats, we need to examine trends in Senate campaign spending since 1974 and analyze the impact of campaign spending on the electoral fortunes of Democratic and Republican candidates.

Trends in Senate Campaign Spending, 1974–1990

Figures 5.1–5.3 display trends in Senate campaign spending by incumbents, challengers, and candidates for open seats between 1974, the first year for which spending data are available, and 1990. Only direct candidate expenditures are included—independent expenditures and coordinated expenditures by party committees are excluded. Spending is measured in constant 1974 dollars to correct for inflation.

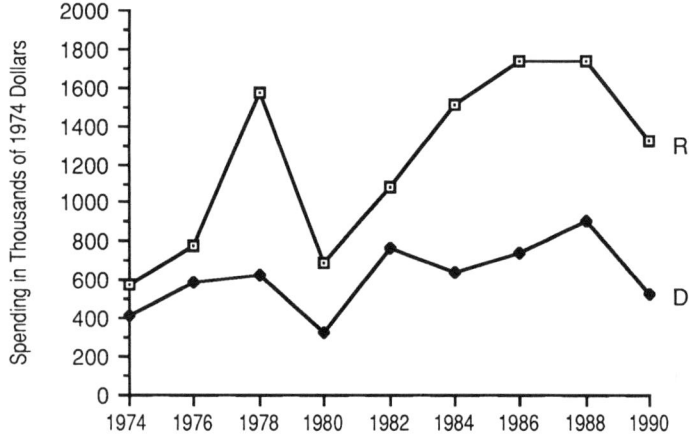

Fig. 5.1. Campaign spending by Republican incumbents and Democratic challengers

Perhaps the most surprising finding that emerges from the data illustrated in the figures is the absence of any clear Republican spending advantage except in races involving GOP incumbents (fig. 5.1). Republican incumbents outspent their Democratic challengers in all nine elections. Only in 1974, 1976, and 1982 did Democratic challengers come close to matching Republican incumbents in campaign spending. In the four most recent elections, GOP incumbents have enjoyed a two-to-one or better spending advantage over their Democratic challengers. For the entire period, Republican incumbents outspent their Democratic challengers by an average ratio of 1.9 to 1.

Despite the Republican party's vaunted fund-raising abilities, however, Democratic incumbents have enjoyed almost as large a spending advantage as their Republican counterparts (see fig. 5.2). The only time that Republican challengers came close to matching the spending levels of Democratic incumbents was in 1978. On average, Democratic incumbents outspent their Republican challengers by a ratio of 1.7 to 1.

A comparison of figures 5.1 and 5.2 shows that Republican incumbents usually spent more money on their campaigns than Democratic incumbents, but Democratic challengers were usually better financed than Republican challengers. These two findings are related. In Senate elections just as in House elections, incumbents tend to spend reactively. The amount of time and effort an incumbent devotes to fund-raising is based largely on the perceived seriousness of the threat posed by the challenger. Therefore, the more money the challenger raises and spends, the more money the incumbent will attempt

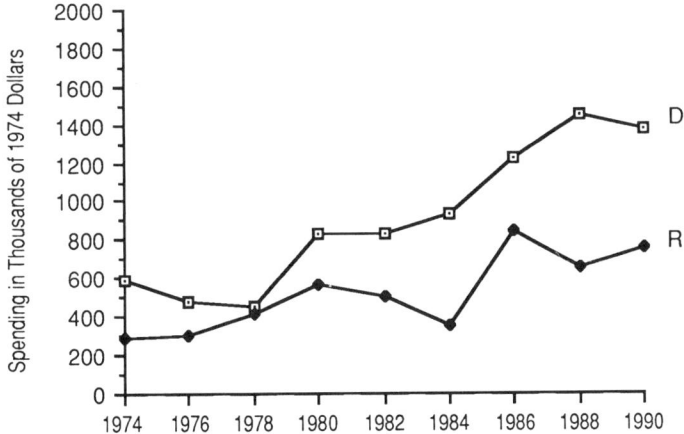

Fig. 5.2. Campaign spending by Democratic incumbents and Republican challengers

to raise and spend.[6] The reason Republican incumbents spent more money than Democratic incumbents was not primarily because they found it easier to raise money, but because they felt that they had to spend more money in order to defend their seats.

The data illustrated in figure 5.3 indicates that neither party has had a consistent spending advantage in contests for open Senate seats. The overall level of spending in these contests varied considerably over time. This is a function of the relatively small number of open Senate seats in most elections. In 1990, for example, there were only three open seats, all in relatively sparsely populated states—Idaho, New Hampshire, and Colorado. In each of these contests, the Republican candidate began the race with a substantial advantage in political experience and visibility. In addition, Idaho and New Hampshire are among the most Republican states in the nation. It is not surprising, therefore, that the Republican candidates for these open seats outspent their Democratic rivals by a substantial margin.

The 1990 election was not typical of the normal spending patterns in open seat races, however. With the spread of two-party competition to more and more states, most of these contests involve two candidates who are well-matched in political experience and financial resources. Overall, the data presented in figure 5.3 indicates that neither party had a consistent advantage

---

6. See Gary C. Jacobson, *Money in Congressional Elections* (New Haven: Yale University Press, 1980), 115–30.

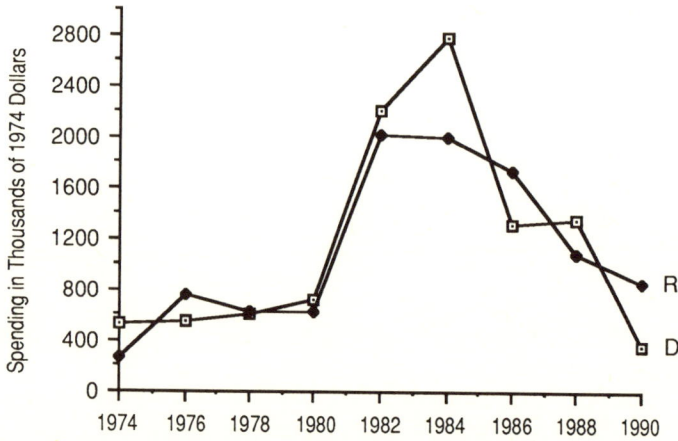

Fig. 5.3. **Campaign spending by candidates for open seats**

in campaign spending in open seat elections. In some years Democratic candidates outspent Republican candidates; in other years, such as 1990, Republican candidates had the advantage. On average, however, Democratic candidates outspent their Republican opponents by a ratio of 1.1 to 1. No trend favoring either party is evident.

What might account for the variation in party spending ratios over time? Given the absence of any central control over the allocation of campaign funds, spending patterns must be the cumulative result of decisions made by thousands of individuals and groups: individual contributors, party committees, PACs, and the candidates themselves.

Jacobson and Kernell have argued that campaign expenditures reflect strategic decision making by candidates and contributors: the quality of each party's challengers and candidates for open House and Senate seats and the ability of these candidates to raise money should reflect perceptions of the parties' prospects in the election. According to this hypothesis, if a party is expected to do well, it will attract many well-qualified candidates and these candidates will raise large campaign war chests; if a party is expected to do poorly, it will attract few well-qualified candidates and its candidates will have difficulty raising adequate campaign funds.[7]

If Jacobson and Kernell are correct, then relative spending by a party's incumbents and challengers in a given year should reflect that party's outlook in the election. When political conditions favor a party, the ratio of challenger

---

7. Gary C. Jacobson and Samuel Kernell, *Strategy and Choice in Congressional Elections* (New Haven: Yale University Press, 1981), 19–48.

to incumbent spending in that party should increase—strong challengers should raise substantial amounts of money while incumbents facing relatively weak opposition should not need to raise large campaign war chests. In contrast, when a party faces adverse political conditions, the ratio of challenger to incumbent spending should decline. Thus, a high ratio of challenger to incumbent spending should reflect an offensive approach to an election, while a low ratio should reflect a defensive approach.

In order to assess relative spending by incumbents and challengers, we can divide the average amount spent by a party's challengers by the average amount spent by a party's incumbents in a given year. A ratio of greater than one indicates that a party's challengers spent more on average than its incumbents while a ratio of less than one indicates that a party's challengers spent less on average than its incumbents. For example, in 1986, the average Republican challenger reported spending $1.9 million while the average Republican incumbent reported spending $3.6 million. Thus, the challenger to incumbent spending ratio for Republican Senate candidates was 0.53.

Table 5.1 displays the challenger-to-incumbent spending ratios for Democratic and Republican Senate candidates between 1974 and 1990. Because of the relatively small number of Senate candidates, the spending ratios are subject to considerable fluctuation due to factors peculiar to each election. Nevertheless, some clear patterns emerge from these data.

There is a striking difference between the two parties in the challenger-to-incumbent spending ratios. Among Democrats, challenger spending generally approached, and occasionally exceeded, incumbent spending. Only

TABLE 5.1. Challenger-to-Incumbent Spending Ratios in U.S. Senate Elections, 1974–90

Year	Democratic Ratio	Republican Ratio
1974	0.80	0.50
1976	1.20	0.30
1978	1.30	0.30
1980	0.40	0.80
1982	0.90	0.50
1984	0.80	0.30
1986	0.60	0.50
1988	0.60	0.40
1990	0.40	0.60
Average	0.78	0.47

Source: Based on data presented in Norman Ornstein, Thomas Mann, and Michael Malbin, *Vital Statistics on Congress* (Washington, D.C.: Congressional Quarterly Press, 1990), 76–77; data on 1990 elections provided by the Federal Election Commission.

twice, in 1980 and 1990, did the average Democratic challenger spend less than half as much as the average Democratic incumbent. In contrast, Republican incumbents almost always outspent challengers by a wide margin. Only in 1980, 1986, and 1990 did the average Republican challenger spend at least half as much as the average Republican incumbent. Over the entire period from 1974 through 1990, spending by Democratic challengers averaged 78 percent of spending by Democratic incumbents, while spending by Republican challengers averaged 47 percent of spending by Republican incumbents.

In order to test the Jacobson-Kernell strategic-spending hypothesis, we can compare each party's challenger-to-incumbent spending ratio under favorable political conditions with its ratio under unfavorable conditions. Between 1974 and 1990 there were two elections—1974 and 1982—in which political conditions seemed to strongly favor the Democratic party. In the aftermath of the Watergate scandal, President Ford's pardon of Richard Nixon, and a recession, the 1974 midterm election was expected to produce widespread Republican losses. In 1982, the Republican party also faced a difficult midterm election: in the midst of a severe recession with a national unemployment rate above 10 percent, President Reagan's approval rating dropped to the lowest level of his entire presidency.

In both 1980 and 1984, political conditions in the United States appeared to strongly favor the Republican party. During 1980 the Iran hostage crisis, double-digit inflation, and rising unemployment led to widespread dissatisfaction with the Carter administration and a bleak electoral outlook for Democratic candidates. Four years later, an economic boom and a popular Republican incumbent running for reelection appeared to favor GOP candidates.

The data in table 5.1 provides only limited support for the Jacobson-Kernell strategic-spending hypothesis. In both 1974 and 1982, which were expected to be good years for Democrats, the challenger-to-incumbent spending ratio was much higher for Democratic candidates than for Republican candidates. In 1980, which was expected to be a good year for Republicans, the challenger-to-incumbent spending ratio was much higher for Republican candidates than for Democratic candidates. In fact, 1980 was the only election in which this was true. Even though political conditions appeared to be highly favorable for the GOP in 1984, the challenger-to-incumbent spending ratio was much lower for Republican candidates than for Democratic candidates. In 1984, the average Republican challenger spent 26 percent of what the average Republican incumbent spent—the lowest challenger-to-incumbent spending ratio during the entire period for either party.

Despite highly favorable political conditions, the spending patterns of Republican candidates suggest that party contributors adopted a defensive orientation in 1984. But this orientation was not peculiar to the 1984 election.

In every election since 1974, with the single exception of 1980, Republican contributors have been much more generous in their support of Republican incumbents than in their support of Republican challengers. In 1984, this defensive approach may have cost the GOP several Senate seats. Despite Ronald Reagan's landslide victory in the presidential election, only one Democratic incumbent lost his seat and there was no net change in the partisan makeup of the Senate.

Sources of Campaign Funds: Who Gives What to Whom?

We may gain a better understanding of spending patterns in Senate elections by examining the sources of funds for different types of candidates. Senate candidates spent almost $200 million on their campaigns in 1988.[8] Sixty-nine percent of this total, or close to $140 million, was contributed by individuals or by the candidates themselves. Another 22 percent of the total, or just under $45 million, was contributed by Political Action Committees. The remaining 9 percent of Senate campaign funds in 1988 came from party committees.

The proportion of Senate campaign funds contributed by individuals and candidates has been gradually declining—falling from 83 percent of total contributions in 1974 to 69 percent in 1988; during the same period contributions by PACs have doubled—going from 11 percent of total contributions in 1974 to 22 percent in 1988. However, PAC contributions still account for a much smaller proportion of campaign funds in Senate races than in House races—in 1988, PAC contributions accounted for 40 percent of all campaign funds in House elections, up from 17 percent in 1974. Party contributions to Senate candidates, including coordinated expenditures made on behalf of candidates, have increased slightly since 1974—going from 6 percent of total contributions to 9 percent in 1986.

Before 1978, Democratic candidates depended on PACs for a larger share of their campaign funds than Republican candidates. Since 1978, however, both Democratic and Republican Senate candidates have received about one-fifth of their campaign funds from PACs. However, Republican candidates have generally received more generous support from party committees than their Democratic opponents. Since 1974, Republican candidates have received an average of 11 percent of their campaign funds from party committees, compared with only 5 percent for Democratic candidates.

In order to compare the levels of support for different types of candidates by different types of contributors, table 5.2 displays the average amount

---

8. This total excludes independent expenditures but includes coordinated expenditures made by party committees on behalf of Senate candidates.

contributed by individuals, party committees, and PACs to Democratic and Republican incumbents, challengers, and open seat candidates, in the 1982, 1984, 1986, and 1988 elections. For example, in 1988, the average Republican incumbent received $1,101,000 in PAC contributions.

The data presented in table 5.2 reveal some striking differences in the behav-

TABLE 5.2. Average Contribution to Senate Candidates by Source, 1982–88

Candidate	Party Committees	PACs	Individuals and Candidates
		1982	
D incumbent	74	413	1,271
R incumbent	205	579	1,570
D challenger	82	187	1,313
R challenger	263	141	832
D open	168	281	4,085
R open	696	616	3,389
		1984	
D incumbent	59	538	1,303
R incumbent	196	670	2,404
D challenger	129	257	1,115
R challenger	154	118	498
D open	372	53	5,295
R open	346	384	3,070
		1986	
D incumbent	159	807	2,098
R incumbent	291	907	2,630
D challenger	127	436	1,261
R challenger	410	243	1,646
D open	141	681	2,196
R open	270	927	2,977
		1988	
D incumbent	142	1,027	2,372
R incumbent	339	1,101	2,794
D challenger	267	388	1,770
R challenger	332	203	1,311
D open	279	557	2,647
R open	386	771	1,810

Source: Based on data presented in Ornstein, Mann, and Malbin, *Vital Statistics*, 88–92.

Note: Contributions in thousands of current dollars.

ior of different types of campaign contributors. Not surprisingly, PACs contributed heavily to incumbents. Candidates for open seats also received rather generous support from PACs. PAC contributions to Democratic candidates for open seats averaged 76 percent of PAC contributions to Democratic incumbents, while PAC contributions to Republican candidates for open seats averaged 84 percent of PAC contributions to Republican incumbents. These findings seem to support the conventional wisdom that PACs are mainly concerned with buying access and, therefore, concentrate their contributions on candidates who have a good chance of winning, regardless of their party affiliation.

While challengers generally got the short end of the stick when it came to PAC contributions, Republican challengers were especially disadvantaged. Whereas the average Democratic challenger received 46 percent of the PAC contributions of the average Democratic incumbent, the average Republican challenger only received 22 percent of the contributions of the average Republican incumbent. In the 1984, 1986, and 1988 elections, the average Democratic challenger received about twice as much money from PACs as the average Republican challenger.

Clearly, the fund-raising difficulties of Republican challengers cannot be attributed to minority party status. Between 1981 and 1987, the Republicans were the majority party in the Senate, but, in all three elections during this period, Republican challengers raised less money from PACs than Democratic challengers. Thus, the findings presented in table 5.2 apparently reflect long-term differences between the contribution strategies of Democratic and Republican PACs.

In contrast to PACs, Democratic and Republican party committees generally concentrated their contributions on open seat candidates and, to a lesser extent, challengers. Republican candidates received about twice as much financial support from party committees as did Democratic candidates. In the four elections between 1982 and 1988, Democratic incumbents received an average of $108,000 in direct and indirect party contributions compared with $151,000 for Democratic challengers and $240,000 for Democratic candidates for open seats. During the same period, Republican incumbents received an average of $258,000 in direct and indirect party contributions compared with $290,000 for Republican challengers and $424,000 for Republican candidates for open seats.

Candidates for open seats led the way in funds contributed by individuals and self-financing. In all four elections, Democratic candidates for open seats received more money from these sources than their party's incumbents; in three out of four elections, Republican candidates for open seats received more money from these sources than their party's incumbents. Democratic open seat candidates received an average of almost $3.6 million in contributions from individuals and self-financing compared with $1.8 million for Democratic incumbents and $1.3 million for Democratic challengers.

Republican open seat candidates received an average of $2.9 million in contributions from individuals and self-financing compared with $2.4 million for Republican incumbents and $1.1 million for Republican challengers. Just as with PAC money, Republican challengers obtained far less money through individual contributions and self-financing than Republican incumbents, while Democratic challengers fared much better compared with their party's incumbents.

PAC contributions now account for a substantial share of all Senate campaign funds. Moreover, the figures included in table 5.2 undoubtedly understate the role of PACs in financing Senate campaigns. In recent elections, a number of PACs have utilized a strategy known as "bundling" in order to avoid the contribution limits imposed by federal election laws. Bundling involves assembling a large number of individual contributions and presenting these as a package to a candidate. In 1985, for example, one insurance industry PAC presented a package of $215,000 in "individual" contributions to Bob Packwood, the chairman of the Senate Finance Committee.[9] Despite the fact that this practice is an obvious attempt to avoid the legal limit on contributions by a single PAC to a Senate candidate, the Federal Election Commission has made no effort to crack down on bundling.

We have seen that PACs tend to concentrate their contributions on incumbents and candidates for open seats and that Republican challengers have been at a disadvantage in receiving PAC funds. However, different types of PACs may follow different contribution strategies in Senate elections. Table 5.3 displays the average contribution to Democratic and Republican incumbents, challengers, and open seat candidates in the 1982, 1984, 1986, and 1988 elections by three types of PACs: business and professional PACs (including PACs run by corporations, trade associations, health organizations, and cooperatives), labor PACs, and nonconnected (primarily ideological) PACs.

In all four elections, business and professional PACs accounted for the large majority of all PAC contributions to Senate candidates. In fact, the business and professional share of PAC contributions rose from 63 percent in 1982 to 65 percent in 1984 and 67 percent in both 1986 and 1988. In contrast, contributions by labor PACs declined from 22 percent of total PAC contributions in 1982 to 16 percent in 1984, 1986, and 1988. Thus, business and professional PACs outspent labor PACs by about a three-to-one ratio in 1982 and by better than a four-to-one ratio in 1984, 1986, and 1988.

Organized labor has not only been declining in its share of workers in the U.S. labor force but also in its share of contributions to congressional candidates. In 1974, labor PACs outspent business and professional PACs and accounted for more than half of all PAC contributions to House and Senate

---

9. Hedrick Smith, *The Power Game: How Washington Works* (New York: Random House, 1988), 260.

candidates. In 1988, labor PACs were outspent by almost a three-to-one ratio by business and professional PACs and accounted for just over one-fifth of all PAC contributions to House and Senate candidates. Moreover, labor PACs have concentrated their contributions disproportionately on House candidates.

TABLE 5.3. Average Contribution to Senate Candidates by PACs, 1982–88

Candidate	Business PACs	Labor PACs	Nonconnected PACs
1982			
D incumbent	225	141	46
R incumbent	492	28	59
D challenger	25	119	187
R challenger	101	1	141
D open	73	145	63
R open	526	9	75
1984			
D incumbent	346	106	84
R incumbent	572	16	82
D challenger	48	125	83
R challenger	115	1	2
D open	198	229	112
R open	319	4	61
1986			
D incumbent	500	178	129
R incumbent	769	27	107
D challenger	162	173	104
R challenger	179	0	59
D open	246	267	168
R open	786	8	133
1988			
D incumbent	637	212	177
R incumbent	931	42	127
D challenger	97	170	121
R challenger	148	0	37
D open	244	174	139
R open	653	30	119

Source: Based on data presented in Ornstein, Mann, and Malbin, *Vital Statistics*, 88–92.

Note: Contributions in thousands of current dollars.

In 1988, for example, labor PACs accounted for 26 percent of all PAC contributions to House candidates, compared to only 16 percent of all PAC contributions to Senate candidates.

Nonconnected PACs accounted for 15 percent of all PAC contributions to Senate candidates in 1982 and this figure rose slightly to 18 percent in 1984, falling to 17 percent in both 1986 and 1988. Between 1974 and 1988, contributions by nonconnected PACs rose from 6 percent of total PAC contributions to House and Senate candidates to almost 13 percent. Moreover, since 1980, nonconnected PACs have concentrated a disproportionate share of their contributions on Senate candidates. This trend probably reflects the growing focus of ideologically oriented PACs on the Senate.

The figures presented in table 5.3 help to explain why Republican challengers have been at a particular disadvantage in receiving PAC contributions. Republican Senate candidates have generally relied very heavily on business and professional PACs for campaign funds, but these PACs have provided much less support for Republican challengers than for Republican incumbents and candidates for open seats. In fact, in all four elections, business and professional PACs gave more than twice as much money to Democratic incumbents as they gave to Republican challengers. In 1988, business PACs gave more than four times as much money to Democratic incumbents as they gave to Republican challengers. Thus, the growing dominance of business and professional PACs in Senate elections has not resulted in a general Republican advantage in Senate campaign finances.

Labor PACs took a much more partisan approach in their campaign contributions than did business and professional PACs. Whereas business and professional PACs gave about one-third of their contributions to Democratic candidates (almost all of which went to incumbents), labor PACs gave less than one-tenth of their contributions to Republican candidates. Moreover, in marked contrast with the approach taken by business and professional PACs toward Republican candidates, labor PACs gave almost as much to Democratic challengers as to Democratic incumbents.

Since 1980, there has been a dramatic shift in the partisan composition of contributions by nonconnected PACs to Senate candidates. In both 1978 and 1980 nonconnected PACs gave almost three-fourths of their contributions to Republican candidates. However, in 1982, the GOP share of nonconnected PAC contributions declined to 50 percent, in both 1984 and 1986 nonconnected PACs gave over half (56 and 55 percent) of their contributions to Democratic candidates, and, in 1988, Democratic candidates received 64 percent of all contributions by nonconnected PACs. It appears that the dramatic and well-publicized successes of conservative ideological PACs in the 1978 and 1980 Senate elections led to a PAC counterattack by liberal interest groups in the early 1980s.

The figures presented in table 5.3 show that, in recent elections, Republican challengers have fared no better with nonconnected PACs than with business and professional PACs. They have received less than half as much from nonconnected PACs as GOP incumbents have received. In contrast, Democratic challengers have received an average of 90 percent as much from nonconnected PACs as Democratic incumbents have received. While the amounts involved are relatively small, the behavior of nonconnected PACs in recent elections has tended to reinforce the proincumbent bias in Senate Republican campaign finances.

A Note on Independent Expenditures

Independent expenditures constitute one of the most controversial aspects of campaign financing today. As a result of the Supreme Court's 1976 decision in *Buckley v. Valeo*, any individual or group can spend an unlimited amount of money to support or oppose a candidate as long as these expenditures are "not made with the cooperation or with the prior consent of, or in consultation with, or at the request or suggestion of, a candidate or any agent or authorized committee of such candidate" (11 C.F.R. 109.1[a]).

Independent expenditures first became a significant factor in congressional elections in 1980, when the National Conservative Political Action Committee (NCPAC) organized a negative advertising campaign aimed at several Democratic Senators, including such prominent liberals as Birch Bayh of Indiana, Frank Church of Idaho, George McGovern of South Dakota, John Culver of Iowa, and Alan Cranston of California. All of the Democrats targeted by NCPAC except Cranston were defeated. Of the $1.7 million in reported independent expenditures in the 1980 Senate elections, over three-fourths ($1.3 million) was spent on negative campaigns aimed at Democratic candidates.

Building on its success in 1980, NCPAC and other conservative groups increased their efforts in the 1982 midterm elections. Independent expenditures in the 1982 Senate elections increased to $4.1 million. Once again, over three-fourths of this total ($3.2 million) were spent on negative campaigns directed at Democratic candidates, including prominent liberals such as Howard Metzenbaum of Ohio, Paul Sarbanes of Maryland, and the bête noir of the conservative movement, Edward Kennedy of Massachusetts. This time, however, the results were different. All of the liberal Democratic Senators targeted by NCPAC were reelected—most by overwhelming margins. Without an unpopular Democratic president in the White House and Ronald Reagan at the head of the ticket, NCPAC's independent expenditure campaign flopped.

Since 1982 there has been a significant shift in the composition of independent expenditures in Senate elections. In 1984, the largest amount of independent expenditures ($2.1 million out of a total of $4.6 million) involved negative campaigns directed at *Republican* candidates; in 1986, the largest amount of money ($3.3 million out of a total of $5.3 million) was spent on positive campaigns on behalf of Republican candidates. In fact, more than three-fourths of all independent expenditures in the 1986 Senate elections were positive. Another change in 1986 was that almost as much money ($4.0 million) was spent on House elections as on Senate elections.

The overall level of independent expenditures in House and Senate elections dropped between 1986 and 1988—from $9.4 million to $7.2 million. Spending in Senate elections declined from $5.3 million in 1986 to $4.4 million in 1988. The pattern of spending in 1988 was very similar to that in 1986, however. There was $3.6 million in positive spending in Senate races compared with only $0.7 million in negative spending. Just over $2.8 million was spent on behalf of Republican Senate candidates compared with $0.8 million on behalf of Democratic candidates.

The shift from negative to positive independent expenditures in 1986 and 1988 may have reflected media criticism of earlier negative campaigns or a perception of growing voter resistance to such tactics. In both 1982 and 1984, negative independent expenditure campaigns met with little success. It remains to be seen whether the new, positive direction evident in 1986 and 1988 will continue in future independent expenditure campaigns.

Except in 1984, independent expenditures in Senate elections have had a strongly pro-Republican tilt. However, independent expenditures still constitute only a small fraction of all Senate campaign expenditures— approximately 2 percent in 1988. It is in presidential elections that independent expenditure campaigns have become a major factor. Independent expenditures came to almost $14 million in 1980, $17.5 million in 1984, and just over $14 million in 1988.

Since each presidential candidate in 1984 was limited to spending approximately $34 million in public funds, independent expenditures constituted a substantial proportion of all spending on the presidential campaign. Moreover, these independent expenditures had an overwhelmingly pro-Republican tilt: over 90 percent of all independent expenditures in the 1980, 1984, and 1988 presidential elections were made on behalf of Republican candidates Ronald Reagan and George Bush. In 1984, Ronald Reagan's campaign received almost half as much financial support through independent expenditures as it received through public campaign funds. Thus, independent expenditures have provided the Republican party with an effective tool for avoiding the spending limits imposed by federal election laws.

These developments raise an important question about proposals to limit spending in Senate elections: what impact would such limits have on independent expenditures in Senate elections? Based on the history of presidential campaign finance, we would expect such spending ceilings to result in a diversion of funds from candidates to independent expenditures. And based on the history of independent expenditures in Senate elections, it is easy to predict which party would benefit from such a diversion.

Campaign Spending and Election Outcomes: Who Benefits?

Perhaps the most important question about campaign spending is how it affects the outcomes of elections. What types of Senate candidates have been most advantaged or disadvantaged in the electoral arena by virtue of their campaign finances? At first glance, the answer to this question might appear to be fairly obvious: candidates who have more money to spend—primarily incumbents—are advantaged, while candidates who have less money to spend—primarily challengers—are disadvantaged. In reality, though, the answer is more complicated. All campaign money is equal, but, when it comes to influencing voters, some campaign funds are more equal than others.

In evaluating the effects of campaign spending on election outcomes, the most important distinction is that between incumbents and either challengers or candidates for open seats. An incumbent Senator running for reelection has already had at least six years to get his or her message across to the voters. What he or she says or does during the campaign is likely to have only a marginal impact on public attitudes toward his or her candidacy. In contrast, a challenger or a candidate for an open Senate seat usually begins the campaign as a relatively unknown quantity to most of the electorate. Even if a candidate has held a statewide office, his or her record may provide voters with very little information about how he or she would perform in the Senate. Therefore, what a challenger or candidate for an open seat says or does during the campaign should have a much stronger influence on public attitudes toward his or her candidacy than we would expect to find in the case of an incumbent.

It follows from the preceding argument that, dollar for dollar, spending by challengers and open seat candidates should produce a greater electoral return than spending by incumbents. In fact, there is a considerable body of evidence supporting this hypothesis in the case of House elections.[10] The results presented in chapter 4 showed that nonincumbents' campaign spending also has a much greater impact than incumbents' campaign spending in Senate elections. In the incumbent support model, the estimated effect of challenger

---

10. See Stanton A. Glantz, Alan I. Abramowitz, and Michael P. Burkart, "Election Outcomes: Whose Money Matters?" *Journal of Politics* 38 (June, 1988): 385–403; Gary C. Jacobson, "The Effects of Campaign Spending in Congressional Elections," *American Political Science Review* 72 (June, 1978): 469–91; Jacobson, *Money*, 136–62.

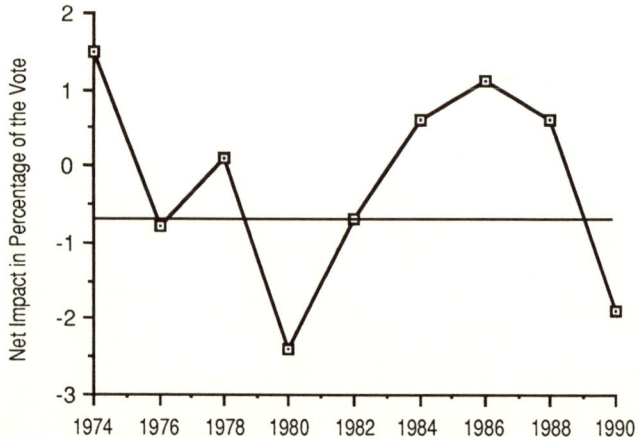

Fig. 5.4. Net impact of campaign spending on the average Democratic vote, 1974–90

spending was three times as great as the estimated effect of incumbent spending and challenger spending was the most influential variable determining election outcomes, far outweighing the partisan and ideological composition of the electorate and national political conditions. In the open seat model, relative campaign spending along with relative candidate experience were by far the most influential determinants of election outcomes.

Between 1974 and 1990, the average Senate challenger increased his or her share of the vote by about 10 percentage points as a result of campaign expenditures while the average Senate incumbent increased his or her share of the vote by about 5 percentage points as a result of campaign expenditures. Combining these estimates, the net impact of campaign spending in an average Senate race was to increase the challenger's share of the vote by about 5 percentage points, even though the average incumbent outspent the average challenger by a substantial margin.

Based on the estimated effects of campaign spending by incumbents, challengers, and open seat candidates, we can measure the net impact of campaign spending on each party's share of the vote in an average Senate race. Figure 5.4 shows the results for each election since 1974. Once again, there is no evidence that either party has consistently benefited as a result of campaign spending patterns. In five out of nine elections, including three of the last four, Democratic candidates had a net advantage as a result of campaign spending. Even though most Democratic candidates were outspent by their Republican opponents in 1986, they got a much higher average rate of electoral return from their campaign dollars because so many of them were challengers. Only twice, in 1980 and 1990, did GOP Senate candidates enjoy a large net advantage (+2.4 percent and +1.9 percent) as a result of campaign spending. In 1980, most of the challengers were Republicans, while, in 1990, the Democrats fielded an exceptionally weak group of challengers and open seat candidates. Combining all nine elections, the net impact of campaign spending was an average Republican advantage of 0.2 percent of the vote.

Evaluating the Consequences of Campaign Spending Limits

What effect would spending limits have on party fortunes in Senate elections? We addressed this question by using the estimates obtained for our incumbent support and open seat models and substituting the spending ceilings proposed in the Boren bill for the actual expenditures of all candidates who exceeded these limits in the 1986 Senate elections. Table 5.4 displays the actual results of all thirty-two contested Senate races in 1986 and the estimated impact of the proposed spending ceiling on each race. These results are based on the assumption that all candidates would have adhered to the spending limit proposed in the bill in order to avoid having their opponents receive public campaign funds.

Even though challenger spending has a much stronger impact on the outcomes of Senate elections than incumbent spending, only six challengers (four Democrats and two Republicans) would have been adversely affected by the Boren bill. This is because very few challengers exceeded the spending ceiling proposed in the bill. In only one race, in South Dakota, does it appear that the proposed spending ceiling would probably have cost a challenger (a Democrat) the election. The average Democratic or Republican challenger would have received an additional 0.1 percent of the vote if the spending ceilings had been in effect.

Democratic candidates for open seats would have been the major beneficiaries if the proposed spending ceilings had been in effect in 1986. They would have gained an average of 1.3 percent of the vote. Overall, Democratic candidates would have benefited slightly from the spending ceilings, gaining an average of 0.3 percent of the vote. However, according to this analysis, not one defeated Democratic candidate would have been elected as a result of the spending limits.

Discussion and Conclusions

Republican opposition to campaign spending limits has been based on the argument that such limits would work to the disadvantage of the minority party, because its challengers would need to spend more than the allowable limit in order to overcome the electoral advantage enjoyed by Democratic incumbents. In 1986 and 1988, however, only four of twenty-four Republican Senate challengers were able to reach the proposed spending limit for their state. In general, Republican challengers have done poorly in terms of fundraising, especially in comparison with their party's incumbents and open seat candidates. Both individual Republican contributors and business PACs have

TABLE 5.4. Estimated Effects of Spending Limits on the Democratic Share of the Major Party Vote in 1986 Senate Elections

State	Incumbent	Actual Vote Percentage	Estimated Effect	Predicted Vote Percentage
Alabama	R	50.2	+0.8	51.0
Arizona	None	39.5	+3.3	42.8
Arkansas	D	62.3	−0.7	61.6
California	D	50.7	+0.9	51.6
Colorado	None	50.8	−0.0	50.8
Connecticut	D	65.1	−1.0	64.1
Florida	R	54.7	−0.5	54.2
Georgia	R	50.9	+0.8	51.7
Idaho	R	48.4	−1.4	47.0
Illinois	D	65.9	NA	65.9
Indiana	R	38.9	+0.3	39.2
Iowa	R	33.7	+1.1	34.8
Kansas	R	30.0	NA	30.0
Kentucky	D	74.4	NA	74.4
Louisiana	None	52.8	+3.3	56.1
Maryland	None	60.7	NA	60.7
Missouri	None	47.4	+1.0	48.4
Nevada	None	52.8	+1.3	54.1
New Hampshire	R	33.9	NA	33.9
New York	R	42.0	+1.5	43.5
North Carolina	None	51.8	+1.0	52.8
North Dakota	R	50.3	+1.1	51.4
Ohio	D	62.4	NA	62.4
Oklahoma	R	44.8	−1.6	43.2
Oregon	R	36.4	+1.8	38.2
Pennsylvania	R	43.2	+0.3	43.5
South Carolina	D	63.4	−0.9	62.5
South Dakota	R	51.7	−3.7	<u>48.0</u>
Utah	R	26.9	NA	26.9
Vermont	D	64.6	+0.9	65.5
Washington	R	51.0	+0.5	51.5
Wisconsin	R	48.2	+1.1	49.3

Source: Almanac of American Politics 1988 and analysis conducted by authors.
Notes: NA = not applicable because neither candidate exceeded proposed spending limit. The predicted result is underlined if the outcome would have been altered by the spending limit.

tended to concentrate their contributions on Republican incumbents and open seat candidates, while largely ignoring GOP challengers even when political conditions appeared promising for the party. As long as this situation continues, spending limits such as those proposed in the Boren bill will have little impact on the campaigns of Republican challengers.

In the long run, spending limits might well work to the advantage of Republican Senate candidates. In the first place, the spending limits would not include expenditures by party committees. Since 1974, Republican Senate candidates have enjoyed a significant advantage in terms of party expenditures. Moreover, as Sorauf has argued, the figures on party contributions and coordinated expenditures undoubtedly understate the benefits that accrue to Republican candidates as a result of the GOP's enormous advantage over the Democrats in party finances—in 1988, local, state, and national Republican committees reported expenditures of $257 million compared with $122 million for Democratic committees.[11]

Independent expenditures may pose an even greater potential threat to Democratic Senate candidates than party expenditures because, unlike contributions and coordinated expenditures by party committees, they are not limited by law. In the last three presidential elections, the Republican candidates enjoyed a huge advantage in the area of independent expenditures. In 1988, almost $13 million was spent on behalf of George Bush's candidacy, compared with less than $1 million on behalf of Michael Dukakis's candidacy. Rising independent expenditures have made the legal spending limits in presidential campaigns virtually meaningless.

If spending limits are imposed on Senate campaigns, then something very similar to what has happened in presidential elections may occur in Senate elections: a diversion of candidate spending into independent expenditures. Based on the history of recent presidential campaigns, the Republican party will probably be much more successful in this venture than the Democratic party. Before Senate Democrats enact a campaign reform law incorporating spending ceilings in Senate campaigns, they would do well to consider the consequences that spending ceilings have had in presidential campaigns.

---

11. Sorauf, *Money*, 153.

CHAPTER 6

Incumbent Winners in Senate Campaigns in the Television Age

In chapter 4 we statistically examined the factors that affect Senate election outcomes. Of particular importance were statewide characteristics (ideology, partisanship, and size), incumbent characteristics (voting record, scandals or controversies, and intraparty competition), challenger characteristics (prior political experience, celebrity status, and campaign expenditures), and national political conditions (the president's approval rating, party competence and the state of the economy, and the presence of a midterm election). We further analyzed campaign finance in chapter 5. Statistics alone, however, do not and cannot tell the entire story of Senate elections. In order to illustrate the analytic findings of the preceeding chapters, and in order to underscore some of the exceptions to these generalizations, chapters 6 and 7 will explore the character of modern Senate campaigns by means of an in-depth examination of four Senate campaigns in 1986: the Cranston-Zschau contest in California, the D'Amato-Green contest in New York, the Hawkins-Graham contest in Florida, and the Abdnor-Daschle contest in South Dakota. We will pay close attention to the factors found important in chapter 4, with special attention to the main use to which campaign revenues are put: television advertising. There is no such thing as a typical Senate campaign, and even four campaigns in the same year cannot do justice to the variety of candidates and circumstances found in Senate contests. Nevertheless, these four campaigns illustrate many of the characteristics of modern Senate elections and some of the variations on these characteristics.

In 1986, Alan Cranston faced the first serious challenge from a Republican candidate since his election to the Senate in 1968. Cranston's advancing years and his disastrous campaign for the Democratic presidential nomination in 1984 contributed to his political problems in 1986. Yet the biggest difference between the 1986 campaign and Cranston's earlier contests was that, in 1986, the Republican party nominated a strong challenger, Congressman Ed Zschau (pronounced like the show in shower). The result was a high-profile, media-based campaign featuring extensive use of negative television advertising by both candidates, a major effort in support of Zschau's campaign by the Republican party, campaign visits by President Reagan, and the expenditure of over $12 million by each candidate. Cranston was reelected by a narrow 51 to 49 margin.

The 1986 Senate campaign in New York was almost the antithesis of the California campaign—the contest was virtually over before it began. By carefully cultivating his politically and ethnically diverse constituency for six years, and by raising an enormous war chest before the 1986 campaign ever began, Alphonse D'Amato, the Republican incumbent, convinced several potentially strong Democratic challengers (including Brooklyn District Attorney and 1980 Senate candidate Elizabeth Holtzman, Congressman Thomas Downey, and former vice presidential nominee Geraldine Ferraro) to stay out of the race. The Democratic primary was won by Mark Green, a liberal, Ralph Nader associate whose only previous campaign experience had been an unsuccessful run for the House of Representatives from Manhattan. Green, who refused to accept donations from political action committees, was unable to raise much money, making it difficult for him to criticize the incumbent's record effectively. Alphonse D'Amato was reelected to a second term by the largest margin of any Republican Senate candidate in New York's history.

The 1986 Florida Senate race was notable for the fact that the Republican incumbent, Paula Hawkins, was the underdog in the contest from the outset. Her challenger, Bob Graham, completing his second term as Florida's governor, was extremely popular with almost all of the state's diverse ethnic groups. Hawkins, after recovering from some gaffes committed early in her term, was also rated quite highly in the polls, but could not match Graham's visibility as governor. Both candidates waged expensive, media-oriented campaigns. The incumbent stressed the problem of crime and her efforts to stem the flow of drugs into the state. Nevertheless, Graham's well-publicized support for the death penalty made it difficult to convince voters that he was soft on crime. Despite campaign visits for Hawkins by President Reagan, Graham won a convincing 55 to 45 victory in the general election.

The 1986 South Dakota Senate campaign differed in several important respects from the Senate campaigns in heavily populated and politically diverse states such as California, New York, and Florida. South Dakota is a sparsely populated state with no major population center, making television advertising a more difficult weapon. Traditionally, states such as South Dakota require personal campaigning and direct contact with voters, yet even here television played a crucial role. In 1980, when the state included two House districts, Congressman James Abdnor, who already represented half the state, succeeded in ousting George McGovern from the Senate. Six years later, Abdnor himself faced a formidable challenge from South Dakota's only congressman, Thomas Daschle. Abdnor was hurt by a depressed farm economy and by his own support for Reagan administration farm policies. The

Democratic challenger defeated the Republican incumbent by a 52 to 48 margin.

The states we have chosen will allow us to examine the crucial features of Senate races across a variety of contexts. The states are geographically diverse: the Northeast, South, Midwest/Plains, and West are all represented. Two of the states have traditionally been dominated by one party; two of the states have a history of strong interparty competition. Three of the races involved experienced challengers and were competitive; one involved a political unknown and was not. In the three competitive states, television advertising, the raison d'être for fund-raising activities, played a major role; in the New York race, the challenger's lack of television expenditures played a major role. The incumbents won two of the races but lost two others. While all races took place in 1986, economic and political conditions varied across the states. California was in the middle of a defense industry boom; South Dakota suffered from a farm economy bust. The heavily Democratic Florida voters loved Ronald Reagan; the heavily Republican South Dakota voters were not so enamored with the president.

California

First and foremost, California is the largest state in the Union, with over 27 million people. More than one out of every nine Americans lives there. After the 1980 census, California received forty-five congressional districts, up from forty-three in 1970, thirty-eight in 1960, and thirty in 1940. It will receive seven more following the 1990 census. Personal appeals to voters are impossible, so incumbents here, more than any other state, are at a relative disadvantage. California is only twenty-sixth in per-pupil education expenditures, but the electorate is highly educated: 43 percent have at least one year of college education and 20 percent have at least four years, ranking California eighth in the country. The ethnicity of the population is quite diverse. Sixteen percent is of Spanish origin, 7 percent black, and 5 percent Asian. Fifteen percent are foreign born. Only 45 percent of Californians were born in the state.[1]

The authors of *The Almanac of American Politics* describe California as follows. "California is not the nation's cultural capital, but it is its entertainment capital; it is not the financial capital, but it is its biggest and strongest

---

1. Much of the background information on the states and candidates discussed herein is derived from Michael Barone and Grant Ujifusa, *The Almanac of American Politics* (Washington, D.C.: National Journal, 1988); Alan Ehrenhalt, ed., *Politics in America* (Washington, D.C.: Congressional Quarterly, 1986); and Alan Ehrenhalt, ed., *Politics in America* (Washington, D.C.: Congressional Quarterly, 1988).

engine of economic growth; it is not the political capital, but it is one place where political trends are made."[2] The major metropolitan area is Los Angeles, with almost 3,000,000 people, followed by San Diego (875,000), San Francisco (680,000), and San Jose (629,000). Ninety-one percent of the people live in urban areas. California is fourth in the nation in violent crime rates. It is tenth in median family income and ninth in per capita tax burden. Its economy is heavily dependent on the military, receiving $40 billion in defense outlays in 1986, more than 17 percent of the nation's total. Over the last dozen years, the biggest changes in California have been the growth of high-tech industries in Silicon Valley and the vast influx of immigrants, mostly Asian and Mexican. "Los Angeles is to the nation today what New York was in 1913: the great entry port of people seeking—and finding—opportunity."[3]

California is a classic two-party state. The Senate seat vacated by Republican Governor Pete Wilson has changed hands between Republicans and Democrats four times since 1958. Cranston's Senate seat was in Republican hands from 1950, when Richard Nixon beat Helen Gahagan Douglas, until 1968, when Cranston defeated Max Rafferty. In the 1960s and 1970s, Republicans and Democrats in California were extremely polarized. The Democrats preferred the most liberal candidates, voting for Robert Kennedy (1968) and George McGovern (1972) in the presidential primaries, while the Republicans chose Barry Goldwater over Nelson Rockefeller (1964). California might be the only state that could elect both Jerry Brown and Ronald Reagan governor. The state now appears to be following a more moderate course: while right-wingers Max Rafferty and Bill Richardson received Republican Senate nominations in 1968 and 1974, moderates Pete Wilson and Ed Zschau received Senate nominations in the 1980s.

California continues its competitive party tradition today. Fifty-one percent of the voters are registered Democrats, 36 percent Republican. The governor is Republican, but both state houses and the congressional delegation are controlled by the Democrats. One U.S. Senator is a Democrat, the other Republican. Voter initiatives radically slashed taxes (Proposition 13) and threw death penalty opponent Rose Bird off the state Supreme Court, but decisively rejected discriminatory proposals against AIDS sufferers.

Twenty-four percent of California voters consider themselves liberal, 26 percent conservative, according to results from ABC election polls.[4] The liberal percentage is the highest among the four states examined here and among the highest in the country. Forty-six percent of those who voted in 1986 considered themselves Democrats, 38 percent Republicans. Yet by a 52 to 48

---

2. Barone and Ujifusa, *Almanac*, 67.
3. Barone and Ujifusa, *Almanac*, 70.
4. ABC News, *The '88 Vote* (New York: Capitol Cities/ABC News, 1989), 403.

margin, Californians felt that the Republican party was better able to cope with the nation's problems. This may be because Californians were relatively happy with the state of the economy. Forty-seven percent considered themselves better off than when Reagan took office; only 20 percent considered themselves worse off. Sixty percent felt the state of the economy was excellent or very good. Given these figures, it is not surprising that Reagan was quite popular in the state. Indeed, 62 percent approved of his performance in office. Overall, the national economic conditions were a wash in 1986: the state populace was relatively more Democratic and liberal than the country as a whole, but voters held Ronald Reagan and the Republican party in high esteem.

Alan Cranston

Alan Cranston was born on June 19, 1914, in Palo Alto, California. He received his Bachelor's degree from nearby Stanford in 1936 and served in the Army during World War II. After the war, Cranston helped form the California Democratic Council (CDC) and served as its first president.

Cranston was first elected to statewide office in 1958, when he became the first Democratic state controller in seventy-two years. After an easy reelection in 1962, Cranston set his sights on the U.S. Senate. Cranston lost a close Democratic primary in 1964 to former White House press secretary Pierre Salinger, who then lost to Republican George Murphy. Two years later, Cranston's political career suffered a further blow when he lost his controller's seat. Two years after that, Cranston again ran for Senate, this time edging out four primary opponents for the Democratic nomination. The Republicans nominated Max Rafferty, the conservative state superintendent of public instruction, who had defeated Senate Minority Whip Thomas Kuchel, a moderate, in a divisive primary. While Rafferty attacked Cranston for his support of a bombing halt in Vietnam and for associations with left-wing organizations such as the CDC, newspaper reports suggested that Rafferty himself had dodged the draft during World War II. Cranston squeaked by in the election with 52 percent of the vote.[5]

Though Cranston quickly aligned himself with the left wing of the Democratic party in Congress, he nevertheless was able to build popularity among business groups.

> Cranston is no doctrinaire foe of business. Indeed, his work on behalf of California business interests has been a major element of his legislative career, and a cornerstone of his political support in the state. . . .

---

5. Barone and Ujifusa, *Almanac*, 75; Ehrenhalt, *Politics*, 1988, 93.

For years Cranston was known among California business people as the man to see for help with the federal government.[6]

Cranston's own aides agree. According to administrative assistant Roy Greenaway, "on some issues Alan has always been more conservative than the stereotype is. For example, he's probably the leading Democratic proponent —has been for years—of a capital gains differential. That's simply where he is politically."[7]

Given his liberal-to-moderate record, Cranston had little trouble in 1974 against his Republican opponent, state Senator and former John Bircher Bill Richardson. Campaign activities by the John Birch Society for Richardson were so out of bounds that even Governor Ronald Reagan joined the criticism. Cranston won handily with 61 percent of the vote. Cranston won easily again in 1980, overcoming the Reagan landslide to win 57 percent of the vote against Proposition 13 coauthor Paul Gann. Cranston unsuccessfully sought the Democratic nomination for president in 1984.

In Congress, Cranston serves on the Veterans Affairs, Banking, Housing and Urban Affairs, Select Intelligence, and Foreign Relations committees. On Foreign Affairs, Cranston was a leader of the Nuclear Freeze movement and has pushed hard to prevent the spread of nuclear weapons. A staunch supporter of Israel, Cranston led the fight against the Reagan administration's plans to sell AWACS radar planes to Saudi Arabia. Cranston's overall voting record is liberal, scoring between 75 and 100 in the ADA ratings and between 79 and 100 in the AFL-CIO ratings since 1971.

Ed Zschau

Cranston's Republican opponent in the 1986 Senate race was Ed Zschau, who, until the Senate race, was a little-known congressman from California's Silicon Valley. Zschau was born on November 12, 1931, in Omaha, Nebraska, more than twenty-seven years after Cranston. Zschau received his B.A. from Princeton and two Master's degrees and a Ph.D. from Stanford.

After completing his degree from Stanford, Zschau remained in Silicon Valley and founded Systems Industries, which became one of the world's largest manufacturers of minicomputer disk storage systems. In 1978, Zschau, then chairman of an American Electronics Association task force, led a successful effort to slash the capital gains tax rate over the opposition of President Carter. With low capital gains rates crucial to raising venture capital, "Zschau

---

6. Ehrenhalt, *Politics*, 1986, 94.
7. Roy Greenaway, personal interview, June 25, 1990.

emerged as a folk hero in Silicon Valley."⁸ Presidential candidate Ronald Reagan named Zschau cochairman of his Business Advisory Panel. After Reagan's inauguration, Zschau became a delegate to the White House Conference on Small Business.

In 1982, Representative Paul McCloskey, a Republican who led a quixotic antiwar challenge to President Nixon's renomination in 1972, resigned from his Twelfth District House seat (Silicon Valley) during an unsuccessful attempt to win the Senate seat held by the retiring S. I. Hayakawa. Zschau quickly entered the race for McCloskey's seat. The Twelfth District is almost perfect for someone such as Zschau, who has demonstrated the high-tech entrepreneurial spirit. The district, dominated by the electronics and computer industries, is strongly Republican and 86 percent white. In the inflated world of California real estate, the Twelfth District has the highest median household value. Zschau was easily elected, winning 63 percent of the vote.

Given his background, it is not surprising that Zschau worked hard in the House to maintain tax breaks for capital gains. Although his voting record has been generally conservative, Zschau showed a great deal of independence from the Republican party, voting against aid to the Contras in Nicaragua and further procurement of the MX missile. In both instances he changed his mind from previous positions. This open-mindedness, though, would hurt him in his Senate race against Cranston.⁹

The Race

Alan Cranston appeared to be one of the Democratic incumbents who could most likely be defeated as 1986 began. The most important reason was Cranston's 1984 presidential campaign, which left Californians with the impression that Cranston was a left-wing ideologue out of touch with California issues. As we demonstrated in chapter 4, a Senator who positions himself or herself too far from his or her constituents can face serious problems in November. Cranston's administrative assistant, Roy Greenaway, made the following comments.

> There were some very serious problems because Alan had in '84 his aborted presidential effort. One of the consequences of that was that it tended to polarize a bit more. Running for president in the Democratic primary means that you have to be very liberal. One of the consequences of the race was to shore up the left, to be sure that we wouldn't have any

---

8. Ehrenhalt, *Politics*, 1986, 131.
9. Ehrenhalt, *Politics*, 1986, 131.

challenges from the left; the other was to kind of knock out some of the more conservative support that Alan always had. Alan had always won with a fairly significant Republican vote. That started in 1968 when, having gotten through a primary, found a general (election) in which Max Rafferty had defeated Tom Kuchel. Rafferty, a very conservative Republican, Kuchel a moderate Republican, and many of the Kuchel supporters supported Cranston in the general, and they did it very openly. They had an organization called GOPocrats for Cranston, and that tradition has continued. So that one of the things that concerned us in '86 was that the presidential race had knocked out that traditionally moderate to conservative Republican group that always voted for us. That was one problem.

The second was that running for president focuses you as a national figure and gives the impression that you've ignored the state, so we felt we were susceptible to the attack that we were out of touch with California. We began early in '85 with a program to get Alan more into the nooks and crannies of California so he wouldn't have to overcome that sort of problem. But that was something we had to do, to overcome, to weather all of this.

The third thing was that there was an increase in his negatives as a result of this. Actually, we went into the campaign with a net unfavorable job rating, which we had to overcome. That's probably partly a consequence of the polarization and partly a consequence of the fact that people felt he wasn't doing a good job because he was out running for president.[10]

Another problem facing Cranston was polls showing the senator to be vulnerable to strong challengers. This in itself could lead to problems, as high-quality Republicans would be more likely to seek his seat. Additionally, conservatives were likely to mobilize during the campaign, due to the movement to oust from office California Chief Justice Rose Bird, who consistently opposed the death penalty.[11] Nevertheless, the senior senator from California opened his 1986 reelection campaign with some advantages. He was a relatively popular incumbent with no challenge from within his party and, for what its worth to an incumbent, $3 million in his campaign chest.[12] Cranston officially declared his candidacy for a fourth term on March 3 in Los Angeles, stressing the environment, child care, and the need to reduce nuclear weapons.[13]

---

10. Greenaway interview.
11. Helen Dewar, "Cranston Out-Distancing Foes," *Washington Post*, March 17, 1986.
12. Keith Love, "Cranston's Campaign Prospers, May Not Get Finance Panel's Help," *Los Angeles Times*, January 9, 1986.
13. Keith Love, "Cranston, His Hat in Ring, Stresses Activist U.S. Role," *Los Angeles Times*, March 4, 1986.

The Republicans, on the other hand, had no shortage of candidates to seek the nomination, many of whom had held public office. But given the size of California, none was well known throughout the state at the time. One of the state's most popular Republicans, Long Beach Congressman Daniel Lungren, bowed out early, citing the difficulties of raising enough money to take on Cranston.[14] Similarly, baseball commissioner and former Olympic Games organizer Peter Ueberroth, a "celebrity" who was perhaps Cranston's strongest potential challenger, refused to run.[15]

Among Republicans vying to take on Cranston were the following: conservative television commentator Bruce Herschensohn of Los Angeles; State Senator and former Los Angeles Police Chief Ed Davis; Congresswoman Bobbi Fiedler; Congressman Ed Zschau; State Assemblyman Robert Naylor; Los Angeles County Supervisor Mike Antonovich; and supply-side economist Arthur Laffer. Naylor and Zschau represented northern California; the remaining candidates were from the southern part of the state. Even without Lungren or Ueberroth, this was a competitive primary pool.

At this point, the Cranston campaign thought someone like Zschau could provide the toughest competition. "The image we were most concerned with would be a moderate Republican with a business background and not a whole lot of political image to him, and Ed Zschau fit that description."[16]

The most bizarre twist of the campaign came early when, on January 24, the *Los Angeles Times* reported that a grand jury had indicted Representative Bobbi Fiedler and Paul Clarke, a top aide, for offering a bribe to State Senator Ed Davis to withdraw from the race. Under California election laws, such offers constitute a felony punishable by up to three years in prison.[17] The activity began in November, 1985, when Fiedler workers approached Davis workers about a financial offer if Davis withdrew from the race. The Davis campaign notified the Los Angeles district attorney, who then began taping conversations between the groups. According to a taped conversation between Clarke and Davis's campaign manager, Martha Zilm, the two specifically discussed the Fiedler campaign paying $100,000 in Davis campaign debts if Davis dropped out of the Senate race. When Zilm questioned the legality of such a transaction, Clarke replied, "I called (a lawyer) and he said it was not illegal if it is not in writing."[18] But the tapes also showed that, at the one face-

---

14. Keith Love, "Lungren Bows Out: It Takes Money to Take on Cranston," *Los Angeles Times*, January 16, 1986.

15. John Balzar, "Ueberroth Says He Won't Be U.S. Senate Candidate," *Los Angeles Times*, January 28, 1986.

16. Greenaway interview.

17. Robert Stewart and Keith Love, "Jury Indicts Fiedler, Aide, in Vote Case," *Los Angeles Times*, January 24, 1986.

18. Robert Stewart and Keith Love, "Fiedler Aide Reportedly Brushed Aside Warning; Legality Discussion was Secretly Taped," *Los Angeles Times*, January 28, 1986.

to-face meeting between Fiedler and Zilm, Fiedler, in agreeing to pay the money, declared "I do think it's important, however, that, uh, this is not a quid pro quo as far as I'm concerned, and I hope you don't consider it as a quid pro quo either. This is something that we're doing because Ed—because Ed and I have been long-standing friends."[19]

Because the evidence against Fiedler was so tenuous, Los Angeles District Attorney Ira Reiner only recommended that Clarke be indicted, but the grand jury chose to indict Fiedler as well.[20] Following Fiedler's indictment, Reiner sought additional information to try to build a case against Fiedler, but was unable to do so. He then told the *Los Angeles Times* that he would recommend that the indictment against Fielder be dismissed.[21]

On February 26, Los Angeles Superior Court Judge Robert Altman dropped the indictments against both Fiedler and Clarke. Fiedler's indictment was dismissed for inadequate evidence, while Clarke was set free because the California statute covers the actual payment of money, not an offer to do so.[22]

Cheered by the legal victory and undaunted by the ethical ramifications of the scandal, Fiedler remained in the campaign only to face yet another controversy. In early March, Fiedler released a series of radio advertisements suggesting that she had the endorsement of President Reagan. One commercial had Reagan declaring, "Do me a favor, on Election Day send Bobbi back to Washington." In another, Reagan states that Fiedler's "doing a terrific job in Congress." Unknown to most listeners, the Reagan spots were from a 1984 campaign rally and not from the 1986 race, where Reagan remained neutral in the primary.[23]

Congressman Ed Zschau, largely unknown outside his Silicon Valley base, received a boost when the House Republican leadership chose him to lead the floor debate on President Reagan's proposal to fund the Nicaraguan Contras. Perhaps because Zschau had previously opposed Contra aid, the leadership felt he could swing the votes of House moderates. One of the results of the publicity that accrued from this was that, by the end of March, Zschau held a decisive fund-raising lead over his six major rivals. Zschau had raised $1.6 million, followed by economist Arthur Laffer with $972,000 and Los Angeles County Supervisor Mike Antonovich with $966,000. Neverthe-

---

19. "The Fiedler Tapes," *Los Angeles Times*, February 6, 1986.

20. Paul Feldman and Terry Pristin, "Dismiss Fiedler case, Reiner Urges," *Los Angeles Times*, February 20, 1986.

21. Feldman and Pristin, "Dismiss"; and Jay Matthews, "DA to drop Fiedler Case, But Will Prosecute Key Aide," *Washington Post*, February 20, 1986.

22. Paul Feldman, "Judge Drops Charges Against Fiedler," *Los Angeles Times*, February 27, 1986; Katharine Macdonald, "Judge Drops Charges Against Fiedler, Aide," *Washington Post*, February 27, 1986.

23. John Balzar, "GOP Foes Attack Fiedler Over Radio Spots Featuring Reagan," *Los Angeles Times*, March 7, 1986.

less, Antonovich had far more cash on hand than Zschau, $578,000 to $257,000. Laffer, consistent with his supply-side ideology, had a campaign deficit of $13,000. On the Democratic side, Cranston was up to $4 million in contributions and had $2.3 million on hand. Most of what Cranston had raised at this point had been put back into direct-mail appeals.[24]

Cranston began to put some of his money into television advertising toward the end of April. Early commercials showed the legs of a man jogging briskly in a park. An announcer (actor Lloyd Bridges) read the following script.

> He's responsible for more new national parks and wilderness areas than anyone since Theodore Roosevelt. He's fought harder for individual liberty than any Californian since Earl Warren. He's worked harder to stop war than any senator since Robert Kennedy. He's responsible for more investment and jobs than any other California senator. That's why he won even more elections in California than Ronald Reagan. [Camera pans up to show 72 year old Cranston.] His name is Alan Cranston.[25]

The commercial served the dual purpose of listing Cranston's accomplishments and suggesting that his age, a potential controversy, was not a political liability.

Another commercial featured testimonials from Cranston's Senate colleagues.

> Gary Hart (D-Colorado): He's a leader in every new issue we face.
> Joe Biden (D-Delaware): He's stopped more wars and started more change than any other senator.
> Ted Kennedy (D-Massachusetts): He cares, and he's not afraid to take a stand.
> Sam Nunn (D-Georgia): And I don't know of anyone who does a better job for his state and for his constituents.
> Biden: Alan Cranston is simply the best senator in the United States.[26]

A third advertisement, featuring famed photographer Ansel Adams, noted Cranston's environmental achievements.

On the Republican side, the nominees began to view Zschau as their

---

24. Keith Love and John Balzar, "Zschau Top Fund-Raiser in GOP Senate Race," *Los Angeles Times*, April 18, 1986.

25. Cranston Commercial no. 1, Center for Political Communications, University of Oklahoma.

26. Cranston Commercial no. 6, Center for Political Communications, University of Oklahoma.

prime competition: Herschensohn called Zschau "the most liberal candidate in the race"; Antonovich, who like Herschensohn was an archconservative, claimed that Zschau had never actively backed President Reagan; Davis's campaign derisively called Zschau "a yuppie dream"; and Fiedler insinuated that Zschau supported legalizing drugs and prostitution.[27] An ultraconservative interest group, Free Congress, targeted Zschau for negative television commercials using a Reagan look-alike. When the White House protested, Free Congress replaced that advertisement with one claiming that Zschau was the one vote the "Stop Reagan Crowd" could count on.[28]

By the middle of May, the three leading contenders were Herschensohn, Davis, and Zschau. A California Poll of 300 Republicans gave Herschensohn 18 percent, up from 12 percent in March, with Zschau receiving 15 percent, up from 11 percent in March and 3 percent the previous November, and Davis also receiving 15 percent, up 1 percent from March.[29] But a larger poll by the *Los Angeles Times* one week later called it a two-person race. The poll gave Herschensohn 16 percent, Zschau 14 percent, and no one else in double digits. While Herschensohn was preferred to Zschau in the poll, California Republicans nevertheless felt that Zschau had the best chance of beating Cranston. Most important, a plurality of California Republicans were still undecided.[30]

Zschau and Herschensohn could hardly have been more different in their views. Zschau, the independent Republican, at various times opposed the MX missile and the Contras, supported the nuclear arms freeze and abortion rights, and was lukewarm about "Star Wars." Herschensohn, representing the right wing of the party, received active support from his political hero, former President Richard Nixon.[31] Herschensohn opposed all arms reductions with the Soviet Union and once replied to charges that Ferdinand Marcos had stolen an election in the Philippines with "so what."[32] His guide to foreign

---

27. Keith Love, "Four GOP Senate Candidates on Attack—Target is Rep. Zschau," *Los Angeles Times*, April 18, 1986; John Balzar, "Fiedler vs. Zschau: Pair Go Two Rounds in GOP Senate Contest," *Los Angeles Times*, May 6, 1986.

28. Keith Love, "White House Shoots Down Anti-Zschau Ad," *Los Angeles Times*, May 23, 1986.

29. Keith Love, "Herschensohn Leads in GOP Senate Race Poll," *Los Angeles Times*, May 14, 1986.

30. George Skelton, "Herschensohn, Zschau Leap Ahead of Field," *Los Angeles Times*, May 22, 1986.

31. Rowland Evans and Robert Novak, "The Bets Against Cranston," *Washington Post*, April 28, 1986.

32. Keith Love, "Herschensohn: A Blunt-Speaking Senate Hopeful," *Los Angeles Times*, April 17, 1986.

policy was "support any friend; oppose any foe."[33] While Herschensohn attacked Zschau as a Cranston Democrat, Zschau attacked Herschensohn as a Jesse Helms Republican.[34]

As the race drew to a close, Zschau continued to lead his Republican rivals in spending. He had also tied Herschensohn in the polls, each receiving 26 percent in the California Poll.

Zschau won the primary with 37 percent of the vote, seven percentage points higher than Herschensohn, in a low turnout primary. Antonovich finished third with only 9 percent of the vote, Davis fourth with 7 percent. Because the conservative vote was so badly split, the moderate Zschau was able to win; it is unlikely that Zschau could have won a two-person race with Herschensohn.[35] Yet by splitting the conservative vote, the Republicans selected the candidate who probably had the best chance of defeating Cranston. Indeed, there were no lasting divisions among the Republican candidates, all of whom backed Zschau in November. Herschensohn declared he would do whatever he could to see Cranston defeated.[36]

Facing a strong moderate challenger for the first time since his election to the Senate, Cranston did not let Zschau bask long in victory. The day after the primary he released a series of negative television commercials portraying Zschau as weak on the environment and flip-flopping on issues. Cranston assistant Roy Greenaway explained their strategy as follows.

> First of all, we laid in our positives in May, even though we had no primary opposition. . . . We started running a series of affirmative ads, the really good ads. The Ansel Adams ad, the ad with the other four senators, and there was a third one about Alan. They were very good, very positive ads. We laid them in during that period with fairly heavy buying, so that we had credibility when we started the negatives, the moment the (primary) election was over. We figured that whoever won had come through a tough primary. He would not be prepared to respond to this.[37]

---

33. John Balzar, "Herschensohn and Zschau Show They're Miles Apart," *Los Angeles Times*, May 13, 1986.

34. Keith Love, "Zschau Takes off the Gloves Against Herschensohn," *Los Angeles Times*, May 17, 1986.

35. Jay Matthews, "Moderate Rep. Zschau Will Challenge Cranston," *Washington Post*, June 5, 1986; Ed Zschau, telephone interview, May 21, 1990. Zschau also believes a regional split helped him as much as the ideological split: Zschau was the only creditable candidate from northern California.

36. Cathleen Decker, "Zschau, Cranston to Debate; Governor, Bradley May Not," *Los Angeles Times*, June 4, 1986.

37. Greenaway interview, June 25, 1990.

Indeed, Zschau was not prepared.

> I never really thought about the general election. I was behind (in the primary polls) the whole time. I was a very inexperienced candidate, not a prepared politician. It was like going from the sandlot to the major leagues. Rather than being ignored, I got more press coverage than I wanted. So I wasn't really ready for the ads from Cranston. I thought, "two Stanford graduates, we could have debates, offer the voters a dialogue on the issues." I was very disappointed in the process.[38]

Debates indeed. One Cranston advertisement had the following script.

> The Great Debates: 1858, Lincoln-Douglas; 1960, Kennedy-Nixon; 1986, Zschau vs. Zschau. Zschau says clean up toxic waste dumps but Zschau voted against tough laws to do it. He voted for the MX missile and against it, against the secret war in Nicaragua, then for it. And Zschau voted against a bill he introduced to ban nuclear tests. That's right. He even flip-flopped on his own bill. Alan Cranston, commitment, courage, California in the Senate.[39]

To stress Zschau's position switching, Cranston declared that Zschau "flip-flops like a flapjack," while serving up flapjacks in front of television news cameras. Not to be outdone, Zschau provided waffles while accusing Cranston of not taking positions on Rose Bird (the controversial state Supreme Court chief justice), the balanced budget amendment, and a farm workers' banana boycott. The media did note that Cranston, the Democrat, personally cooked and served the flapjacks, while Zschau, the millionaire Republican, had his waffles catered.[40]

Zschau also began to sound what would be the theme of his campaign. Relying on his youth and business experience, he offered a better future for California. "While I have been creating jobs, Alan Cranston has been creating more government," Zschau told a press conference the day after his primary victory.[41] Zschau, after spending close to $3.5 million to win the primary, had only $30,000 left. Cranston, with no primary opposition, had increased his campaign war chest to $1.4 million.[42] Included among Cranston's donations

---

38. Telephone interview, Ed Zschau, May 21, 1990.
39. Cranston Commercial no. 12, Center for Political Communications, University of Oklahoma.
40. Keith Love, "Charges Hot Off the Griddle," *Los Angeles Times*, June 17, 1986.
41. Keith Love and John Balzar, "Zschau Basks in Role of Winner," *Los Angeles Times*, June 5, 1986.
42. Jay Matthews, "Cranston-Zschau Battle Becomes TV Spectacle," *Washington Post*, July 20, 1986.

were tens of thousands of dollars given for various purposes by Charles Keating, chairman of the now infamous Lincoln Savings Bank.[43] The California Poll gave Cranston an early, nine-point lead over Zschau.[44]

If Senate elections are to be responsive to the desires of voters, then issues must play an important role in the campaign. One leading issue was Proposition 65, a clean-water voter initiative that would ban numerous pesticides, many of which farmers viewed as essential to their survival. Cranston strongly supported the measure; Zschau was unable to make up his mind, and eventually opposed it. According to Zschau, "Prop 65 was a bill to make those who cared about the environment but were reasonable look bad."[45]

Foreign policy issues also received their due. Toward the end of June, the Cranston campaign sought to strengthen its support among Jewish voters by attacking Zschau's lack of support for Israel. Cranston long supported Israeli policy and was a frequent floor leader of efforts to block arms sales to Arab countries. Alternatively, Zschau supported arms sales to Saudi Arabia and had occasionally voted to cut foreign aid to Israel. As a result, Cranston received ringing endorsements from four former presidents of the Jewish Federation Council of Los Angeles, who referred to Cranston as "one of the strongest and most effective friends Israel has." The object here was not so much votes, as California has a small Jewish population, as money, both in and out of state.[46] Zschau, on the other hand, was described as "unfriendly toward Israel."[47] In an attempt to boost Jewish support, Zschau left California for a few days in early July for an official visit to Israel.

When Zschau returned from Israel he hosted a luncheon featuring Vice President George Bush. Bush argued that defeating Cranston was crucial if the Republicans were to retain their control of the Senate. Reagan loyalist Bush praised the 70 percent of the time that Zschau had backed the president, claiming "nobody asks for 100 percent."[48]

Meanwhile, the Cranston campaign continued to attack Zschau's flip-

---

43. Lincoln Savings went bankrupt in 1989, at a cost that might exceed $2 billion to the taxpayers. The cost got out of control because Cranston and four other Senators (to whom Keating made campaign contributions) allegedly pressured the Federal Home Loan Bank Board to go easy on Keating. The five Senators, Cranston and Dennis DeConcini (D-Arizona), John Glenn (D-Ohio), John McCain (R-Arizona) and Donald Riegle (D-Michigan) were investigated by the Senate ethics committee. See "Damage Control Gets Harder In Lincoln Savings Probe," *Congressional Quarterly Weekly Report*, November 11, 1989, 3029–35.

44. Maralee Schwartz, "Cranston Sets the Pace," *Washington Post*, August 10, 1986.

45. Zschau interview.

46. Greenaway interview.

47. Marylouise Oates and Keith Love, "Zschau's Positions on Israel Spur Criticism from L.A. Jewish Leaders," *Los Angeles Times*, June 28, 1986.

48. John Balzar, "Zschau Seeks a Bridge to Conservatives Within GOP," *Los Angeles Times*, July 13, 1986.

flops, as well as his stands on the environment, Israel, and, more recently, South Africa. According to the Cranston campaign, Zschau's company was conducting business with the apartheid regime. Zschau flatly denied the charges, and, indeed, Cranston's staff no longer stands by its accusations.[49]

Toward the end of July, the Zschau campaign finally realized that it could not win by daily reactions to Cranston's charges; the campaign needed to do a better job of controlling the media. Toward that end, they chose to focus consistently on three issues: fiscal austerity, "leadership for the future," and the campaign to unseat California Chief Justice Rose Bird.[50] The early results from this new strategy were not overwhelming. A California Poll from the beginning of August showed Cranston had a 51 to 38 lead over Zschau, a 4 percentage point increase over June.[51]

National political conditions explicitly influenced the campaign when President Ronald Reagan made the first of two visits to California to help the Zschau campaign. The Reagan fund-raiser added $1.3 million for Zschau, who had raised $6.2 million since the primary. Yet he was losing ground to Cranston. A *Los Angeles Times* poll put Cranston's lead at 15 points, 39 to 24. Furthermore, according to the California Poll, only 56 percent of the voters had even heard of Zschau, compared to 95 percent for Cranston.[52]

Given this comfortable lead, Cranston refused to debate Zschau. The League of Women Voters offered to sponsor three debates, but Cranston refused unless three minor party candidates, none of whom were receiving any support in the polls, were allowed to participate. Obviously, a one-on-one debate would dramatically increase voters' knowledge of Zschau. In addition, pundits speculated that "the gaunt seventy-two-year-old senator fears side-by-side comparison with his sandy-haired forty-six-year-old challenger."[53]

Zschau, who had heretofore avoided personal attacks and negative advertising, started to go on the offensive. He released a 1983 article on Cranston that had accused him of the following: offering a newspaper editor in 1964 pictures of a political opponent in a hotel room with a woman who was not his wife; labeling Ronald Reagan a front man for the right-wing John Birch society in 1966; and suggesting in 1983 that Reagan's arms control negotiator supported the use of nuclear weapons against blacks in South Africa. Zschau

49. Zschau interview; Greenaway interview.
50. Keith Love, "Advice to Zschau After Campaign's Rocky Beginning: Be Yourself," *Los Angeles Times*, July 27, 1986.
51. Schwartz, "Cranston Sets Pace"; Keith Love, "Cranston Lead Over Zschau is Growing, Poll Indicates," *Los Angeles Times*, August 7, 1986.
52. Jay Matthews, "California GOP Amassing Millions, But Cranston's Lead Grows Wider," *Washington Post*, September 16, 1986; George Skelton, "Cranston Holds 15 Percent Lead; Zschau Seen as an Enigma," *Los Angeles Times*, September 12, 1986.
53. John Balzar, "Debates, Prop. 65 Will Play Role in Senate Race," *Los Angeles Times*, September 12, 1986.

released his own commercial attacking Cranston for his opposition to the death penalty, even for terrorists who kill innocent civilians.[54] Another commercial, attacking Cranston's opposition to the death penalty for drug dealers who murder, took on the guise of a news report, complete with a silver-haired ex-anchorman as the announcer.[55] Cranston responded to the latest shift in Zschau campaign tactics by calling his opponent a "liar" and permanently refusing to debate.[56]

The change in tactics plus a one month, $2.5 million television campaign appeared to be paying off for Zschau. By mid-October, Cranston's lead was down to 7 percentage points, half what it had been in September. The biggest shift came from Republicans and conservative Democrats. In September, less than half of polled Republicans supported Zschau, while in October over two-thirds supported him.[57] Cranston's support among conservative Democrats dropped from 61 to 32 to 43 to 33.[58]

During the final month, Cranston worked to shore up liberal support, bringing in luminaries such as Ted Kennedy. While Cranston already had the support of two-thirds of Latino voters and 90 percent of black voters, bringing in popular Democrats with long-standing ties to these groups was calculated to help increase voter turnout.[59] Alternatively, Zschau worked to increase his tenuous support among conservative voters. Though Cranston never took a stand on the bid to remove Rose Bird, Zschau constantly linked the two death penalty opponents. When asked whether he was running against Cranston or Bird, Zschau replied, "it's hard to tell the difference between the two."[60]

By the final week of the campaign, the California Poll showed Zschau trailing Cranston by only 1 percentage point, while other polls showed a slightly larger Cranston lead. In an attempt to shift the balance in the closing days, the Republican campaign again brought President Reagan to California. Reagan delivered his toughest attack of the midterm campaign, claiming that Cranston "plays fast and loose with the lives of those who protect us . . . and

---

54. Matthews, "California GOP."
55. Keith Love, "Stations Protest Zschau TV Ads as Misleading," *Los Angeles Times*, October 9, 1986.
56. Keith Love, "Cranston Calls Zschau Liar; Won't Debate," *Los Angeles Times*, September 27, 1986.
57. Maralee Schwartz, "Rep. Zschau Cuts Cranston's Lead in California Race," *Washington Post*, October 21, 1986; George Skelton, "Zschau's Momentum Paring Cranston Lead," *Los Angeles Times*, October 19, 1986.
58. Maralee Schwartz and Paul Taylor, "Sen. Cranston Losing Support Among Conservative Democrats," *Washington Post*, October 8, 1986.
59. Keith Love, "Gloves Come Off in Race for Senate," *Los Angeles Times*, October 22, 1986.
60. John Balzar, "Gloves Come Off in Race for Senate," *Los Angeles Times*, October 22, 1986.

looks at your take-home pay as his personal treasury. . . . I cannot think of a single member of the Senate who has a record as antimilitary, antipreparedness, antisecurity as Ed's opponent."[61] Reagan did not mention that Zschau, like Cranston, supported a 3 percent cut in military spending in 1987, opposed the MX missile, and wanted less spending on Star Wars than did Reagan. "It's a wonder Cranston survived" Reagan's attacks.[62]

In these final days of the campaign, perhaps fearing voter backlash, Cranston began to use more positive television advertisements. One Cranston advertisement attacked Zschau's position taking, but another featured a constituent claiming that Cranston's legislative efforts on emergency medical assistance saved her father's life.[63] Zschau officials also claimed that the negative advertisements were being cut back, but a new commercial criticized Cranston on spending and budget issues.[64] Zschau even got "Bartles and Jaymes" to do a commercial attacking Cranston for missing votes and not taking a stand on Rose Bird.[65]

Cranston held on to his narrow lead on election day, winning by 116,000 votes out of over seven million cast. The final percentages were 49 to 48.[66] In the end, according to Cranston aide Roy Greenaway, Zschau may have proven to be an easier opponent than Herschensohn. "We beat Zschau because of his record as a Congressman. The whole flip-flop issue, which was our major theme, was based on our analysis of Zschau's voting record. We couldn't have done that with Herschensohn. . . . The miracle isn't that he [Zschau] almost won; it's that he lost."[67]

Survey Results

According to ABC News (see table 6.1), the most important issues Californians cited in determining for whom to vote were the national economy (42 percent), keeping the United States out of war (39 percent), reducing unemployment (36 percent), and the budget deficit (35 percent).[68]

---

61. Lou Cannon, "Reagan Attacks Cranston," *Washington Post*, November 2, 1986; John Balzar, "The Senate Campaign: It's Down to the Wire," *Los Angeles Times*, November 2, 1986; Gerald Boyd, "Reagan Urges Californians to Protect Gains of G.O.P.," *New York Times*, November 2, 1986.

62. Greenaway interview.

63. Cranston Commercial no. 17, Center for Political Communications, University of Oklahoma.

64. E.J. Dionne, Jr., "Last-Ditch Flurries on Final Weekend," *New York Times*, November 3, 1986.

65. Zschau Commercial no. 1, Center for Political Communications, University of Oklahoma.

66. "State Election Returns," *Los Angeles Times*, November 5, 1986.

67. Greenaway interview.

68. ABC News, *The '88 Vote*, 403.

TABLE 6.1. California Exit Poll Results (in percentages)

	All Voters	Cranston Voters	Zschau Voters
Gender			
Male	51	52	47
Female	49	58	38
Race			
White	85	51	46
Black	6	93	6
Other	9	63	32
Ideology			
Liberal	24	89	9
Conservative	26	21	77
Party			
Democrat	46	86	12
Independent	12	58	38
Republican	38	15	83
Other	3	67	20
Better cope			
Democrats	48	90	6
Republicans	52	20	76
Personally better off than when Reagan took office			
Better off	47	34	63
About the same	33	65	33
Worse off	20	83	14
Reagan job performance			
Approve	62	33	64
Disapprove	38	89	8
State of economy			
Excellent	6	18	82
Good	54	41	56
Not so good	34	77	20
Poor	7	83	15
Important items (selected)			
National economy	42	56	42
Local economy	31	56	41
Reagan performance	30	51	47
Candidates' party	22	51	47

Source: ABC News, *The '88 Vote* (New York: Capitol Cities/ABC News, 1989), 403.

ABC exit polls showed Cranston winning 55 percent of the vote, though he only won with 49 percent. Nevertheless, the polls should be useful in determining the sources of Cranston's support. As was true in all four races, the Democrat, Cranston, did better among women than among men. This is consistent with the well-known "gender gap," whereby women are more likely to hold liberal positions than men, and are more likely to identify as and vote for Democrats.[69] The most Democratic demographic group in the country is black voters, and they voted for Alan Cranston by a 93 to 6 margin. While the exit polls show Cranston winning 51 percent of the white vote, given black support and Cranston's 51 percent overall total, Zschau no doubt captured a majority of the white vote. Not surprisingly, Cranston carried Democrats (86 percent) while Zschau carried Republicans (83 percent); Cranston carried self-declared liberals (89 percent), Zschau, self-declared conservatives (77 percent).

The exit polls support the argument that Senate races are not merely personal popularity contests, that issues and national concerns can have a large impact.[70] For instance, on the hotly contested environmental issues, 78 percent of those who call themselves environmentalists voted for Cranston. Of those who generally thought the Democrats better able to cope with the nation's problems, 90 percent voted for Cranston. Only 20 percent who favored the Republicans did so. As stated previously, the national economy was listed by more Californians as an important issue than any other factor. Of those who thought the state of the economy was excellent, 82 percent voted for Republican Zschau; of those who thought the state of the economy was poor, 83 percent voted for Democrat Cranston. Similarly, 63 percent of those who considered themselves better off than when Reagan took office voted for Zschau, while 83 percent of those who considered themselves worse off voted for Cranston. Finally, Zschau received the votes of 64 percent of the Reagan supporters, while Cranston received the votes of 89 percent of those who disapproved of the president's performance.

Conclusions

Using our framework from chapter 4, we see that state characteristics, which can give candidates from one party or another a decided advantage across the country, had little influence in California, a classic two-party state. Though it is relatively more liberal and Democratic than the rest of the country, it has often elected Republicans to statewide office. Neither Cranston nor Zschau had a substantial built-in partisan advantage. Cranston had no scandals or controversies to drag him down and was unencumbered by intraparty competition. His main weakness was the leftward shift that accompanied his failed

---

69. See, e.g., Paul Abramson, John Aldrich, and David Rohde, *Change and Continuity in the 1980 Elections* (Washington, D.C.: Congressional Quarterly, 1983); Robert Erikson, Norman Luttbeg, and Kent Tedin, *American Public Opinion* (New York: Macmillan, 1988).

70. The data available from the exit polls do not allow us to control for other factors, so the findings here are in and of themselves not definitive. In chaps. 4 and 5, we provide more systematic evidence for the effect of issues and economic conditions on voter choice and election outcomes.

1984 presidential campaign. Cranston faced a high-quality opponent in Zschau, a moderate Republican congressman who was able to raise enormous amounts of money. Moreover, many of the national political conditions favored Zschau in 1986. The voters by and large considered the economy to be healthy, they felt that they personally were better off, and they largely approved of the Republican president. But all this left Zschau just short of the votes he needed to upset Cranston. Cranston, a popular incumbent, used television effectively to portray Zschau as inconsistent on the issues. Though spending by incumbents has not previously been found to have a significant impact on the vote, the negative advertisements placed by Cranston kept Zschau on the defensive. Cranston, of course, had a huge advantage in name recognition, as Zschau was largely unknown outside his congressional district before the campaign. That Zschau came as close as he did exemplifies the competitiveness of Senate races: seats held by popular incumbents are not necessarily safe when challenged, as they so frequently are, by highly qualified, well-financed challengers.

New York

New York is the second largest state in the union, behind only California. From 1810 until 1970, New York had more Congressional districts than any other state. From a peak of forty-five districts in the 1930s and 1940s, New York now has only thirty-four, a figure that will drop to thirty-one following the 1990 census. New York is second in the nation in per-pupil expenditures and fourteenth in the proportion of residents with college degrees (18 percent). The voting-age population is 12 percent black, 8 percent Spanish, and 2 percent Asian. Fourteen percent are foreign born and 69 percent were born in the state.[71]

Any discussion of the State of New York must begin with the City of New York, which has over 7 million residents, plus millions more in the surrounding metropolitan area. New York, with its famous Wall Street, is the financial capital of the world, and, with Broadway and innumerable museums, may be the cultural capital of the world.[72] The city, which nearly went bankrupt in 1975, recovered through the 1980s only to face setbacks once again following the stock market crash of October, 1987. Additionally, the city is faced with social problems unheard of in earlier years, including crack and AIDS.

Upstate New York is not always treated kindly by its downstate giant.

---

71. Background information on New York and its Senate candidates is derived from Barone and Ujifusa, *Almanac*; Ehrenhalt, *Politics*, 1986; and Ehrenhalt, *Politics*, 1988.
72. Barone and Ujifusa, *Almanac*, 784.

Former Mayor Koch's statement that life upstate is sterile no doubt hurt him in his race against Mario Cuomo for the governorship. Buffalo, upstate's largest city, has suffered from the same economic stagnation as have many industrial cities in the Northeast. But "upstate has its assets. It has high-tech industries and a highly skilled labor force. It has a fine physical environment—green hills, majestic mountains, (and) glistening lakes. . . . Upstate's biggest problem may be that it gets little attention: in the state it is overshadowed by New York City."[73]

Outside of New York City, the state's largest cities are Buffalo (358,000), Rochester (242,000), and Yonkers (195,000). Eighty-five percent of the people live in urban areas and New York is second in the violent crime rate nationally. New York is nineteenth in median family income, but sixth in tax burden per capita.

Like California, New York is a two-party state, though it leans more toward the Democrats. New York City is heavily Democratic, its suburbs and upstate (except for the few larger cities) are normally Republican. Overall, 47 percent of the state's registered voters are Democrats, 32 percent Republicans. The Senate seat held by D'Amato has been Republican since Jacob Javits first won it in 1956. The other seat has been won in the past thirty years by Republican Kenneth Keating (1958), Democrat Robert Kennedy (1964), Conservative James Buckley (1970), and Democrat Daniel Patrick Moynihan (1976, 1982, and 1988). Governor Mario Cuomo is a Democrat, as are a majority of the congressional delegation and State Assembly. The State Senate is controlled by the Republicans.

The ABC exit polls show New Yorkers to be less liberal than Californians.[74] Seventeen percent of New Yorkers categorized themselves as liberal, 22 percent conservative. Similarly, the Democratic party is not quite as strong: 42 percent of New Yorkers voting called themselves Democrats, compared to 46 percent in California. Thirty-eight percent of voting New Yorkers were Republican. Like Californians, New Yorkers in 1986 believed the Republican party better able to cope with the nation's problems by a narrow margin, 51 to 49. Fifty-six percent thought that the economy was in excellent or good shape and almost twice as many people considered themselves better off than worse off compared to when President Reagan took office. Sixty-four percent of New Yorkers approved of Reagan's job as president, slightly higher than in his home state of California. As in California, New York presents a relatively Democratic, relatively liberal state that felt good about Ronald Reagan and the Republican party in 1986.

---

73. Barone and Ujifusa, *Almanac*, 786.
74. ABC News, *The '88 Vote*, 443.

Alphonse D'Amato

New York's junior senator was born in Brooklyn on August 1, 1937. He attended Syracuse University, where he received his Bachelor's and Law degrees. D'Amato's political career began with the Nassau County Republicans, who control one of the nation's last remaining political machines. In 1977, D'Amato was elected presiding supervisor of Hempstead Township and appeared to be a likely candidate for county executive.

In 1980, against the advice of Nassau County political boss Joseph Margiotta, D'Amato announced his candidacy for the Republican U.S. Senate nomination against the popular incumbent, Jacob Javits (see chap. 3). D'Amato was the surprising victor of the bitter campaign, in which he attacked Javits as too old, too ill, and too liberal. Much to the benefit of D'Amato, Javits remained on the Liberal party line, siphoning support from the Democratic candidate, Congresswoman Elizabeth Holtzman. Holtzman attacked D'Amato's relationship with the corrupt Nassau County machine.[75] Unfortunately for Holtzman, Javits drew enough votes away from her on election day to enable D'Amato to squeak by with 45 percent of the vote.

D'Amato serves on the Appropriations, Banking, Housing and Urban Affairs, Small Business, and Joint Economic committees. Unlike Javits, who prided himself on his work on civil rights and foreign affairs, D'Amato used his opportunities on Capitol Hill to emphasize casework and constituent service. D'Amato consistently and effectively uses his position on the Appropriations committee to bring federal funds back to New York. In 1986, less than a month before the election, D'Amato brought the government of the United States to a standstill in order to prevent the Senate from halting production of an Air Force airplane built on Long Island. By holding up a Goldwater (R-Arizona) amendment stopping production, D'Amato prevented the passage of an omnibus appropriations bill. Without the bill, the government could not spend money, so nonessential services were shut down and federal workers sent home. D'Amato won a temporary reprieve for the aircraft, but, after the election, funding for the airplane was rescinded.

D'Amato was also highly visible in the war against drugs. In one highly publicized event, D'Amato dressed in army fatigues and went undercover to participate in a drug buy in Manhattan.

D'Amato has been conservative in his voting record, but that conservatism moderated significantly as the 1986 election approached. From an ADA score of 15 in 1981, D'Amato's liberal rating climbed steadily until it reached

---

75. The following year, party boss Margiotta was convicted of fraud and extortion; the entire party apparatus was later convicted of involvement in a kickback scheme.

35 in 1986. D'Amato also does not let his conservatism interfere with representing his constituents; he is among the leading supporters of mass transit aid and urban development grants on Capitol Hill.[76]

D'Amato's representation of constituents, particularly those who donate campaign funds, may be the undoing of the senator. Though largely exonerated of influence peddling by the Senate Ethics Committee, D'Amato continues to be connected to several criminal investigations.

Mark Green

Mark Green was born on March 15, 1945, in Brooklyn, New York. He received a Bachelor's degree from Cornell in 1967 and a J.D. from Harvard Law School in 1970, where he edited the *Civil Rights-Civil Liberties Law Review*, a liberal alternative to the more traditional *Harvard Law Review*. Green entered the political arena under the tutelage of consumer advocate Ralph Nader. Among Green's responsibilities was the directorship of Congress Watch, a consumer lobbying organization involved in the lawmaking process. His achievements there include a lawsuit that enabled gas stations to give discounts to cash customers and another that required the Commerce Department to release the names of U.S. companies complying with the Arab boycott of Israel.[77]

In addition to his efforts for Congress Watch and other organizations, Green is a prolific writer, having written or edited a dozen books, including the influential *Who Runs Congress* (1972), with James Fallows and David Zwick. In the tradition of the muckrakers, the book examines the power structure in Congress, the pervasive impact of special-interest campaign financing on the legislative process, and even criminal activity among members of Congress. Green is also well known for his verbal skills. According to conservative commentator William F. Buckley, Green "articulates the liberal position better than most anyone around."[78]

Mark Green first sought elective office in 1980, running for Congress in New York's wealthy "silk stocking" district on the East Side of Manhattan. The heavily Democratic district was represented by Ed Koch until his election as mayor of New York in 1977. In 1978, Republican Bill Green (no relation to Mark) defeated liberal Democrat Bella Abzug in a special election to fill the Koch vacancy. Bill Green then won the regularly scheduled election in November by spending more money, $1.6 million, than any other congressional candidate in the nation.

---

76. Barone and Ujifusa, *Almanac*, 791; Ehrenhalt, *Politics*, 1988, 1025.
77. Michael Kramer, "Is Anybody Listening," *New Yorker*, November 3, 1986, 37.
78. Kramer, "Anybody Listening," 48.

Mark Green easily won the 1980 Democratic primary, overwhelming two other candidates with 81 percent of the vote. In the general election, Mark Green challenged Bill Green to voluntarily limit campaign spending. Given Bill Green's independent wealth—as heir to the Grand Union supermarket chain he is worth millions—and his willingness to spend that money on his campaigns, observers were surprised when he agreed to a $236,000 spending limit.[79] A moderate Republican in earlier years, Bill moved even more strongly to the left as the 1980 campaign developed: his ADA ratings increased from 68 in 1979 to 94 in 1980. With a week left in the campaign, the *New York Times* endorsed Bill Green, stating that "We would like to see Mark Green in Congress, but loosing Bill Green would be too high a price to pay."[80] Bill Green defeated challenger Mark Green with 57 percent of the vote.

The Race

New York's junior senator, Alphonse D'Amato, may at first have seemed quite vulnerable. He is a Republican in a Democratic state; he won in 1980 by less than 1 percent of the vote, and that was only because Jacob Javits remained on the Liberal party line; and he came up through the ranks of a political machine whose leader had recently been imprisoned. D'Amato responded as effectively to these problems as a politician could. He worked hard to downplay ideology, particularly later in his term, and instead emphasized federal projects he brought to New York. He seized on the drug issue and became a vociferous supporter of Israel. And, perhaps most important, he accumulated a massive campaign war chest. By April, 1986, D'Amato had raised over $6 million.[81]

Whatever the direct effects of incumbent spending may be, in this election, D'Amato's treasury clearly had an indirect effect: many of the strongest Democrats chose not to enter the race.[82] Brooklyn District Attorney Elizabeth Holtzman, the former congresswoman who lost a narrow race to D'Amato in 1980, felt she could not raise the amount of money needed to wage a successful campaign. Former vice presidential candidate Geraldine Ferraro declined the opportunity, citing the Justice Department's investigation of her congressional campaign finances.[83] Entertainer and civil rights activist Harry

---

79. Joyce Purnick, "Two Greens in House Race Agree To Limit of $236,145 on Spending," *New York Times*, October 15, 1980.

80. "For the House From New York," *New York Times*, October 27, 1980.

81. Frank Lynn, "New York GOP Plans a Busy Week," *New York Times*, April 14, 1986.

82. See, generally, Gary Jacobson and Sam Kernell, *Strategy and Choice in Congressional Elections*, 2d ed. (New Haven: Yale University Press, 1983).

83. Michael Oreskes, "Levitt Declines to Challenge D'Amato," *New York Times*, January 19, 1986.

Belafonte held conversations with Democratic officials about a possible campaign but ultimately rejected their overtures, citing professional and personal commitments.[84] Other prominent Democrats choosing not to take on D'Amato included Arthur Levitt, Jr., chairman of the American Stock Exchange, and Tom Downey, a popular congressman from Long Island. Beyond whatever explanations the potential candidates gave for not running was "the widespread perception that Mr. D'Amato will be hard to defeat."[85]

In the absence of a more experienced and visible challenger, Governor Cuomo and Democratic party leaders gave their backing for the Senate nomination to John Dyson, a member of the State Power Commission. A former State Commerce commissioner, Dyson had conceived the enormously successful "I Love New York" advertising campaign. Also endearing Dyson to party leaders was the fact that Dyson, a multimillionaire, promised to spend up to $3 million—a figure that later jumped to $6 million—of his own money in the campaign.[86]

Unduanted by Dyson's money and connections, Mark Green announced his candidacy on April 21. Green offers this account of his decision to seek the Senate.

> I had worked ten years in Washington with Ralph Nader. I had written *Who Runs Congress*. I had met hundreds of congressmen and senators, which led me to two conclusions: (1) it made me exuberant to play a role in high-level public policy, and (2) it led me to believe that I was at least equal in skills and dedication to the people who ended up getting elected. So it gave me more confidence perhaps than I deserved. I came back to New York and ran for Congress in 1980. I lost to a popular incumbent. Looking back, it was a noble but perhaps foolish venture. We now see in the 1980s that 98 percent of incumbent congressmen win unless they're senile or in a scandal.
>
> In 1985, I realized that the best members of the New York congressional delegation wouldn't run against D'Amato, who was both high in the polls and high in dollars. Why? In a large, populated state, no congressman can get known in the other congressional districts, so you're an emperor in your own district and an unknown in the other

---

84. Frank Lynn, "Belafonte Says He Won't Run for Senate Seat," *New York Times*, March 4, 1986.

85. Frank Lynn, "Green, Seeking to be Senator, Steps Up Effort," *New York Times*, February 3, 1986.

86. Frank Lynn, "Cuomo Pushing Dyson to Seek D'Amato Seat," *New York Times*, April 15, 1986; Frank Lynn, "With Eye to November, Dyson Stresses Wealth," *New York Times*, August 26, 1986.

thirty-three, unlike South Dakota, where Tom Daschle is known statewide because he's the only congressman [see chap. 7].

One last point: I feel very comfortable and confident on television, and I thought that my ability to discuss issues electronically could enable me to be competitive, if not win a primary. If there were no top-ranking opponent, like a Geraldine Ferraro, like a [State Attorney General] Bob Abrams, like a [Congressman] Steven Solarz, and that in a general election against Al D'Amato I was one scandal away from winning. I thought there were a lot of time bombs in his past that could explode in his face.[87]

Attending Green's announcement were noncandidates Elizabeth Holtzman, Geraldine Ferraro, and Harry Belafonte.[88] Dyson officially announced his candidacy on May 31 with a strong attack on D'Amato's connections to special interests. While Dyson avoided criticism of Green, Green denounced Dyson as a conservative.[89] Ironically, with the support of Governor Cuomo, Dyson received the official backing of the Liberal party.[90] Three days later, the Democratic State Committee endorsed Dyson for senator, but Green received enough support, 34.7 percent, to ensure a spot on the primary ballot.[91]

The early campaign strategy of Dyson consisted of a relatively large television budget, $1.2 million—later increased to $3.0 million—to be used largely to attack D'Amato. Green, on the other hand, had no personal fortune and refused to accept donations from political action committees. Though Green estimates his stand cost him up to $500,000 through the entire campaign, he felt he had little choice but to decline such contributions.

> I did it for two reasons. One, I'd been such a prominent critic of how PACs corrupted politics that I thought it inconceivable that I accept the gifts I'd criticized. If nothing else, I had to be consistent with my personal history. Second, politics is not a business where virtue is its own reward, you need a majority or else why bother, and I'd hoped the public, if not small donors, would reward me for taking this principled if

---

87. Mark Green, personal interview, March 23, 1990.

88. Frank Lynn, "Mark Green Joins Race to Oppose D'Amato," *New York Times,* April 22, 1986.

89. Peter Kerr, "Dyson Announces Bid for U.S. Senate," *New York Times,* June 1, 1986.

90. Despite its name, the Liberal party exists more to receive patronage from cross-endorsements than to support the campaigns of liberal or progressive candidates. "No doubt the Liberal party began as a group of dedicated idealists, but few today doubt that its dedication to principle has given way to obsession with patronage" (Howard Scarrow, *Parties, Elections and Representation in the State of New York* [New York: New York University Press, 1983], 74).

91. Frank Lynn, "Cuomo Attains Party Backing by Acclamation," *New York Times,* June 3, 1986.

painful stand. And my guess is I did get a number of small donors who I urged to give to me since the fat cats weren't, and so I ended up with 18,000 contributors, which is an extraordinary number for a first-time candidate. But the media ignored the issue. They treated it as just a gimmick or ignored it all together. . . . The issue is large, legislatively interested money. Now, accepting PAC money is not immoral, and it's certainly not illegal. I just went beyond the legal minimum to try to make a point. Now, accepting PAC money and then in effect arm twisting government to enrich your PAC donors is unethical and should be illegal, and that's why I did ultimately file my ethics complaint against Senator D'Amato.[92]

Through June, Green had raised a total of only $350,000 and had little money for television. While he condemned D'Amato's voting record, he also criticized Dyson for recent flirtations with the Republican and Conservative parties and for ties with companies that do business in South Africa.[93]

Green's attacks on Dyson continued at an August 12 debate in upstate Oneonta, New York. Green charged that two Dyson family businesses had participated in the Arab boycott of Israel. Green labeled millionaire Dyson "elitist, arrogant," and "a closet Republican." Dyson spent more of his time attacking D'Amato and Reagan, but managed to criticize Green's lack of experience in government as well.[94] The sniping continued at a *New York Times*–sponsored forum. Dyson argued that there were few policy differences between the candidates and emphasized, instead, that Green had no record of government service. Green declared that there were real differences between him and Dyson, particularly with respect to the environment, South Africa, and Reaganomics. Finally, Green accused Dyson of "a ten-year imitation of Al D'Amato."[95]

As the primary approached, Dyson continued his lead in the polls.[96] Through the end of August, Dyson had put just under $5 million of his own money into the primary campaign and had already spent $4.7 million. Budgeted into the last days of the primary campaign was $550,000 per week for radio and television advertisements. On the other hand, Green had raised only

---

92. Green interview.

93. Frank Lynn, "Rivals for Senate Differ on Strategy," *New York Times*, June 16, 1986; Lynn, "Eye to November"; Ronald Smothers, "Dyson Holdings Spark Exchange Over Apartheid," *New York Times*, July 17, 1986.

94. Frank Lynn, "Mark Green and Dyson Trade Barbs," *New York Times*, August 13, 1986.

95. "Accomplishments Are a Key Issue in Senate Democratic Primary Debate," *New York Times*, August 20, 1986; Frank Lynn, "Green and Dyson Exchange Accusations," *New York Times*, August 20, 1986.

96. Lynn, "Eye to November."

$570,000 and spent merely $465,000. He budgeted $40,000 per week for radio for the closing days of the primary.[97] By the end of the primary campaign, Dyson had spent $6 million, Green, but $800,000.[98]

With Dyson ahead in the polls, Green's lone shot at victory would be a low turnout. The explanation for this is quite simple: it is only those who are most interested in politics who vote in primaries; and those who are most interested in politics are more likely to be more extreme in their views than those less interested.[99] The lower the turnout, the more ideologically extreme the electorate. This is exactly what happened in the New York primary. With Al D'Amato appearing unbeatable and no other interesting races, fewer than a half-million of New York's 3.8 million eligible Democrats voted. Of these, just under 54 percent voted for Green, who, given the low turnout, won by 34,000 votes.[100] Green won by three to two margins in New York City and won 58 percent of the vote in the highly populated suburbs. While Dyson won upstate by nearly two to one, this accounted for only 25 percent of the votes cast.[101]

On the Republican side, D'Amato was not standing still waiting for the Democrats to choose a candidate. D'Amato's campaign received early boosts through separate visits by Vice President Bush and President Reagan in April. Reagan's speech at a D'Amato fund-raiser roundly praised the senator, emphasizing bipartisan issues. "There are two areas where Al D'Amato's leadership and total—that is *total*—commitment have made a major and immediate impact. I'm referring to the problems of drugs and crime."[102]

D'Amato officially announced his campaign on May 6 in Manhattan. With Senate Majority Leader Robert Dole at his side, D'Amato dedicated his second term in office to fighting "the scourge of drugs." In a state where Democrats outnumber Republicans by more than one million voters, D'Amato chose the nonpartisan "Getting it Done" as his campaign theme, and highlighted praise by Democrats Ed Koch and Mario Cuomo in his campaign brochure and news releases.[103]

---

97. Frank Lynn, "Dyson Reports Spending $4.7 Million on Campaign," *New York Times*, August 30, 1986.

98. Frank Lynn, "Mark Green Beats Dyson in Primary," *New York Times*, September 10, 1986.

99. See, e.g., Jack Walker, "The Primary Game," *Wilson Quarterly* 12 (1988): 64–77; Nelson Polsby, *Consequences of Party Reform* (New York: Oxford University Press, 1983).

100. "Results of Balloting in New York and Connecticut," *New York Times*, September 11, 1986.

101. "The Senate Race, County by County," *New York Times*, September 10, 1986; Lynn, "Green Beats Dyson."

102. Frank Lynn, "Reagan Lauds D'Amato at Waldorf Luncheon," *New York Times*, April 19, 1986.

103. Frank Lynn, "D'Amato Announces for Second Term," *New York Times*, May 17, 1986.

In an effort to prevent either Democratic candidate from cutting into his sizable lead, D'Amato unveiled a series of commercials produced by Roger Ailes, who later ran George Bush's 1988 media campaign. The 1986 Ailes was kinder and gentler than the 1988 Ailes, who brought Willie Horton to the nation's attention. Ailes's advertisements emphasized D'Amato's accomplishments as senator and never mentioned Mark Green, directly or indirectly. One commercial noted D'Amato's efforts in getting funds for Mother Hale, the Harlem woman who treated drug-addicted infants and children in her home.[104] Another noted D'Amato's efforts in freeing Jewish émigrés from the Soviet Union.[105] The theme throughout the commercials was simple and nonideological: "Al D'Amato, Getting It Done."

Other commercials sought a more personal appeal. One showed an elderly couple at Ellis Island, where immigrants to the United States landed at the turn of the century. An announcer read the following script.

> Ellis Island. They [the couple] are part of the American dream. Their parents came here as immigrants so many years ago, to raise a family, to be free. They came with few belongings, but a willingness to work hard, a faith in God, and a belief in America's promise. Times weren't always easy but this couple has lived the American dream, and they still believe. Today, their son is a United States senator. His name is Al D'Amato.[106]

D'Amato continued his massive fund-raising efforts throughout the primary season. Through the end of August he had raised $7.4 million and had $3.0 million on hand. An additional $1.2 million was expected from the Senate Republican Campaign Committee.[107]

Meanwhile, whatever boost Green may have received from his upset victory over Dyson was short lived. First, Dyson vowed to run an active campaign on the Liberal line. Dyson claimed to be giving the people a choice between "a right-wing ideologue, a left-wing Warren Beatty—Jane Fonda liberal and a moderate Democrat."[108] Then, the day after the primary, Democratic New York Mayor Ed Koch told a news conference that D'Amato had been a "superb senator." While not formally endorsing D'Amato, Koch de-

---

104. D'Amato Commercial no. 5, Center for Political Communications, University of Oklahoma.
105. D'Amato Commercial no. 15, Center for Political Communications, University of Oklahoma.
106. D'Amato Commercial no. 14, Center for Political Communications, University of Oklahoma.
107. Lynn, "Dyson Reports Spending."
108. Maralee Schwartz, "Green Has Not Won the Hearts of Leading N.Y. Democrats," *Washington Post*, September 12, 1986.

clared that he could never endorse Green, given Green's liberal philosophy.[109] Looking back on Koch's opposition, Green made the following remarks.

> If Ed Koch had not been the mayor in 1986, I of course still would have lost, and probably by a comparable margin. However, there is no doubt he took the wind out of my sails the day after what should have been a catapulting win. Instead of the front page of the *Times* saying "Green takes initiative against D'Amato's ethics," in effect, the headline was "Koch pulls the rug out from under Green."
>
> In the country in 1986, I think there was perhaps one prominent Democratic officeholder who endorsed a Republican for senator, at a time when the majority of the Senate was, of course, at risk. It was, of course, Ed Koch. He and D'Amato had a kind of back-scratching compact: D'Amato helped Koch; Koch helped D'Amato. Ed Koch was free to endorse D'Amato and I was free to point out that Koch was, in effect, a Republican helping Republicans retain control of the Senate, and three years later returned the favor. I spent a year *pro bono* with David Dinkins making sure that Koch would be a private sector Republican rather than a public sector Republican. Mission accomplished.
>
> Koch consistently attacked me during the general election. This created an insuperable problem. I had to focus 150 percent of my time on a highly favored, well-funded incumbent who was ahead in the polls. That was challenge enough. But with Koch biting at my heel, when Koch attacked me, I couldn't spend any money or effort in answering him. Then I'd be taking on the leading Italian Republican and the leading Jewish Democrat in the state, and the combination proved extremely difficult to handle.[110]

Two weeks after the primary, close to three dozen Democratic leaders endorsed D'Amato. At the same time, D'Amato's polls showed him winning 50 percent of the Democratic vote.[111] The same factor that helped Green most in winning the primary, his liberalism, was beginning to hurt him in the general election.

Green was able to pick up support from Governor Cuomo, though. Following a poll showing Dyson with only 8 percent of the vote on the Liberal line, Cuomo started to question Dyson's candidacy.[112] By the end of September, Cuomo was actively criticizing D'Amato for the first time. D'Amato was

---

109. Frank Lynn, "Mayor Commends D'Amato as Being 'Superb' Senator," *New York Times*, September 11, 1986.
110. Green interview.
111. "D'Amato is Endorsed by Some Democrats," *New York Times*, September 23, 1986.
112. "Cuomo Questions Dyson Senate Bid," *New York Times*, September 19, 1986.

"bad for New Yorkers," who would be better off with a Democrat.[113] Yet it is also the case that Cuomo's dissatisfaction with D'Amato was not strong enough to stop the governor from using a complimentary quote from D'Amato in a Cuomo campaign commercial.

Following the primary, the front-running D'Amato sought to avoid any mention of his opponent's name, though he did at one point note Green's view, from the 1960s, that marijuana should be legalized.[114] Green, on the other hand, was not at all reluctant about attacking D'Amato. On September 27, Green accused the D'Amato campaign of accepting illegal campaign contributions from investment firms E. F. Hutton and Drexel Burnham Lambert. According to Green, there was "probable cause to believe that fraud, forgery, misrepresentation and other violations of Federal and state law were committed by Senator D'Amato [and] his campaign."[115] In addition to illegality, Green also claimed impropriety on D'Amato's part. Drexel Burnham, which pioneered junk bonds, hosted a fund-raiser for D'Amato after D'Amato amended a bill to delete federal restrictions on the bonds. On September 30, Green called D'Amato a "senator for sale or rent," noting that D'Amato received $1.3 million from special-interest Political Action Committees. After noting contributions from certain groups, Green asked "Why in the world would he vote for the used-car lobby, the big oil lobby, the National Rifle Association and the chemical industry, were it not for the influence of thousands of dollars in solicited donations."[116] In October, Green charged that D'Amato used his position as chairman of the Senate Subcommittee on Securities to make money on the stock market.[117] The D'Amato campaign consistently denied all charges made by Green, and by and large the charges did not pick up much publicity.

Green finally unveiled a modest, $150,000 television advertising campaign in mid-October, using Cuomo's voice and still pictures. Another advertisement, featuring Green himself, attempted to make D'Amato's conservatism an issue.

> I'm Mark Green, the Democrat running against Al D'Amato. Here's what his commercials don't tell you. He's against handgun control; you and I are for it. He's against a woman's right to choose; you and I support

---

113. Jeffrey Schmalz, "Cuomo Criticizes D'Amato's Record," *New York Times*, September 30, 1986.

114. "Green Shifts on Marijuana," *New York Times*, October 13, 1986.

115. Frank Lynn, "Mark Green Seeks Inquiries Into D'Amato Campaign Gifts," *New York Times*, September 28, 1986.

116. "Green Study Says Special Interests Donated $1.3 Million to D'Amato," *New York Times*, October 1, 1986.

117. "Dyson and Green Begin Advertising in Race with D'Amato," *New York Times*, October 10, 1986.

it. He's voted sixteen times to cut social security and student loans. Would you have done that? And he's taken a million bucks from big special interests. I don't take any of their money. Now, if you don't agree with Al D'Amato, why vote for him. I'm Mark Green.[118]

Based on the data in chapter 4, perhaps $10 million would have enabled Green to wage an effective campaign in a state the size of New York. The feeble amount spent was far too little to be of effective use by a challenger against a popular incumbent.

In Green's continued efforts to damage D'Amato, Green noted a *New Republic* article in which an anonymous source stated that D'Amato had referred to those who lived in a low-income housing project as "animals." D'Amato's campaign called the charge a fabrication.[119] With Ralph Nader at his side, Green later charged D'Amato with participation in a Nassau County kickback scandal, whereby employees were required to give 1 percent of their salary to the Republican party.[120] In late October, Green's latest charge centered around campaign contributions to D'Amato by convicted racketeer, Philip Basile. D'Amato, in fact, was Basile's sole character witness at Basile's trial.[121] By and large, though, the media, and the public, paid little attention to Green's charges. The reason, according to New York media guru David Garth, is that "Green has been coming across as too shrill."[122]

Three weeks before the election, John Dyson, with less than 10 percent support and at the behest of Governor Cuomo, dropped out of the race and endorsed Green. Green, in return, surprisingly dropped his opposition to research into the Star Wars space defense system. However, polls still showed D'Amato with up to 60 percent support, and Green hovering in the low 20s. D'Amato even took exception to a *Washington Post* story claiming that D'Amato had a 2 to 1 lead. According to the *Post*, D'Amato did not want Green, "a young man I am increasingly growing to dislike," to believe the race was closer than it was.[123] Through mid-October, D'Amato had spent over $4.5 million and had over $2.5 million on hand. Green had spent $1.1 million, had only $49,000 cash on hand, and had $75,000 in debts.[124]

---

118. Green Commercial no. 3, Center for Political Communications, University of Oklahoma.
119. Robert McFadden, "Green Notes Magazine Article That Laid a Slur to D'Amato," *New York Times*, October 14, 1986.
120. Frank Lynn, "After Feud, Dyson Plans to Endorse Green," *New York Times*, October 16, 1986.
121. "Green Links D'Amato to Convict," *New York Times*, October 20, 1986.
122. Kramer, "Anybody Listening," 37.
123. Maralee Schwartz, "Postscript," *Washington Post*, October 17, 1986.
124. Lynn, "After Feud"; Frank Lynn, "Dyson, Despite Differences, Endorses Green for Senate," *New York Times*, October 17, 1986.

D'Amato agreed to two debates with Green, but given the Senator's lead in the polls it is not surprising that he sought to minimize their impact. Therefore, the debates were scheduled, at D'Amato's insistence, only fourteen hours apart from each other. Furthermore, D'Amato scheduled the first debate for October 21 in Albany only after it was clear that it would be competing for attention with the game 3 of the World Series, which featured the New York Mets.[125] D'Amato stated that his wish was "for the Mets to win in seven. That will delay people's attention to just a few days before the election."[126]

Consistent with the rest of the campaign, both Green and D'Amato focused on D'Amato's record during the debate. Green decried D'Amato's connection with the Nassau County Republican political machine, his support for the Contras in Nicaragua, his opposition to gun control, and his opposition to abortion rights. D'Amato highlighted his record of delivering federal funds to New York in mass transit, senior citizen housing, and urban development grants. D'Amato's only reply to any of Green's charges was to deny that he had voted against South African sanctions.[127] The debate the next morning in New York City was little different. Green attacked D'Amato's voting record, his connections to alleged mobsters, and his support for the interests of his campaign contributors. The senator's only mention of Green was to criticize the challenger's reversal on Star Wars. Later, D'Amato declared that the debate was "about a very bright ideologue trying to incite me and my doing everything in my power to remain senatorial. I had to hold my tongue and stare straight ahead."[128]

Perhaps the cruelest blow to Green during the campaign came on October 29, when the liberal *New York Times* endorsed D'Amato. The *Times* acknowledged the claims of D'Amato's critics, including "his incredible testimony that he didn't know, as a Long Island official, that the Republican party required the faithful to kick back 1 percent of their salaries," and his role as "the sole character witness for a man convicted of conspiring with an organized crime figure." And the *Times* even denied charges that Green was a "doctrinaire liberal." Yet, D'Amato, the "Pothole Senator," brought home hundreds of millions of dollars in federal aid. "Measured by his practical achievements, Senator D'Amato has earned another term."[129]

---

125. Frank Lynn, "In Initial Debate, D'Amato Ignores Green and Criticism," *New York Times*, October 22, 1986.

126. Kramer, "Anybody Listening."

127. "Excerpts from D'Amato-Green Debate in Albany," *New York Times*, October 22, 1986; Lynn, "Initial Debate."

128. Kramer, "Anybody Listening," 36–41.

129. "For the Senate From New York," *New York Times*, October 29, 1986.

Green blames much of his problems on John Vinocur, then metropolitan editor of the *Times*.

> [Vinocur] was a conservative who loved D'Amato and didn't like me. He refused to cover the race. His reporters later complained to me that "he wouldn't let us cover the race."[130] Because the *Times* covered it very little, because John Vinocur had no interest in investigative reports which exposed D'Amato, and because D'Amato was so far ahead in the polls a month out that he looked like the inevitable winner, it is not surprising that a paper like the *Times* went with the likely winner rather than the interesting, distant underdog.
>
> Now there's not much I can say about this without sounding self-serving, so let me limit my remarks to these few. . . . I think it's fair to say that a lot of people were shocked that a great liberal, ethical newspaper like the *New York Times* would endorse someone who was not, shall we say, a great, ethical senator. I think it fair to say that that was in another administration of the *New York Times*. There is now a different executive editor, there is now a different editorial page editor, there is now a different metropolitan editor. The ownership is the same. My guess is, everyone would agree, that the *New York Times* in 1990, based on all their editorials agreeing with my ethics complaint against D'Amato, would not now endorse him over me. In fact, after the editorial endorsed my ethics complaint, and after the ethics committee decided to investigate D'Amato, a friend of mine in journalism called me up and said "The *New York Times* did endorse you in your senate race, three years too late."[131]

If nothing else, the 1986 *Times* was backing a sure winner. The final preelection poll by the Marist Institute showed D'Amato with 56 percent, Green with 29 percent, and Dyson, who could not remove his name from the Liberal line, at 4 percent.[132]

The campaign ended with D'Amato releasing Kennedyesque commercials of the senator playing football with his kids. Green received a last

---

130. Frank Lynn, who covered the race for the *Times*, denies making or even thinking such comments. According to Lynn, any lack of coverage was a combination of competition from the Wedtech trial in the Bronx and the lack of competition in Senate race (Frank Lynn, personal interview, May 3, 1990).

131. Green interview.

132. Esther Fein, "D'Amato Seeks Wide-Based Support," *New York Times*, November 1, 1986.

minute shot of cash from a benefit by rock group Crosby, Stills and Nash, but this hardly made a difference.

D'Amato won the Senate election with 58 percent of the vote, the most by any Republican in New York State history. Green received 41 percent, and Dyson received 1 percent. While Green won overwhelmingly Democratic New York City with 57 percent, D'Amato won 64 percent of the vote outside the city. D'Amato won every county outside the city except one, including heavily Democratic Albany and Erie Counties.[133]

To Green, his loss was due to no money and low visibility. When asked whether his liberal positions hurt him, he made the following comments.

> Conceivably they could have if people had known of them. What hurt me was that people didn't know who I was. Every candidate who loses comes up with exonerating reasons, so that might look like an alibi, but it also happens to be true. I was a little-known nominee. If I had been, say, a well-known state attorney general, or if I had $14 million, as Lew Lehrman did when he ran for governor in 1982, to advertise my values, then you could say that I was rejected because of my policies or my personality. But spending under $2 million and being little known at the start and relatively at the finish . . . basically, people were satisfied with the incumbent. In fact, my values are not substantially different than Mario Cuomo's values, you know, a good FDR, John Kennedy, Mario Cuomo Democrat. So the variables were not ideology, the variables were money and visibility.
>
> I had assumed the free media would play up a race between a Nader Democrat and a [jailed Nassau County Political leader Joseph] Margiotta Republican. Wrong. The major papers, with the exception of *Newsday*, bought into the incumbent's mind-set, and never covered the race because they thought it wasn't a race, which predetermined that it wasn't a race. I hope this doesn't sound like bellyaching but I think it's documentingly true.[134]

Survey Results

According to ABC News (see table 6.2), New Yorkers cited illegal drugs as an important issue in determining for whom to vote (43 percent), followed by the national economy (42 percent), social security (40 percent), and reducing unemployment (39 percent).[135]

---

133. "Tallies for U.S. Senator and Statewide Offices," *New York Times*, November 6, 1986.

134. Green interview.

135. ABC News, *The '88 Vote*, 444.

D'Amato beat Green by a 58 to 41 margin (57 to 40 in the ABC data). He did so by sweeping every age category, white-collar workers and blue-collar workers, union and nonunion households, and people of all income categories. D'Amato won 60 percent of the male vote and 55 percent of the female vote. He won 62 percent of the white vote and a relatively high 24

TABLE 6.2. New York Exit Poll Results (in percentages)

	All Voters	Green Voters	D'Amato Voters
Gender			
Male	50	38	60
Female	50	42	55
Race			
White	90	36	62
Black	6	74	24
Other	4	58	34
Ideology			
Liberal	17	74	22
Conservative	22	17	81
Party			
Democrat	42	65	33
Independent	17	44	50
Republican	38	9	89
Other	3	27	63
Better cope			
Democrats	49	68	28
Republicans	51	12	86
Personally better off than when Reagan took office			
Better off	39	24	74
About the same	40	40	57
Worse off	21	65	32
Reagan job performance			
Approve	64	21	77
Disapprove	36	69	28
State of economy			
Excellent	4	19	81
Good	52	26	72
Not so good	36	53	43
Poor	8	70	28
Important items (selected)			
National economy	42	40	57
Local economy	34	41	57
Reagan performance	26	35	64
Candidates' party	15	43	54

Source: ABC News, The '88 Vote, 442.

percent of the black vote. D'Amato also failed to capture the Jewish vote (11 percent of those who voted in New York), losing to Green 64 to 34, but his strong support for Israel gave him a fairly high level of support against his liberal Jewish opponent. Though there are more Democrats than Republicans in New York, D'Amato upset that advantage by carrying 89 percent of the Republicans and holding Green to just 65 percent of the Democrats.

While demographic factors of course affected the race, D'Amato was able to overcome the obstacles facing Republicans in New York by winning over some of the traditionally Democratic groups (union workers, blue-collar workers, and the poor) and doing reasonably well among others (blacks and Jews). Thus, these factors were not as strong predictors of the vote as they traditionally have been.

On the other hand, national issues clearly divided D'Amato and Green supporters. D'Amato won 81 percent of the conservative vote, while Green won 74 percent of the smaller, liberal vote. Among those who thought the Democrats could better cope with the nation's problems, 68 percent voted for Green, while 86 percent of those who thought the Republicans could better cope voted for D'Amato. Those who were better off compared to when Reagan took office voted for D'Amato by a 74 to 24 margin, while those who were worse off voted for Green 65 to 32. Crucial to D'Amato, those who were better off outnumbered those who were worse off 39 to 21. Similarly, D'Amato overwhelmingly won among voters who thought the economy was excellent or good (81 percent and 72 percent, respectively) and lost among voters who thought the economy was not so good or poor (43 percent and 28 percent, respectively). But again, those who thought the economy was at least good outnumbered those who did not, 56 to 44. Finally, D'Amato won the votes of 77 percent of those who approved of Reagan's job performance, but only 28 percent of those who disapproved. But those who approved outnumbered those who disapproved 64 to 36.

Conclusions

Like California, New York is a two-party state. Though there are far more Democrats than Republicans, and though there are a relatively large number of liberals compared to the rest of the country, Democrats do not and have not dominated the political landscape. There is, perhaps, a slight advantage to being a Democrat in statewide races, but that advantage can be easily overcome. D'Amato, though more conservative than most New Yorkers, built his legislative career and political campaign around nonpartisan issues and constituent casework. He ran what must be considered a classic campaign, emphasizing the federal dollars he brought back to New York, rather than the conservative issues he often supported. The issues he did emphasize, support for Soviet Jews and opposition to illegal drugs, are hardly stands that would alienate voters. Though incumbent spending has only a marginal direct effect on votes (see chap. 4), D'Amato's war chest appears to have kept many strong Democrats out of the race. Mark Green, on the other hand, was, in some senses, one of the weakest possible candidates that D'Amato could have faced. He has never held elective office, and despite frequent appearances on political talk shows in no way can be considered a celebrity. Green was unable to raise anything near the amount of money he needed to attack D'Amato's record forcefully. He relied on the free media to relay his charges about D'Amato's behavior, but the news organizations would not bite. Moreover, the forces that enabled Green to capture the Democratic nomination, notably his strong liberal stand, worked to his disadvantage in the general election as traditional Democratic groups and many Democratic elites supported D'Amato. Finally, examining national political conditions, D'Amato ran with the active support of a popular Republican president during relatively prosperous times. This was far more than a challenger without a great deal of personal popularity or wealth could overcome.

We examine two senators less fortunate than Cranston and D'Amato when we continue with the analyses of the Florida and South Dakota elections in chapter 7.

CHAPTER 7

Incumbent Losers in Senate Campaigns in the Television Age

In chapter 6 we examined the 1986 Senate races in California and New York. In the New York race, Senator D'Amato faced a weak challenger and easily won reelection. In the California race, Alan Cranston held his seat despite a strong challenge from Congressman Ed Zschau. In chapter 7, we examine two Republican incumbents, Paula Hawkins of Florida and Jim Abdnor of South Dakota, who, like Cranston, faced strong challengers; the former faced a popular governor, the latter a populist Congressman. Abdnor's loss to Tom Daschle was largely due to the depressed farm economy, while Hawkins's loss to Bob Graham was largely due to the enormous popularity of the governor.

Florida

Florida is currently the fifth largest state in the Union, with almost twelve million inhabitants. It is also the fastest growing state. Following the 1950 census, Florida was allotted eight seats in the House of Representatives. It now has nineteen, and that number will increase to twenty-three following the 1990 census. Between 1970 and 1980, Florida's population grew by 44 percent. Between 1980 and 1986 its population increased by 20 percent. Due in large part to the age of the electorate, Florida is only twenty-ninth in the proportion of persons with college degrees. It is twenty-eighth in per pupil education expenditures. Florida's population is "as diverse as any in America," including native Floridians (only 31 percent of the population), northern Protestants and Jews, who began to migrate there in the 1940s and 1950s, respectively, and refugees from Cuba (1960s) and other Latin American countries (1980s). Fourteen percent of the population is black; 9 percent is Hispanic; 11 percent is foreign born. Though 84 percent of the population lives in urban areas, there is no single metropolis that dominates the state. The largest city, Jacksonville, has only 540,000 people. Miami is second with 345,000, and Tampa third with 271,000. Due largely to drug dealing, Florida has the highest violent crime rate in the country.[1]

---

1. Much of the background information on the states and candidates is derived from Michael Barone and Grant Ujifusa, *The Almanac of American Politics* (Washington, D.C.:

The *Almanac of American Politics* describes Florida in the 1940s as "a steamy, sparsely populated backwater, one of the least developed parts of the Deep South. . . . The state's few citizens were mostly poor, disease-ridden, uneducated, insular, and bigoted."[2] Due in no small part to the invention of air conditioning, Florida's population jumped from two million in 1940 to twelve million today.

As one cohort of older Americans after another has migrated from the cold industrial belt to . . . the Florida peninsula, a new megastate has grown. . . . Hundreds of square miles of swampland have been drained, miles and miles of roads and parking lots have been laid down, shopping centers and restaurants and luxury resorts and trailer parks have been built. For millions of Americans, Florida has been a chance to start over, . . . to build if not a city on the hill then a suburb in what until quite recently was a swamp.[3]

Florida, like all of the former Confederacy, was a solid, one-party Democratic state until recently. From the end of Reconstruction until 1968, Florida never elected a Republican to the U.S. Senate. Of the 180 House races from 1896 until 1965, 172 were won by Democrats.[4] Southern Democratic politics was, of course, conservative politics, but, according to V. O. Key, "while the state's politics was by no means free of Negro-baiting, the dominant attitude on the race question is comparatively mild."[5] Unlike many southern states, Florida did not vote for Strom Thurmond in 1948, nor for George Wallace in 1968. But like the other southern states, as the national Democratic party became more and more associated with civil rights, Florida increasingly voted Republican. Indeed, while 57 percent of the voters are registered Democrats, Republicans have outregistered Democrats by a 2 to 1 margin since 1980.[6] Florida elected its first post-Reconstruction Republican to the U.S. Senate in 1968 and, except for Jimmy Carter in 1976, has consistently voted Republican in presidential contests since then.

Based on statewide characteristics and national political conditions, Florida was a state that should have been made for the Republicans in 1986.

National Journal, 1988); Alan Ehrenhalt, ed., *Politics in America* (Washington, D.C.: Congressional Quarterly, 1986); and Alan Ehrenhalt, ed., *Politics in America* (Washington, D.C.: Congressional Quarterly, 1988).

    2. Barone and Ujifusa, *Almanac*, 235.

    3. Barone and Ujifusa, *Almanac*, 235.

    4. Harold Stanley and Richard Niemi, *Vital Statistics in American Politics* (Washington, D.C.: Congressional Quarterly, 1988), 86–87.

    5. V. O. Key, *Southern Politics* (New York: Vintage, 1949), 85.

    6. Ehrenhalt, *Politics*, 1986, 292.

Though the Democrats held an edge over Republicans in party identification, 46 to 35, there were more than twice as many self-identified conservatives (29 percent) as liberals (13 percent).[7] Floridians thought Republicans better able to cope with the nation's problems by an impressive 58 to 42 margin. By more than a 5 to 2 ratio, Florida voters considered themselves better off in 1986 than when Reagan took office. Their approval rating for Reagan, 71 percent, was among the highest in the nation. Sixty-five percent thought the economy excellent or good, while only 36 percent considered it not so good or poor.

Paula Hawkins

Paula Hawkins was born on January 24, 1927, in Salt Lake City, Utah. She attended Utah State University from 1944 to 1947 and received an honorary degree from the same in 1982. Hawkins was one of the first post-Reconstruction Republicans elected to statewide office in Florida when, in 1972, she was selected by the voters to serve on the state Public Service Commission. When Hawkins was returned to her seat in 1976, she became the first Republican since Reconstruction to be *reelected* to statewide office. On the commission, Hawkins took a populist stand, opposing rate hikes by telephone and utility companies.[8]

Hawkins ran unsuccessfully for higher office in 1974, when she sought the Republican nomination for U.S. Senator, and again in 1978, when she tried for the lieutenant governorship. In 1980, she again sought the Republican U.S. Senate nomination and finished at the top of a crowded field. Because Hawkins won with less than a majority of the vote, 48 percent, she was forced into a runoff with former Congressman Lou Frey, who finished second with 27 percent. Hawkins won the runoff handily, winning 62 percent of the vote. On the Democratic side, state Insurance Commissioner Bill Gunter defeated incumbent Richard Stone (see chap. 3). In winning the nomination, Gunter split the Democratic party and depleted his campaign treasury.[9] Aided by the coattails of Ronald Reagan, who won 55 percent of the vote in Florida to 39 percent for President Carter, and the split in the Democratic party, Hawkins won the election with less than 52 percent of the vote. She thus became only the second Republican to be elected to the U.S. Senate from Florida since Reconstruction.

Hawkins's Senate career got off to what can only be considered a shaky start. At the now infamous "steak and jail lunch," she served steak, asparagus, and fresh strawberries to guests while announcing plans to send food

---

7. ABC News, *The '88 Vote* (New York: Capitol Cities/ABC News, 1989), chap. 3.
8. Ehrenhalt, *Politics*, 1986, 292.
9. Ehrenhalt, *Politics*, 1986, 292.

stamp cheaters to prison. She also suffered from severe health problems, including backaches and migraines.

In 1984, Hawkins drew national attention when she revealed that she had been sexually abused as a child. As much as anything else, Hawkins's disclosure focused the public spotlight on this horrible problem.

In the Senate, Hawkins served on the Agriculture, Labor, and Aging committees. More than any other Senator, she devoted her energies to the nation's children. Hawkins wrote the 1982 Missing Children Act, which established a national system for locating missing children. She has also specialized in antidrug efforts. Hawkins founded the Drug Enforcement Caucus and sponsored a Senate amendment that cuts off foreign aid to countries that do not reduce narcotics production.

In 1985, Hawkins filmed a series of advertisements that showed Floridians Hawkins's special role in the Senate. A testimonial from Senator John Chafee (R-Rhode Island) stated that "the men in the Senate had not given much thought to missing children and child abuse until Paula Hawkins came along."[10] Senator Orrin Hatch (R-Utah) thanked "God that we have Paula Hawkins here, because some of us men would never understand all the problems that women have to go through and confront."[11] As Bob Graham later told us, "Senator Hawkins had identified with a group of Americans and a set of issues that had not been as forcefully advocated previously, particularly lost and abandoned children and some issues related to women and children. She was a strong and effective campaigner."[12]

Despite these efforts, Hawkins also developed a reputation in the Senate for impulsiveness. Her child abuse revelation came in a public speech, before even her husband knew. In 1982, she asked to leave the Labor Committee to join Banking. After assignments were set, she reversed herself and asked to be put back on Labor. This was accomplished only after numerous other senators had their assignments rearranged.

Hawkins's voting record had been consistently conservative, as one would expect a Florida Republican's to be. In no way could she be considered out of touch with her constituents. Her ADA ratings were in the teens and twenties. She was strong on defense, voting for the MX missile, chemical weapons production, and military aid to El Salvador. On domestic issues, she was opposed to abortion, for school prayer, and against the Equal Rights Amendment. Of course, as a senator from Florida, she consistently supported

---

10. Hawkins Commercial no. 7, Center for Political Communications, University of Oklahoma.

11. Hawkins Commercial no. 9, Center for Political Communications, University of Oklahoma.

12. Bob Graham, personal interview, June 27, 1990.

Social Security. In 1985, she helped lead the fight against Reagan's plan to trim cost-of-living increases for Social Security recipients.

Bob Graham

Bob Graham was born on November 9, 1936, in Coral Gables, Florida. He received a B.A. from the University of Florida in 1959 and an LL.B. from Harvard Law School in 1962. Graham grew up in a political family: his father was a state senator and an unsuccessful candidate for governor in Florida; his half-brother, Phil, was publisher of the *Washington Post*. After amassing a fortune of over $8 million in the business world, Bob turned toward public service. In 1966, Graham won a seat in the Florida House of Representatives and was reelected in 1968. In 1970, Graham was elected to the state Senate and was later reelected there as well.

In 1978, Graham entered the race for the Democratic nomination for governor as a relative unknown against three candidates holding statewide office: Attorney General Robert Shevin, Lieutenant Governor Jim Williams, and Secretary of State Bruce Smathers. During the campaign, Graham, the attractive, Harvard-educated multimillionaire, developed a gimmick to help him appeal to the average voter: he spent much of the campaign working in menial jobs across the state. Graham garnered an enormous amount of free and favorable publicity from these "work days," enabling him to finish second in the primary to Shevin. Graham beat Shevin in the runoff and then defeated Republican candidate Jack Eckerd with 56 percent of the vote.[13]

Like Paula Hawkins in Washington, Bob Graham got off to a slow start in Tallahassee. He was seen as overly cautious and indecisive. The *St. Petersburg Times* called him "Governor Jell-O." Democratic State Senator Dempsey Baron called Graham "the worst governor in the history of the world."[14]

Graham's fortunes began to change in 1982, just in time for his reelection campaign. A new staff helped him push his proenvironment agenda through the state legislature. Graham easily defeated Republican gubernatorial candidate Skip Bafalis with 65 percent of the vote.

As governor, Graham submitted eight consecutive balanced budgets. Graham won support for his proposals to raise taxes–a dangerous task during the Reagan years—by earmarking the money for such specific purposes as education. Like Hawkins, Graham championed the cause of the elderly. His "Community Care for the Elderly" program claimed credit for keeping

---

13. Barone and Ujifusa, *Almanac*, 238; Ehrenhalt, *Politics*, 1988, 290.
14. Ehrenhalt, *Politics*, 1986, 289.

many Floridians in their communities and out of nursing homes.[15] In Paula Hawkins's words, "Bob Graham is a good, decent, dedicated public official. He's a fantastic individual."[16] As the popular governor of the state, he was the quintessential high-quality challenger.

The Race

The Florida race is the only of the four we examine in which there was no serious primary challenge in either party.[17] The early story of the race instead involved what we would consider a serious controversy, the health of Senator Hawkins. As far back as 1960, Hawkins required surgery to fuse disks in her neck after a car accident. The injury was aggravated in 1982 when a backdrop fell on her head during an interview on WESH-TV, knocking her unconscious. In January, 1986, Hawkins filed suit against the television station, claiming that she had "suffered physical handicap and *her working ability was impaired*" (italics added). The suit further alleged that her injuries "are either permanent or continuing in nature and (she) will suffer such losses and impairment in the future."[18]

On February 6, while her staff was announcing that Hawkins had left Washington for an early vacation, Hawkins secretly entered Duke University Medical Hospital. This followed a week in which she canceled interviews with three reporters and failed to preside over scheduled hearings of her subcommittee.[19] A press conference scheduled by Republican Congressman Connie Mack III a few hours before one by Hawkins's doctor led to unfounded speculation that Hawkins was dropping out of the race. Though Mack denied any intention of running, Hawkins's lack of forthrightness about her hospital stay turned her health into the biggest issue of the early campaign.[20]

Hawkins left the hospital ten days later, declaring that she was "in good health and good spirits." Oddly, she declared that "the good news is that I

---

15. Graham for U.S. Senate Press Release, January 28, 1986.

16. Paula Hawkins, telephone interview, September 5, 1990.

17. Graham was challenged by gay rights activist Bob Kunst. Kunst's fifteen minutes of fame came when he led the battle against Anita Bryant over the 1980 Dade County gay rights vote. Hawkins was challenged by John Larsen Shudlick, mayor of the tiny town of Ocean Ridge (population 1500). Kunst received 15 percent of the vote against Graham, Shudlick received 11 percent of the vote against Hawkins.

18. Gregory Spears and R. A. Zaldivar, "Sen. Hawkins' Health is Good, Her Aides Insist," *Miami Herald*, January 12, 1986.

19. R. A. Zaldivar and Tom Fiedler, "Hawkins Quietly Enters Hospital," *Miami Herald*, February 8, 1986; Gregory Spears and Tom Fiedler, "Hawkins May Require Neck Surgery," *Miami Herald*, February 13, 1986.

20. Bill Peterson, "Hawkins Health is Biggest Campaign Issue," *Washington Post*, February 16, 1986.

don't have cancer," even though previous reports made no mention of the disease. She did admit that she might have to return to the hospital for surgery at a later time.[21]

Health issues aside, Hawkins started 1986 in good financial shape but questionable political shape. Though trailing Graham in early polls, Hawkins raised more than $2.5 million in 1985, thanks in large part to fund-raisers with President Reagan in March and Vice President Bush in November. Graham, on the other hand, had raised only $1.4 million through the end of 1985.[22]

Graham unofficially announced his intention to challenge Hawkins in a letter to 14,000 campaign contributors mailed during the first week of January. Graham wrote, "I wanted you to be among the first to know that I have decided to run for the United States Senate. . . . I will make my announcement in the next few weeks." The letter was signed Bob.[23] According to Graham, the decision to run

> was not an easy decision because I wasn't certain that I wanted to serve in the Senate. There's almost an assumption of some political people that after you've been governor you automatically want to serve in the Senate. That increasingly is less true. People like Dick Lamm, for instance, in Colorado, had a relatively open opportunity, decided that wasn't what he wanted to do.
>
> I went through some of that analysis. I finally decided that I wanted to serve in the Senate for several reasons. There were some issues that I'd been involved with as governor that I understood were going to require a sustained federal interest in order to be positively advanced, and those ranged from drug issues to the U.S. role in Latin America.
>
> Also I was impressed with the new people who had entered the Senate who seemed to share the same kind of values that I did, people like Dick Lugar (R-Indiana), Bill Bradley (D-New Jersey), just to mention a couple. So I made a decision in the summer of 1985 that I was going to run for the Senate. I knew that it was going to be a very contested campaign but I thought that I would be successful if we conducted ourselves in office in a satisfactory way to maintain levels of positive feelings about our governorship and conducted a quality campaign.[24]

Graham, the popular incumbent governor, hoped that his success as governor could translate into votes for Senator. "The most important thing that

---

21. Tom Fiedler, "Hawkins Back on Job, May Have Surgery Later," *Miami Herald*, February 18, 1986.
22. Paul Anderson, "Nearly $1.4 Million Raised in '85 for Graham's Senate Campaign," *Miami Herald*, January 24, 1986.
23. "I'm Running for Senate, Graham Says," *Miami Herald*, January 10, 1986.
24. Graham interview.

had to be done was we had to continue to do a good job as governor. As an incumbent, your major credential for the office was the quality of the performance you had and were turning out. So that was the cornerstone of our strategy."[25]

In the middle of January, Graham released a series of television advertisements highlighting the governor's "work days," in which Graham worked various blue-collar jobs to "keep in touch" with the average citizen.

Hoping to deflate some of the momentum Graham would receive from the impending formal announcement of his candidacy, Hawkins released a series of commercials attacking Graham for supporting the carrying of oil through the Transgulf pipeline. An announcer in one spot read the following script.

> Maybe you don't know it but some of Florida's most beautiful lake country is in danger and so is the water that supplies our communities. This is where the Transgulf pipeline runs beneath our state. Right now it carries only natural gas, but the oil companies want it to carry oil. Is the pipeline safe for oil? After all, its an old pipeline, twenty-five years old. It's had sixteen leaks in Florida already. Could you imagine the pollution if it began to leak oil? In 1982, a concerned Florida legislature voted for a total review of the project, but Governor Bob Graham vetoed the bill. He said current regulations were good enough. Florida's Senator Paula Hawkins disagrees with Graham.[26]

Hawkins then announced Senate hearings to examine the environmental implications of the pipeline. Interestingly, representatives of Florida's two leading environmental groups, the Florida Sierra Club and the Florida Audubon Society, denounced the commercials as "a disservice to the environment and to the people of the state of Florida" by "repeating old and disputed charges against the pipeline."[27] Nat Reed, a Republican environmentalist who served under Presidents Nixon and Ford, later endorsed Graham.[28] The hearings that were eventually held were denounced by Senate Democrats as politically motivated, and only one other Senator, committee chair Orrin Hatch (R-Utah) showed up.[29]

---

25. Graham interview.
26. Hawkins Commercial no. 11, Center of Political Communications, University of Oklahoma.
27. Paul Anderson, "Two Environmental Groups Defend Graham Against Hawkins TV Ad," *Miami Herald*, January 28, 1986.
28. Graham for U.S. Senate Press Release, October 9, 1986.
29. Mona Z. Browne, "Hawkins Challenge to Pipeline Gets Flak on Capitol Hill," *Miami Herald*, February 19, 1986.

Graham did not gain the expected momentum from his formal announcement, but this was not a result of Hawkins's television advertisements. Graham's announcement was tragically timed for January 28, 1986. Shortly after his announcement, space shuttle *Challenger* exploded following takeoff from Cape Canaveral, Florida. Graham decided to cancel his first week of television advertisements, campaign appearances, and fund-raisers.[30]

Returning to the campaign trail in mid-February, Graham toured the state, receiving enthusiastic support throughout.[31] In his speeches, Graham took a moderate approach to issues: he called for environmental protection, more services for the elderly, and a balanced federal budget. On foreign policy, he called for stronger support for Israel and the "freedom fighters" in Nicaragua, thus appealing to Florida's large Jewish and Hispanic populations.[32]

Graham's television commercials stressed his accomplishments as governor.

> Announcer: After eight years as governor, Bob Graham has earned the smile on his face. Model community care centers for our seniors, day care for the children of working mothers, school standards raised, with test scores up. Florida, doing more for the environment than ever. And taxes, lower than forty-six other states, and with a balanced budget.
> Graham: In Florida, we balance our budget every day. That's a lesson Washington can learn.
> Announcer: Keep Bob Graham working for Florida in the United States Senate.[33]

By the beginning of March, a Graham-sponsored poll showed the governor leading Hawkins by 17 percentage points.[34] A *Miami Herald* poll taken two weeks later showed Graham with a smaller, but still significant, 8 percentage point lead. According to the poll, 64 percent of the voters approved of Hawkins's job as Senator, but 76 percent approved of Graham's job as governor. Crucially, voters thought Graham could do a better job on two of the issues Hawkins campaigned hardest on, crime/drugs and the environment.[35]

---

30. Graham interview; Paul Anderson, "Graham Kicks Off Race," *Miami Herald*, January 29, 1986.

31. Paul Anderson, "Graham's Senate Campaign Takes Off; He's in Rare Form," *Miami Herald*, February 11, 1986.

32. Anderson, "Graham Kicks Off Race."

33. Graham Commercial no. 3, Center for Political Communications, University of Oklahoma.

34. "Graham's Poll Shows Him with Big Senate Race Lead," *Miami Herald*, March 6, 1986.

35. Tom Fiedler and Richard Morin, "Graham's Ahead But Is Beatable, Survey Indicates," *Miami Herald*, March 16, 1986.

Three days later, Hawkins's pollster released a poll showing the Senator only 4 percentage points behind the governor.[36]

The Graham campaign suffered through some embarrassing medical news when it was reported that, until 1978, Graham had a phobia of blood, needles, and medical exams, for which he began seeing a clinical psychologist.[37] But the medical news for Hawkins was much worse. Hawkins had to return to the hospital in early April for more tests on her back. On April 8 and again on April 21, Hawkins underwent major orthopedic surgery. The operations kept her from campaigning until June 1.[38] Nevertheless, Hawkins made the most of her hospital stay. Rather than hide from the press, as she had in February, Hawkins allowed daily photographs, held a press conference, and even appeared live via satellite on a Tampa news show.[39] Senate colleagues read her speeches for her on the Senate floor.[40]

Hawkins now admits how seriously incapacitated she was by her injuries. "I don't remember very much about the campaign. The medication for pain made me forget appointments and my train of thought. . . . The medication dulls the pain but it also dulls your memory."[41] Referring to her desire to seek reelection, she declared, "When I had any lucid, clear moments, I thought the record was one to be proud of."[42]

The hospitalization also hurt Hawkins's ability to raise funds. The senator, who originally had expected to outspend Graham by 2 to 1, raised $600,000 during the first three months of 1986, compared to $875,000 for Graham.[43] By the end of March, Graham had raised a total of $2.2 million and had spent less than $1.0 million.[44] Hawkins's total raised was up to $3 million, but she had less than half the cash on hand that Graham had.[45]

Vice President Bush came to Florida on May 19 to host a fund-raiser for Hawkins, even though Hawkins was unable to attend. Bush called Hawkins "a tiger" and called on Florida Republicans to help continue the Reagan

---

36. Paul Anderson, "Hawkins Poll: It's 'Dead Heat' in Race," *Miami Herald*, March 19, 1986.

37. "Florida Governor Once Treated for Phobias," *Washington Post*, March 31, 1986.

38. Steve Sternberg and Tom Fiedler, "Hawkins to Have Two Disk Fusions, Shoulder Surgery," *Miami Herald*, April 8, 1986; Tom Fiedler, "Hawkins Recovering from Second Spinal Surgery," *Miami Herald*, April 22, 1986.

39. Bill Peterson, "Hawkins Changes Publicity Strategy," *Washington Post*, April 7, 1986.

40. Robert Lystad, "Hawkins Misses Not a Step, Despite Her Stay in Hospital," *Miami Herald*, April 20, 1986.

41. Hawkins interview.

42. Hawkins interview.

43. "Graham:$875,393; Hawkins:$600,000," *Miami Herald*, April 12, 1986.

44. Paul Anderson, "Disney Boosts Graham Campaign," *Miami Herald*, April 16, 1986.

45. Gregory Spears, "Hawkins Drive Faces 'Serious Crisis,'" *Miami Herald*, May 30, 1986.

revolution by reelecting Hawkins and other Republican contenders.[46] But Bush's visit did not forestall Hawkins's continuing decline in fund-raising. On May 21, the National Republican Senatorial Committee mailed out an urgent appeal for donations, admitting that contributions had dropped "to a critical level" following Hawkins's hospitalization.[47] Contributions still did not pick up significantly. Between April and June, Hawkins raised $731,000, while Graham raised $1.2 million. Hawkins's overall lead in money raised was down to $0.5 million, while Graham retained a sizable lead in money on hand, $1.5 million to $828,000.[48] Graham continued his lead in the polls as well. A *Miami Herald* poll showed Graham with 49 percent and Hawkins with 38 percent. Only 10 percent of respondents were undecided, a low number for so early in the campaign.[49]

The influence of national politics was felt strongly in July when President Reagan agreed to appear at a Hawkins fund-raiser, allegedly in return for Hawkins's vote to confirm Daniel Manion to the Court of Appeals.[50] Reagan came to Miami on July 23. Hawkins was at his side when Reagan stepped off *Air Force One*, and she accompanied him to a "boisterous political rally" and fund-raiser that earned the Hawkins campaign $300,000. Reagan called Hawkins a "gutsy lady" who "may be recovering, but . . . still knows how to twist arms."[51] The Hawkins campaign began to revive.

While Hawkins thought the Reagan visit crucial to her electoral efforts,[52] Graham downplayed the direct influence of the Reagan visit in the campaign at hand, believing it was more important in terms of raising money than switching votes.

> The main thing that a president can do is give a big infusion of dollars. I don't think in terms of changing people's votes it was significant. This is

---

46. Paul Anderson, "Bush Sees Republicans Making Election Gains," *Miami Herald*, April 20, 1986.
47. Spears, "Hawkins Drive."
48. "Hawkins Surgery Caused Fund-Raising Gap, Aides Say," *Miami Herald*, July 17, 1986.
49. Tom Fiedler and Richard Morin, "Graham Maintains Solid Lead Over Hawkins," *Miami Herald*, July 20, 1986.
50. Paul Anderson, "Hawkins: Reagan Is Coming to Fund-Raiser," *Miami Herald*, June 26, 1986. Manion, a conservative Republican, had been criticized for a stunning lack of intellectual ability. To prove the point, drafts of letters he had written containing egregious spelling and grammatical errors were released to the press. Senator Slade Gorton (R-Washington) also apparently traded his vote on the Manion nomination for White House favors. Gorton's trade became a crucial issue in his reelection race, which he lost to former Transportation Secretary Brock Adams.
51. Tom Fiedler, "Reagan Rouses Miami Crowd," *Miami Herald*, July 24, 1986.
52. Hawkins interview.

a case where you have two candidates who were very well known. Paula had been elected statewide two times and I had been elected statewide two times. The public had pretty much formed an opinion of us that they were going to make based on information available to them rather than deferring to a third party, even the president of the United States, for advice.[53]

Hoping to capitalize on the momentum of the Reagan visit, Hawkins released a statewide television blitz focusing on a speech Hawkins gave during a 1985 Reagan visit. The speech captured the fundamental nature of what Hawkins sought to be as a Senator. With her eyes glistening and her voice cracking, she declared that

> I want to continue to be the Senator for people who don't have a Senator. For parents desperately searching for missing children, for a sick person who would rather be cared for at home than be institutionalized, for the single mother trying to make ends meet, for an abused child, seeking guidance and protection, for parents trying to keep drugs out of America and away from their children. A Senator for the people that the bureaucrats have forgotten, but for people this Senator will never forget.[54]

The advertisement was backed by others featuring heart-rending testimonials from typically "forgotten" constituents, including the father of a missing boy and a teenage girl who had overcome drug addiction. Both effusively praised the efforts on their behalf of Senator Hawkins.[55]

By the beginning of September, Hawkins was finally beginning to catch Graham. The *Tampa Tribune* reported the two running neck and neck while the *Palm Beach Post* gave Graham a slim, 4 percentage point lead.[56] Toward the middle of September the gap was narrower still. Statewide polls released on September 26 showed Hawkins anyplace from thirteen points down to eight points ahead.[57] Hawkins also increased her lead in fund-raising. Through the middle of August, Hawkins had raised a total of $5 million, while Graham had raised a total slightly over $4 million.[58]

---

53. Graham interview.
54. Hawkins Commercial no. 18, Center for Political Communications, University of Oklahoma.
55. Hawkins Commercial no. 1 and no. 26, Center for Political Communications, University of Oklahoma.
56. "Hawkins Declares U.S. Senate Fight a 'Tie Race,'" *Miami Herald*, September 9, 1986.
57. Maralee Schwartz and Sidney Blumenthal, "Politics," *Washington Post*, September 27, 1986.
58. R. A. Zaldivar, "Hawkins Working All Angles to Keep Money Coming In," *Miami*

As Graham's lead narrowed, the governor's hands-off policy, in which he lauded his own accomplishments without attacking Hawkins, came to an end. In the middle of September, Graham, following the strong advice of his media consultant, Bob Squier, began to attack Hawkins's role in the war on drugs.[59] It was Hawkins who sponsored the "Hawkins Amendment," which cut off aid to countries that produced drugs for export to the United States. Hawkins also called for mandatory drug testing for all state and federal workers.[60] She had even visited China in a purported effort to stop the export of methaqualone, the generic form of the brand name drug Quaalude. In one commercial, Senator Bob Dole (R-Kansas) called Hawkins "the Senate's general in the war on drugs." [61]

Graham, taking the offensive, released a commercial accusing Hawkins of talking tough on drugs but voting to cut drug education and Coast Guard enforcement.[62] (The votes in question were, in fact, votes on larger spending bills that included those provisions.) Hawkins then counterattacked, calling Graham a liar.

> Announcer: There's an ad on T.V. that tells us who the real Bob Graham is. It's so false you wonder why it was allowed on the air. He tries to make it seem that Paula Hawkins opposed money for the Coast Guard and drug education. Those statements are false. . . . Now if Bob Graham is trying to make Paula Hawkins look soft on drugs, on drugs!, what will he try to do next?[63]

The attack intensified as Graham accused Hawkins of fabricating a meeting with Chinese leader Deng Xiaoping. According to one of Hawkins's commercials,

> Senator Hawkins undertakes a very difficult mission of one-woman diplomacy. She travels to China and meets personally with Chinese leader

---

Herald, September 14, 1986; Paul Anderson, "Graham Campaign to Exceed the Cost of Last Two Combined," *Miami Herald*, September 14, 1986.

59. Bill Peterson, "Candidates Fight Over War on Drugs," *Washington Post*, September 23, 1986; Paul Anderson, "Image-Maker Seeking to Rev Up Graham's Bid," *Miami Herald*, September 21, 1986.

60. Hawkins Commercial no. 16, Center for Political Communications, University of Oklahoma.

61. Hawkins Commercial no. 5, Center for Political Communications, University of Oklahoma.

62. Graham Commercial no. 4, Center for Political Communications, University of Oklahoma.

63. Hawkins Commercial no. 34, Center for Political Communications, University of Oklahoma.

Deng Xiaoping. She writes to him with the facts on methaqualone exports. Then the announcement comes. China agrees to stop the manufacture and shipment of methaqualone.[64]

Unfortunately for Hawkins, the story just was not true. She did meet with Deng, but that was nine months before she learned about the "China methaqualone connection," according to her staff.[65]

In an attempt to recapture the offensive, Hawkins launched a series of advertisements accusing Graham of supporting parole for drug pushers. (Graham had signed a law that allowed all criminals ten days off for every thirty days served if they were well behaved. This is considered "good time" and differs in function and purpose from parole. Another law signed by Graham actually eliminated parole for all felons entering the Florida penal system after October 1, 1983.) The commercials were filmed on October 1, a week after an Indian River Sheriff's deputy had been shot and killed.[66] The first advertisements shown made no mention of the killing, but, instead, primed the public to the issue of parole for drug pushers. The commercials noted that, under the Graham administration, pushers are "getting off early to stalk our neighborhoods and kill our kids."[67] Following this came commercials with unidentified police officers blasting Graham for his parole policy. One officer declared "a deputy sheriff near Vero Beach just got killed. And they say a dealer out on parole did it."[68] (In fact, the alleged killer was released after serving his sentence for drug dealing; he was not out on parole.)[69]

Then came the clear forerunner of the infamous Willie Horton commercials used by the Republican national campaign in 1988.

> Deputy Sheriff Richard Raczkoski [camera shows picture of slain sheriff, who is white] of Vero Beach is dead, killed two weeks ago by William Reaves [camera shows picture of Reaves, who is black, and apparently strung-out on drugs], a drug pusher on parole [*sic*]. Why do we parole

---

64. Hawkins Commercial no. 2, Center for Political Communications, University of Oklahoma.

65. R. A. Zaldivar, "Hawkins Aide Backs Off TV Claim on China," *Miami Herald*, October 3, 1986.

66. Gregory Spears, "Hawkins Unleashes More TV Ads," *Miami Herald*, October 16, 1986.

67. Hawkins Commercial no. 33, Center for Political Communication, University of Oklahoma.

68. Hawkins Commercial no. 36, Center for Political Communications, University of Oklahoma.

69. Spears, "Hawkins Unleashes."

drug pushers? In Washington, Paula Hawkins is leading the fight to stop paroling pushers, but in Florida Bob Graham signed the law letting parole for drug pushers continue. If drug pusher William Reaves [picture] had not been paroled [sic], Deputy Sheriff Richard Raczkoski [picture] would be alive today. Bob Graham, when will we stop letting pushers go free?[70]

Willie Horton, though, was far more devastating to Michael Dukakis than William Reaves was to Bob Graham. One reason, perhaps, is that it was easy to believe that the liberal governor of Massachusetts was "soft on crime." Bob Graham, on the other hand, was a vocal supporter of the death penalty who signed numerous execution warrants while governor. "I just don't think you're going to get people in Florida to believe that Bob Graham is soft on crime," said Graham campaign manager Jim Eaton.[71] According to Graham, the attacks "didn't have any credibility. I've been a very strong advocate of our criminal justice system. On the issue of the death penalty, I've signed over 100 death warrants. I've substantially increased the funding for law enforcement and most of the leaders in law enforcement were supportive."[72] Indeed, Graham was endorsed by the statewide Fraternal Order of Police, the Hispanic Officers Association, and by numerous sheriffs statewide.[73] For her part, Hawkins states that she "didn't choose the [crime] issue, the 'experts' did. . . . The issues are selected by the pollsters. You're supposed to stick to the script."[74]

The television advertisements showed up not only as commercials, but in news broadcasts as well. According to Michael Putney, a Florida television reporter, "You keep trying to report the issues. You keep trying to report what the candidates are talking about. But we keep getting drawn back to the ad wars."[75] Indeed, between September 21 and October 20, eleven out of seventeen stories in the *Miami Herald* were about the candidates' television advertisements.[76]

Television was indeed crucial in the Florida race. According to Hawkins,

---

70. Hawkins Commercial no. 43, Center for Political Communications, University of Oklahoma.
71. R. A. Zaldivar, "Hawkins May Be Walking a Thin Line in Drug Ads," *Miami Herald*, October 19, 1986.
72. Graham interview.
73. Graham for U.S. Senate Press Release, September 16, 1986; Graham for U.S. Senate Press Release, October 7, 1986.
74. Hawkins interview.
75. Bill Peterson, "In Thirty-Second Bursts, TV Ads Shape the Campaign," *Washington Post*, October 27, 1986.
76. Peterson, "Thirty-Second Bursts."

television "was the whole campaign."[77] Senator Graham offered the following explanation.

> Florida is a state that both requires and lends itself to the extensive use of television. Required because we have a very mobile population. Every year about 450,000 people move into the state of Florida, 150,000 move out, leaving a net growth of 300,000. So over the eight years that I was governor, roughly 3.0 to 3.5 million people had moved into the state. So television is the most effective way to introduce yourself to those new people. Also, Florida has a relatively low penetration level of newspapers, that is, the percent of families who subscribe. So the alternative means of communicating are less effective.
>
> Florida lends itself to television because of its peninsula shape. When you buy time on the Tampa television station you pay for that time in terms of the numbers of households reached, and every one of those households is a Florida household. In contrast, for instance, if you were running in New Jersey, which is almost another extreme, when you buy New York City television, 80 percent of the households for whom you're paying aren't households that have a [New Jersey] voter, so Florida is an efficient state for television.[78]

The two candidates squared off for a contentious debate, the only one of the campaign, on October 20 in Orlando. Hawkins accused Graham of supporting a limit on social security increases, of allowing abused children in the custody of the state to die, and of supporting parole for drug dealers. She reportedly made faces at him while he answered questions. Graham, discussing Hawkins's alleged meeting with Deng Xiaoping, referred to the senator's premier accomplishment as "a fantasy." Hawkins noted her support for Ronald Reagan and Graham's labeling Reagan "a simpleton." Then, noting Graham's role at the 1980 Democratic Convention, she said "I know its a great honor to second Jimmy Carter. I personally would have declined."[79]

Graham appeared to be the victor of the campaign's only debate. A *Miami Herald* poll taken before and after the debate, showed Graham increasing his narrow lead from 47 to 43 to 47 to 40. Among those who had seen, heard, or read about the debate, 45 percent thought Graham had won, while

---

77. Hawkins interview.
78. Graham interview.
79. Bill Peterson, "Graham-Hawkins Debate Follows Dramatic Script," *Washington Post*, October 22, 1986; "Highlights From Debate Between Hawkins and Graham," *Miami Herald*, October 21, 1986; R.A. Zaldivar and Paul Anderson, "Charges Fly in Tense TV Debate," *Miami Herald*, October 21, 1986.

only 23 percent thought Hawkins had won.[80] Hawkins, then still ill, basically agrees with that assessment. "I was so pleased that I did not fall down during the debate. I couldn't remember some of the questions. In previous debates I was spunky and gave it back as soon as I got it. I was just glad I made it through. I was deathly ill."[81] Graham later said that "for most practical purposes the campaign ended the night of the debate. There was not much at that point forward that she could have done to redeem herself or we could have done to change the result."[82]

The debate did not stay in the headlines for long, thanks in large part to a statement Hawkins made to a radio call-in show the next day. Referring to U.S. immigration problems, Hawkins declared that "Mexico gums up everything because they walk over at night. And they're not patriots by and large. They're not patriots like the . . . Cuban Americans." Even after time to reflect, she stated that "quite a large group" of Mexican immigrants do not like the United States.[83]

Then, on October 23, the ghost of Joseph McCarthy entered the race when Hawkins declared that the Soviet Union wanted Graham to win. The Soviet Union was not alone though. Domestic Communists also supported Graham. According to Hawkins, "The Young Communists League of America said Senator Hawkins should be defeated. Now I don't know who they're for, but there are only two people in this race."[84]

In an attempt to save her foundering campaign, Hawkins called on the enormously popular President Reagan. "To beat Graham," declared columnists Evans and Novak, "Paula Hawkins needs to make Ronald Reagan the issue."[85] Though Reagan declined to sign a drug bill in Florida, he did film two, thirty-second commercials and appeared at a Tampa rally. The commercials had a simple theme, Reagan's need of Hawkins (and other Republicans) in the Senate. In the second commercial, Reagan declared that

> I have a simple message for the people of Florida. Reelect Paula Hawkins to the Senate. Paula has been one of my strongest supporters in our economic recovery. She has steadfastly supported my foreign and de-

---

80. Tom Fiedler and Richard Morin, "Graham Leads, Hawkins Stalls, Poll Finds," *Miami Herald*, October 26, 1986.
81. Hawkins interview.
82. Graham interview.
83. R. A. Zaldivar, "Hawkins: Cubans Are 'Patriots,'" *Miami Herald*, October 22, 1986.
84. Gregory Spears, "Hawkins: Communists for Graham," *Miami Herald*, October 24, 1986; the Young Communists League USA refused to comment.
85. Rowland Evans and Robert Novak, "Playing the Reagan Card in Florida," *Washington Post*, October 24, 1986.

fense policies as we have restored America to world respect and brought the Soviets to the negotiating table. In this critical time I need the support of a Republican Senate. Paula Hawkins's reelection is essential to make that happen. Please vote on Tuesday to send Paula back to the Senate.[86]

At the October 24 rally in Tampa, Hawkins opened by telling the audience that Reagan needs Republican control of the Senate to complete his work. Reagan agreed, saying, "We need the Republican Senate. We need Paula Hawkins."[87] Reagan, who had not mentioned Graham in his previous appearances for Hawkins, specifically criticized the governor by name. "I can't help but think that if you liked Jimmy Carter as president, you'll love Bob Graham as senator. . . . When it comes to raising taxes, he's a real pro. He's got lessons that even the Washington crowd could learn."[88]

Reagan's final boost for Hawkins during the campaign came on October 27, when he signed the drug bill in Washington. With Hawkins on the podium, Reagan singled out the role of the Florida Republican, calling her a "driving force" in the war on drugs.[89]

The last major controversy during the campaign involved Graham's alleged support at a governor's conference for a cost-of-living freeze for Social Security recipients. During the debate and later that week, Graham called the charges "a lie. I was there. I know how I voted. . . . What is the fantasy land in which this lady operates?"[90] But newspaper accounts from the 1984 convention cited the proposal being approved 28 to 10, with only Republicans voting no. A videotape released by the Hawkins campaign apparently showed Graham raising his hand to vote yes on the proposal.[91] After failing to link Graham to the oil pipeline, dying children under state care, and "paroled" drug dealers, Hawkins finally found "an effective attack" on the governor.[92] Unfortunately for Hawkins, the issue was a classic example of too little too late.[93] Graham won the election with a sizable 55 to 45 majority.

---

86. Hawkins Commercial no. 44, Center for Political Communications, University of Oklahoma.

87. R. A. Zaldivar and Tom Fiedler, "Reagan Boosts Hawkins, Rips Graham's 'Liberalism,'" *Miami Herald*, October 25, 1986.

88. Zaldivar, "Reagan Boosts Hawkins."

89. Tom Bowman, "Reagan Calls Hawkins 'A Driving Force' in War on Drugs," *Miami Herald*, October 28, 1986.

90. Paul Anderson, "Hawkins in 'Fantasy Land,' Graham Says," *Miami Herald*, October 28, 1986.

91. Anderson, "Hawkins in 'Fantasy Land.'"

92. R. A. Zaldivar, "Hawkins Hits at Graham's Benefits Vote," *Miami Herald*, October 30, 1986.

93. Hawkins no longer considers her defeat unfortunate. Because of her loss, she was able to devote herself full time to her convalescence, and she now reports that she is fully recovered

Survey Results

According to the ABC exit polls (see table 7.1), the most important issues to Floridians, not surprisingly, were social security and the illegal drug problem, both mentioned by 52 percent of the respondents, followed by the national economy (45 percent) and the budget deficit (42 percent).[94]

Given these numbers, the popular governor may have been the only Democratic candidate who could have beaten Paula Hawkins. Graham won with 55 percent of the vote, the same margin as in the ABC News exit poll. According to the exit poll, Graham won 52 percent of the male vote and 57 percent of the female vote. The gender gap clearly applied to the parties of the candidates, not their sex. Graham won 53 percent of the white vote and 80 percent of the black vote, but only 38 percent of Florida's conservative Hispanic vote.[95] Graham's sweep was very much like D'Amato's. He won across every age level, every education level, and virtually every income level. His "work days" no doubt helped him capture union households by a large margin (66 to 34 percent), but he captured nonunion households as well (54 to 46 percent). Though Hawkins captured the Protestant vote (52 to 48 percent), Graham swept the Catholic (58 to 42 percent) and Jewish vote (77 to 23 percent).

Unlike Republicans elsewhere, Hawkins did not do as well as she needed to among those satisfied with Reagan and the economy. She won only 63 percent of those who were better off under Reagan, but lost 82 percent of those who were worse off. She won only 70 percent of those who thought that Republicans could better cope with the nation's problems. Her Republican counterparts in California, New York, and South Dakota won 76 percent, 86 percent, and 82 percent of that vote, respectively. Similarly, she garnered the votes of but 59 percent of the Reagan supporters, compared to 64 percent, 77 percent, and 71 percent in the above-listed states. Graham, on the other hand, won 82 percent of those who were worse off under Reagan, 87 percent of those who thought the Democrats could better cope with the nation's problems, and 89 percent of those who disapproved of Reagan's job performance. Graham also won 56 percent of those who thought social security an important issue. Despite Hawkins's battles against illegal drug use, her misstatements about her trip to China and Graham's support for the death penalty no doubt softened her support. She won only 51 percent of those who listed

---

from her injuries. She recently told a citizen who told her he voted for Graham, "You did me a favor, buddy" (Hawkins interview).

94. ABC News, *The '88 Vote*, 412.

95. In the ABC polls, respondents are asked whether they are white, black, or some other race. They are later asked for their ancestry. It is from the ancestry question that the responses of Hispanics are taken.

TABLE 7.1. Florida Exit Poll Results (in percentages)

	All Voters	Graham Voters	Hawkins Voters
Gender			
Male	49	52	48
Female	51	57	43
Race			
White	92	53	47
Black	6	80	18
Other	2	56	38
Ideology			
Liberal	13	80	20
Conservative	29	34	66
Party			
Democrat	46	78	21
Independent	15	60	39
Republican	37	24	76
Other	1	58	37
Better cope			
Democrats	42	87	12
Republicans	58	30	70
Personally better off than when Reagan took office			
Better off	47	37	63
About the same	35	67	33
Worse off	18	82	18
Reagan job performance			
Approve	71	41	59
Disapprove	29	89	10
State of economy			
Excellent	7	33	67
Good	58	45	55
Not so good	30	75	25
Poor	6	82	17
Important items (selected)			
National economy	45	52	48
Local economy	31	54	46
Reagan performance	33	40	60
Candidates' party	20	52	48

Source: ABC News, *The '88 Vote* (New York: Capitol Cities/ABC News, 1989), 411.

illegal drugs as an important issue. Clearly, the favorable economic and political conditions in Florida were not enough for Hawkins to overcome the enormous popularity of Governor Graham.

Conclusions

Florida was made for the Republican party in 1986. Although the state's voters, like those in the rest of the South, are overwhelmingly Democratic in party identification, it is also overwhelmingly conservative in political orientation. Since 1968, Floridians have shown little reluctance in voting for the party of Abraham Lincoln. On the national level, Floridians loved Ronald Reagan, thought the economy was in excellent condition, and thought Republicans better able to handle the country's problems than Democrats.

In Paula Hawkins, the Republicans had a popular incumbent. Her voting record was in line with the views of her constituents and she faced no primary competition. She did, however, suffer from a significant controversy, her failing health. In the popular governor, Bob Graham, Hawkins faced an opponent we described earlier as a quintessential high-quality challenger. Unlike many Senate races, Graham was able to keep attention away from national political conditions (Ronald Reagan and the economy) and on the two candidates themselves. The voters loved Ronald Reagan, but that does not mean they would let him choose their senator, when the opponent was well known and well respected.

South Dakota

South Dakota is by far the smallest of the states whose 1986 Senate races we examine in detail. Though South Dakota is sixteenth in land area, with only 708,000 people it is only the forty-fifth largest state. Until 1980, South Dakota had two Congressional Districts; today it has only one. Education is not a top priority in South Dakota: it is thirty-sixth in the proportion of persons with college degrees (14 percent) and thirty-seventh in per-pupil expenditures. South Dakota is forty-ninth in per capita tax burden and forty-eighth in median family income. On the other hand, it is forty-ninth in its violent crime rate. There is little diversity in South Dakota's ethnic breakdown: it is 93 percent white and 7 percent native American, the highest in the nation. Seventy-one percent of South Dakotans were born there and only 1 percent were foreign born.

The South Dakota economy is overwhelmingly based on farming and ranching: 93 percent of its acreage is farm land. The largest city, Sioux Falls, has only 81,000 people. The state is split in two by the Missouri River: the eastern half is fertile farm land; the western half contains sparse plains more suitable for ranching.[96]

Like Florida, South Dakota has historically been a one-party state, but, unlike Florida, that party has been Republican. Between 1938 and 1970, Democrats controlled the governorship for only two years. George McGovern was the only Democrat elected to the Senate during that period. From 1896 until 1965, Democrats won only ten of eighty-one Congressional elections.[97] In the last ten presidential elections, South Dakota voted for the Democrat only once, choosing President Johnson in his 1964 landslide victory over Barry Goldwater. Forty-nine percent of the registered voters are Republicans, 43 percent are Democrats.

As McGovern's Senate elections attest, the state is willing to vote for Democrats on occasion. At various times prior to 1973, Democrats actually controlled the governorship, both Senate and House seats, and the state legislature. In the 1970s, South Dakota turned to the right, with Republicans recapturing both House seats, the state legislature, and, in 1980, defeating George McGovern.

Exemplifying the decreasing importance of partisanship in modern Senate elections, South Dakota's political climate was not favorable to the Republican party in 1986. South Dakota voters offered a unique contrast to voters in virtually all other states at that time. Though they were disproportionately Republican (45 to 42 percent over Democrats) and conservative (23 to 12 percent over liberal), President Reagan and the Republican party were not popular. By a 53 to 47 margin, South Dakotans thought the Democratic party better able to cope with the country's problems. Reagan's job approval, 53 percent, was lower in South Dakota than any other state surveyed by ABC News. The reason for this is abundantly clear: South Dakota's farm economy. Only 28 percent of South Dakotans thought themselves better off than when Reagan took office, versus 37 percent who said they were worse off. Only 35 percent thought the economy was excellent or good, against the 65 percent who thought the economy not so good or poor. Right behind the budget deficit, which South Dakotans ranked first in terms of important issues (49 percent), were the state of the national economy (47 percent) and the state of the local economy (46 percent). Compared to virtually every other state, South Dakotans disapproved of Reagan, felt that their own economic well-being had fallen, thought the economy in general was doing poorly, and thought the local economy was an important issue in the campaign.[98] In a sense, South Dakota was the mirror image of Florida, where Democratic voters felt more favorably toward the Republican party than toward their own.

---

96. Barone and Ujifusa, *Almanac*, 1093.
97. Stanley and Niemi, *Vital Statistics*, 86–87.
98. Survey data are from ABC News, *The '88 Vote*, 458.

James Abdnor

James Abdnor was born on February 13, 1923, in Kennebec, South Dakota. He received a B.A. from the University of Nebraska in 1945. Abdnor served briefly in the army at the end of World War II. After working many years on his family's ranch, Abdnor entered politics. He was elected to the South Dakota Senate in 1957, where he served for eleven years, eventually becoming president pro tempore. In 1969, Abdnor was elected lieutenant governor, where he served until 1971. In 1970, Abdnor was upset in his bid to win the Republican nomination for the Second (of two) Congressional District. Two years later, Abdnor won both the nomination and the general election. In the House, Abdnor, like most congressmen, focused heavily on constituent affairs.[99] In 1974, despite a Watergate-based Democratic landslide throughout the country, Abdnor easily won reelection. Opposition was similarly limited in the 1976 and 1978 campaigns, and Abdnor won these races handily. Even his opponents recognized his immense statewide popularity. According to Daschle campaign manager Peter Stavrianos, Abdnor "is about as South Dakota as you can get."[100]

In 1980, Abdnor left the House in a bid to unseat Senator George McGovern. It was a good year for such a challenge. Prior to 1980, McGovern had a solid hold on the Democratic nomination for the Senate. In 1980, a conservative, antiabortion Democrat received 40 percent of the vote in the primary against McGovern. Though McGovern won the primary, he was an easy target for Abdnor, the well-known conservative congressman. Adding to McGovern's woes was a highly publicized negative campaign by the National Conservative Political Action Committee (NCPAC). Under a campaign-finance loophole, NCPAC was able to spend unlimited amounts of money against McGovern as long as it did not act in concert with Abdnor. This legal separation was helpful to Abdnor, as NCPAC came under heavy criticism for its strident attacks. Nevertheless, NCPAC put McGovern's extremely liberal voting record in the spotlight and, thus, put McGovern on the defensive. Additionally, Ronald Reagan handily defeated the unpopular incumbent, Jimmy Carter, in the South Dakota presidential race. In the end, Abdnor won an easy victory with 58 percent of the vote.

In the Senate, Abdnor served on the Appropriations, Environment, Indian Affairs, and Joint Economic committees. On the Environment Committee, Abdnor held the crucial post of chairman of the Water Resource Subcommittee. Few issues are of greater importance to western farmers and ranchers than water use.

---

99. Ehrenhalt, *Politics*, 1986, 1422.
100. Peter Stavrianos, personal interview, June 25, 1990.

In 1981, President Reagan proposed a new council, to be headed by Interior Secretary James Watt, that would establish guidelines for determining which water projects to build. Abdnor, fearful of budget cutting by the administration, proposed an independent board that would report to Congress and the president. The result was a stalemate between Congress and the administration that left Congress in its traditional role of dominance over water projects.

The problems of farmers went beyond water, though. Low prices for their products and high interest rates had led to a depressed farm industry. In 1985, the Reagan administration opposed a Democratic farm credit bill. Abdnor, a loyal Reaganite, faced intense pressure from home to vote for the bill, which he eventually did. Nevertheless, Abdnor continued to defend the unpopular Reagan farming program, and later voted for the Reagan farm bill that eventually became law.

Abdnor's voting record was consistently conservative in both the House and the Senate. His ADA scores ranged between zero and twenty, consistent with the preferences of conservative South Dakota. He voted against abortion rights, for school prayer, and against a national holiday to commemorate the birth of Martin Luther King, Jr. On defense, he voted for chemical weapons and the MX missile and for military aid for El Salvador.[101]

Despite an overall voting record popular in South Dakota, Abdnor would face two serious obstacles in the campaign. First, he would be challenged for his party's nomination by the popular governor of the state, William Janklow. Moreover, he would involve himself in a serious political controversy by supporting lower prices for farm products.

Thomas Daschle

Thomas Daschle was born on December 9, 1947, in Aberdeen, South Dakota. He received a B.A. from South Dakota State University in 1969 and served in the Air Force from 1969 to 1972. Daschle's start in politics came as a legislative aide to Senator James Abourezk (D-South Dakota).

In 1976, Daschle moved back to South Dakota from Washington to help prepare for Abourezk's reelection campaign and to prepare for his own run for Congress. (Abourezk later chose not to seek reelection.) In the primary, Daschle upset former Congressman Frank Denholm, largely as a result of tireless campaigning. Daschle and his wife rang more than 40,000 doorbells, no easy task in rural South Dakota.[102] Meanwhile, the First District's incumbent, Republican Larry Pressler, decided to seek Abourezk's Senate seat. The

---

101. Ehrenhalt, *Politics*, 1986, 1422.
102. Ehrenhalt, *Politics*, 1986, 1427.

Republicans then chose former Vietnam prisoner of war Leo Thorsness to run for the House seat. Thorsness had tried to unseat George McGovern in 1974 and had received 47 percent of the vote. Daschle's nonstop campaigning brought him an early advantage, but Thorsness effectively used Daschle's support of abortion rights and opposition to right-to-work laws against him. The initial results had Thorsness winning, but a recount gave the election to Daschle by a slender 139-vote margin.

Daschle easily won reelection in 1980 (66 percent of the vote), but faced a difficult fight in 1982, when South Dakota lost its second Congressional seat and Daschle had to run against fellow incumbent Clint Roberts. Roberts, a rancher who dressed the part even in Congress, charged Daschle with being part of the "Eastern Establishment." Daschle, though, raised and spent $150,000 more than Roberts, and was better known even in parts of Roberts's old district.[103] Daschle won the election by less than 9,000 votes. Daschle won an easier victory in 1984, garnering 57 percent of the vote against Dale Bell.

In Congress, Daschle served on the Agriculture, Select Hunger, and Veterans' Affairs committees. From his position on Agriculture, he became one of the most outspoken protectors of farmers. In his first term, Daschle championed the cause of gasohol and other energy sources derived from grains. He was author of the 1985 multibillion dollar farm credit bill that was eventually vetoed by President Reagan. His constant attempts to give extraordinary aid to farmers have been labeled demagogic by critics,[104] but Daschle replies that the more he asks for originally, the more he ends up with after compromising. As an Air Force veteran on the Veterans' Affairs Committee, Daschle helped write legislation to compensate veterans for damage due to exposure to the defoliant Agent Orange. A slightly watered-down version of his bill was signed into law.

As a challenger to Abdnor, Daschle would have to rank highly on any candidate quality scale. Like Ed Zschau of California, Daschle was a congressman at the time of his Senate race. But in an important sense his position was closer to that of Governor Graham of Florida, for Daschle represented his entire state, whereas Zschau represented only 2 percent of California.

The Race

South Dakota is the only state we examine in which the incumbent senator faced a serious challenge for his party's nomination. Abdnor's weak position stemmed from the fact that he supported Ronald Reagan's farm policies,

---

103. Ehrenhalt, *Politics*, 1986, 1426.
104. Ehrenhalt, *Politics*, 1988, 1392.

which, rightly or wrongly, were blamed for South Dakota's devastated farm economy. Perhaps the most crucial day of the 1986 campaign came in 1985, when Abdnor voted for the Reagan farm bill. It was a vote that would haunt him throughout the campaign.

The election year began with the three potential candidates for senator, Republican incumbent Jim Abdnor, Republican Governor William Janklow, and Democratic Congressman Tom Daschle, offering legislative goodies to farmers. Abdnor proposed a farm credit bill that would lower interest rates and allow banks to forgive loan principals; Janklow called for a one-year moratorium on farm foreclosures; and Daschle revived his farm bill, which Reagan had vetoed.[105] Both Janklow and Daschle told a farm crisis conference sponsored by the University of South Dakota that Reagan's 1985 farm bill, supported by Abdnor, would not give farmers the help they needed.[106] Support for this position came two weeks later when a team of agricultural economists released a study saying that farm income would drop from $26.6 billion in 1985 to $21.8 billion in 1989 under the 1985 law.[107]

Abdnor, the incumbent and a Republican, should have had a fund-raising advantage over Daschle. He particularly needed such an advantage, as much of what he raised would be needed in an expected primary challenge by Janklow. Through the end of 1985, Abdnor had raised $600,000 and spent $500,000. Daschle, on the other hand, was able to raise slightly more than Abdnor, $675,000, and had spent $450,000. Because Janklow had not yet established an official campaign, he was not required by federal law to report money raised.[108]

Abdnor officially announced his candidacy on February 11, declaring that he wanted to continue "fighting and winning for South Dakota." Abdnor, despite having voted for the 1985 farm bill, stressed all he had done for South Dakota's farmers, including four amendments to the farm bill and his work to save the Rural Electrification Administration.[109]

Janklow told reporters at a February 15 news conference that "I'm going

---

105. Brenda Wade, "Farm Credit," *Sioux Falls Argus Leader*, January 28, 1986; "Janklow Calls for Moratorium," *Sioux Falls Argus Leader*, January 15, 1986; Doug Cunningham, "Two See Way to Stave Off Farm Crisis," *Sioux Falls Argus Leader*, January 8, 1986.

106. Todd Murphy, "Janklow, Daschle, Trade Jabs over Farm Crisis," *Sioux Falls Argus Leader*, February 1, 1986.

107. "Study: Law Will Bite into Farm Income," *Sioux Falls Argus Leader*, February 14, 1986.

108. Mireille Gates, "Abdnor Money," *Sioux Falls Argus Leader*, February 6 1986; "Daschle Campaign Spent $451,648 in 1985," *Sioux Falls Argus Leader*, February 6, 1986.

109. Todd Murphy, "Abdnor: I Want to Keep Fighting," *Sioux Falls Argus Leader*, February 12, 1986.

to run."[110] His official announcement was slated for February 22. A fiery, blustery orator, Janklow offered a sharp contrast to the quiet, behind-the-scenes Abdnor, who talked with a mild speech impediment. While Abdnor was a staunch Reagan loyalist, Janklow offered a decidedly anti-Washington campaign. He once declared that the Soviet Union could bomb the District of Columbia and "half of America wouldn't care."[111] His official announcement hardly strayed from this course. "You probably expected I'd come here tonight and start bashing Congress. I'm going to disappoint you. I'm going to disappoint you. I'm not going to bash any organization that has figured out how to get paid for twelve months and only work six." Then, turning his acid tongue on Daschle and Abdnor, he remarked, "They say they get along in Washington. Maybe it's time we sent somebody to Washington who didn't get along with Washington. . . . They have twenty-two years of seniority. Somebody tell me what South Dakota has got for that besides three post offices and a bridge."[112]

Democrat Tom Daschle announced his bid for Abdnor's seat on March 6. Behind the decision lay two factors, winnability and increasing dissatisfaction with life in the House.[113] In a four-and-a-half-minute television speech, Daschle noted that he could accomplish far more as one of a hundred senators than as one of 435 congressmen. He then examined Janklow's and Abdnor's chances of achievement. "It's not enough to shout and scream and point fingers at Washington. And it's not enough just to complain and make excuses for this administration. Our forefathers knew that leadership is judged neither by the volume of one's voice, nor the number of one's excuses."[114]

Back on the Republican side, after several weeks of wavering, Abdnor officially announced that he would not debate Janklow. Abdnor had not debated an opponent since his run for Congress in 1978, including his 1980 campaign to unseat George McGovern. While Abdnor said his refusal had nothing to do with his speech impediment, Abdnor's administrative aide admitted that

> if this debate is something that shows who is the most articulate, who is the quickest on his feet, best able to twist an argument in his favor,

---

110. Richard Bale, "Janklow Warms up Campaign Rhetoric," *Sioux Falls Argus Leader*, February 16, 1986.

111. Peter Bragdon, "Abdnor-Janklow Match Tamer Than Expected," *Congressional Quarterly Weekly Report*, May 17, 1986, 1113.

112. Todd Murphy, "Janklow Makes It Official," *Sioux Falls Argus Leader*, February 23, 1986.

113. Stavrianos interview.

114. "Politics," *Congressional Quarterly Weekly Report*, March 8, 1986, 581; Todd Murphy, "Daschle Tunes In to Senate Campaign," *Sioux Falls Argus Leader*, March 7, 1986.

we have no problem attributing those things to Governor Janklow. . . . Jim is a reasonable thoughtful listener. Tell me how a debate demonstrates that. Jim's style works in Washington. The governor's works on television.[115]

Abdnor did, however, agree to debate Daschle if Abdnor won the primary.

Janklow, well aware of the advantages of debating Abdnor, appeared uninvited at Flandreau and Rapid City congressional hearings sponsored by Abdnor. Mike Freeman, Abdnor's press secretary, acknowledged that "Bill [Janklow] can walk in and in five minutes, steal the thunder." Abdnor had to accept the fact that Janklow's tactics worked. "He got most of the credit at Flandreau."[116]

Such campaign tricks were necessary for Janklow, who was running his campaign on a shoestring budget. Janklow, a maverick from the start of his political career, had never been popular among the Republican party leadership. His decision to challenge the likable Abdnor and risk splitting the party made relationships even worse.[117] The schism made fund-raising a difficult burden for Janklow. During the first quarter of 1986, Janklow raised $130,000 and spent a paltry $27,334. Abdnor, in contrast, raised about $350,000 and spent close to $200,000, while Daschle, who was not even involved in a primary race, raised over $400,000 and spent nearly $500,000.[118]

While the polls in April showed Abdnor with a lead over Janklow, it was difficult to tell how large the lead was. A poll commissioned by Abdnor showed the Senator leading the governor by a whopping 24 percentage points, while Janklow's poll showed the governor trailing by only 6 percentage points.[119] Daschle's poll showed him leading a race against Abdnor by 48 to 35 percent and leading a race against Janklow by a nearly identical 48 to 36 percent.[120]

Janklow's financial fortunes began to pick up during April and May. Between April 1 and May 14, Janklow narrowly surpassed Abdnor's fundraising, $183,000 to $182,000, and Janklow outspent Abdnor, $206,000 to

---

115. Todd Murphy, "Abdnor Refuses to Debate," *Sioux Falls Argus Leader*, March 23, 1986.

116. Todd Murphy, "Janklow Stirs Up Hearings," *Sioux Falls Argus Leader*, April 6, 1986.

117. "South Dakota," *Congressional Quarterly Weekly Report*, February 22, 1986, 423–25.

118. Todd Murphy, "Janklow Cuts Corners on Campaign," *Sioux Falls Argus Leader*, April 20, 1986; Todd Murphy, "Campaign Trail," *Sioux Falls Argus Leader*, May 4, 1986.

119. "Abdnor Pulls for His Poll," *Sioux Falls Argus Leader*, April 20, 1986. See Alan Ehrenhalt, "Poll Fever Infects 1986 Campaign Coverage," *Congressional Quarterly Weekly Report*, April 5, 1986, 779, on how politician-sponsored polls, and Abdnor's in particular, are easily manipulated to favor the sponsor.

120. James Dickenson and Maralee Schwartz, "Politics," *Washington Post*, May 6, 1986.

$149,000.[121] An independent poll taken by South Dakota University May 8–11 showed Abdnor with a 10 percentage point lead, 47 to 37, though many professional politicians believed "that Janklow has the momentum and that the race is about even."[122]

One of the few controversies in what was generally a high-road campaign developed over $100,000 in independent expenditures by the National Association of Realtors on behalf of Abdnor. Any contribution that large in a state the size of South Dakota would raise ethical suspicions. The expenditure equaled 10 percent of what Abdnor's own campaign was spending. On a per capita basis, it is the equivalent of a $1.7 million expenditure in Florida, or a $3.8 million expenditure in California. More interesting than the size of the expenditure is that, according to Janklow, the three principals behind the decision were former advisers to Jimmy Carter, Ted Kennedy, and the Democratic Senate Campaign Committee. Janklow charged that Abdnor was a dupe of the realtors: they were helping him so the weaker candidate would face Daschle in the November election.[123]

Five days before the primary, the two candidates were interviewed separately on South Dakota public television. Both candidates stressed their support for President Reagan and their belief that improving the economy was more important to helping farmers than congressional legislation. They disagreed, though, on how much help Congress had delivered over the past six years and the role of South Dakota's senators in fighting for that help. Janklow, for instance, argued that South Dakota was not getting its share of federal funds, while Abdnor claimed that South Dakota was among the leading states in per capita federal funding. Janklow argued that his aggressive approach would accomplish the most, while Abdnor spoke of the value of compromise.[124]

Abdnor won the June 3 primary by a surprisingly comfortable 54 to 46 margin. According to *Congressional Quarterly*, Janklow "found himself overmatched by the incumbent's fund-raising and organization and by the national Republicans who flocked to Abdnor's side."[125] Todd Murphy, of the *Sioux Falls Argus Leader*, agreed: "In the end, the result of the race may have been

---

121. Chet Brokaw, "Janklow Gains in Campaign Spending," *Sioux Falls Argus Leader*, May 23, 1986.

122. James Dickenson, "Abdnor Trying to Fend Off Governor's Challenge," *Washington Post*, May 31, 1986. See also Bragdon, "Abdnor-Janklow Race," 1113–15.

123. Dickenson, "Abdnor Trying"; Todd Murphy, "Some Local Realtors to Back Janklow," *Sioux Falls Argus Leader*, May 27, 1986; Hank Klibanoff, "Will Be-Bop Beat Out Bland?—It's Up to the GOP Voter," *Miami Herald*, May 31, 1986.

124. Todd Murphy, "Abdnor, Janklow Air Views," *Sioux Falls Argus Leader*, May 30, 1986.

125. Peter Bragdon, "Abdnor Exceeds Expectations in South Dakota Primary," *Congressional Quarterly Weekly Report*, June 7, 1986, 1284.

determined less by issues and personalities than by each campaign's organization and whose supporters voted. Abdnor's was widely considered the better organization."[126] Janklow, who ran a campaign far less belligerent than expected by the media, offered his support to Abdnor after conceding the election. The following day, Janklow's leading supporters did the same.[127]

The conventional wisdom is that a strong primary challenge will hurt an incumbent. Anyone who has heard Jimmy Carter speak about Ted Kennedy knows that Carter holds Kennedy more responsible for his defeat by Ronald Reagan than he does the Ayatollah Khomeini.[128] Similarly, Abdnor feels that Janklow's challenge hurt his campaign tremendously. "South Dakota is a very loyal state to its supporters. We had a very, very popular governor who split our party right down the middle. The fallout was tremendous. That was our biggest single problem."[129] This is entirely consistent with the systematic results on the influence of divisive primaries reported in chapter 4.

An alternative view of the effect of the primary comes from Daschle campaign manager Peter Stavrianos.

> We thought, and we continued to say throughout, that there was [an advantage to Daschle from the primary]. The truth of the matter was that the way it came out, if anything Abdnor was helped by that primary in our view. That was because of the specific problems he faced in facing Daschle . . . . Jim Abdnor's only problem in South Dakota is "is he aggressive enough and tough enough and capable enough to do the job for us in a pinch in the Senate?" There was never any problem with is he a nice guy, is he like us, do we like him, do we like him personally? He is about as South Dakota as you can get.
>
> So he has one problem: is he tough enough? He takes on the toughest guy ever to come into South Dakota politics and beats him in the primary. He rose eighteen points after winning the primary, in our poll anyway, in our tracking against Daschle, and it wasn't just a typical, one-day, two-day, three-day, "gee you won, that's neat," you go up for a while then you drop right back. It went to the question of is Jim Abdnor able to mix it up with the big boys, which was people's only doubt about him, so it helped him.
>
> It wasn't something he wanted. He was hurt by spending a lot of money, though that's very replenishable in a very important Senate race.

---

126. Todd Murphy, "U.S. Senate Race: The Battle That Never Was," *Sioux Falls Argus Leader*, June 4, 1986.

127. Todd Murphy, "'Nice Guy' Abdnor Finishes First," *Sioux Falls Argus Leader*, June 4, 1986; Todd Murphy, "The Day After," *Sioux Falls Argus Leader*, June 5, 1986.

128. Jimmy Carter, personal conversation, October 7, 1987.

129. James Abdnor, telephone interview, August 24, 1990.

Maybe it's too glib to say it helped him, but it definitely didn't hurt him as much as you would think it would, as we thought it would, or as it normally would.[130]

The polling evidence mentioned by Stavrianos showed Daschle's commanding 15 percentage point lead before the primary evaporate into a 3 percentage point deficit following the Republican election.[131]

Despite the polling evidence, Abdnor strongly disagreed with Stavrianos's assertions.

Well, when you take a guy like Bill Janklow, who was a very, very popular governor you get a lot of support. What the hell, I mean this guy won with the biggest majority we ever had in the state. He was a good governor. . . . My opponent [Daschle] didn't have anyone running against him in the primary. He spent something like a million dollars. I had a tough race in the primary. I had to go long and hard and tough, but if you think Bill Janklow and I were smiling at each other you're wrong. We're friends now and all that but it was a tough race. We were speaking out on what we thought and answering each other.[132]

Whatever momentum Abdnor may have received from the primary victory was short-lived, for three weeks following the primary Abdnor made the biggest campaign mistake of any of the candidates we examined. Speaking before a Huron forum sponsored by the nonprofit group Communicating for Agriculture, Abdnor was asked how to revive the farm export market. He replied, "and maybe we do have to sell below cost for a while, but I think that until we regain the market, that's the way we're going to have to go."[133] Whatever the long-term economic merits of such a proposal might be, this was politically less astute than Walter Mondale's 1984 promise to raise taxes.

Though the media originally downplayed the statement—the *Argus Leader*, for instance, buried it on page 3b—the Daschle campaign did not. Their cameras were filming the forum, including Daschle's reply: "I think it's a big mistake. By the time we have the export market back half the people in the audience won't be there any more. That to me is the difference, we've got to have a price; we've got to have income."[134] One week later, Abdnor's statement that economically depressed farmers should sell below cost for a

---

130. Stavrianos interview.
131. Stavrianos interview.
132. Abdnor interview.
133. Daschle Commercial no. 9, Center for Political Communications, University of Oklahoma.
134. Daschle Commercial no. 9.

while and Daschle's reply were released as a thirty-second advertisement for Daschle.

Though the tape makes it clear that Abdnor called for lower prices, Abdnor released advertisements claiming that Daschle was misrepresenting Abdnor's position and letters calling Daschle a liar. In one mailing, Abdnor claimed that he was actually calling for lower interest rates, not lower prices. The campaign quickly admitted error.[135] Though Abdnor still argues that he was misunderstood, that is, that lower prices does not mean lower subsidies, he recognizes that the statement hurt him. "No one told me they were going to allow [Daschle to film the conference]. I thought it was all for public television. How wrong I was. It didn't help me. I guarantee that got it [the campaign] off to a bad start and lasted right up to the election. When things are bad it's awful easy to convince people."[136]

Another Daschle commercial, released July 14, assailed Abdnor for his vote for the 1985 Reagan farm bill.

> Announcer: The '85 farm bill. Not apples and oranges, but the legislation that governs farm prices for the next five years. Now it's law. Wheat prices will fall ($3.30 to $1.95), corn prices will fall ($2.55 to $1.57), farm income will fall ($25.7 billion to $20.0 billion). That's the guaranteed result. It's the same failed policies that's brought six years of declining exports and the first farm trade deficit in twenty-seven years. Jim Abdnor voted yes to lower prices. Tom Daschle voted no and that's the fundamental difference.[137]

Polls taken by Information Associates before the advertisements showed Daschle with a 9 percentage point lead, 46 to 37. Daschle spokesman Roy Behr claimed that polls taken by Daschle after the media blitz showed a 15 percentage point edge.[138]

When Abdnor continued to object to the advertisements as unfair characterizations of his views, Daschle replied with a unique proposition: In return for both candidates giving up all television and radio advertising, Abdnor would agree to debate Daschle six times. Abdnor turned the proposal down, but did not rule out the possibility of debating Daschle.[139]

---

135. Richard Bale, "Abdnor Misquoted, Campaign Aide Says," *Sioux Falls Argus Leader*, August 15, 1986.

136. Abdnor interview.

137. Daschle Commercial no. 10, Center for Political Communications, University of Oklahoma.

138. James Dickenson, "'Nice Guys' Talk Tough in South Dakota Race," *Washington Post*, August 23, 1986; Bob Imrie, "Polls, Candidates Disagree about U.S. Senate Race, *Sioux Falls Argus Leader*, August 11, 1986.

139. Brenda Wade, "Daschle to Abdnor: Drop Ads for Debates," *Sioux Falls Argus Leader*, July 18, 1986.

Debate over the content of the campaign continued when Abdnor accused Daschle's surrogates of portraying him as anti-Semitic and a bigot. The materials in question accused Abdnor, who is of Lebanese descent, of being "100% against Israel" and "allied with the Moral Majority and radical right."[140] The mischaracterization, according to Abdnor, is because he consistently votes against foreign aid for Israel and all other countries. "I just don't vote for foreign aid. People go wild about it, giving money to the World Bank but not to farmers."[141]

Debate over proposed debates continued as well. An August 27 meeting between aides for Daschle and Abdnor broke down after just thirty minutes. Daschle wanted six to eight debates, Abdnor only two. According to Daschle's aides, they were willing to negotiate, but Abdnor's side was not. Tom Mason, Abdnor's administrative aide said, "We have said we will do two debates, and we'll stand by that."[142] On September 4, the Daschle campaign gave in to Abdnor's insistence and agreed to just two debates with the incumbent.[143]

Meanwhile, the Abdnor camp was being criticized by Republicans for having remained on the defensive ever since the Huron "below cost" remarks. State Senator Majority Whip George Shanard (R-Mitchell) told the *Argus Leader* that Daschle's candidacy poses "an altogether different race than (Abdnor) has ever faced—someone much younger, and certainly more liberal than anyone he has ever met, even George McGovern." Abdnor needed to go on the offensive.[144]

The decision to go on the offensive came toward the end of September. Frank Thieman announced that the Abdnor campaign would start to focus on Daschle and his record. Foreshadowing an upcoming campaign advertisement, Thieman said "You can kind of tell a guy by the friends he keeps." The friend in question was Jane Fonda, once known as "Hanoi Jane" because of her friendly visit to North Vietnam's capital during the Vietnam War.[145] Fonda, along with Robin Williams, Jack Nicholson, and other luminaries, had attended a $5,000 per couple fund-raiser for Daschle and five other Democrats at Barbra Streisand's ranch in Los Angeles. Fonda had also testified at Daschle's request at congressional hearings on the farm problem.[146] The

---

140. Dickenson, "'Nice Guys' Talk Tough."
141. Dickenson, "'Nice Guys' Talk Tough."
142. Jim Rasmussen, "Abdnor, Daschle, Debate Talks Break Off," *Sioux Falls Argus Leader*, August 28, 1986.
143. Jim Rasmussen, "Abdnor OKs Debate," *Sioux Falls Argus Leader*, September 5, 1986.
144. Chuck Raasch, "Shanard Criticizes Abdnor Campaign," *Sioux Falls Argus Leader*, August 23, 1986.
145. Todd Murphy, "Abdnor Staff Ready to Take the Offensive," *Sioux Falls Argus Leader*, September 21, 1986.
146. Maralee Schwartz, "Politics," *Washington Post*, September 24, 1986; "Money Girl,"

commercial that eventually ran tied in these hearings to another side of Fonda, her pronouncements against red meat.

> Announcer: Jane Fonda's been associated with more radical causes than almost anyone in America, including warning people against *red meat* [emphasis in commercial]. So when the Democratic task force on agriculture held hearings, guess who Tom Daschle invited. That's right, Jane Fonda. Instead of inviting someone from South Dakota, Daschle invites the same Jane Fonda who writes and speaks against eating beef and pork, our state's biggest farm products. Tom Daschle talks big for South Dakota, but who can you really trust to put South Dakota first?[147]

When Daschle complained about the advertisement, Thieman replied that "Tom Daschle has done nothing but cry and complain and wimp about ag issues ever since he got to Congress."[148]

The "Fonda campaign" carried over to the newspapers. An Abdnor print advertisement said Fonda

> seems to like Tom's liberal style. She and her Hollywood friends have a strong agenda for the United States, and she believes Tom will see it through.
> That's why just a month ago Jane Fonda paid $2,500 just to have dinner with Tom and other Democrats in Hollywood.
> These days, more and more people are realizing that Tom's song and dance for South Dakota's farmers is just like a Hollywood prop: a lot of show and little substance.[149]

Daschle was not the only candidate receiving support from Hollywood stars. On September 29, President Reagan came to Sioux Falls in an effort to save the troubled Abdnor campaign. Reagan gave his usual Senate speech, extolling the local candidate, Abdnor, who Reagan called a workhorse, criticizing his opponent (a "show horse," and a "razzle-dazzle liberal" who supported Reagan administration programs less than Ted Kennedy [D-Massachusetts]) and urging South Dakotans to help keep the Republicans in control of the Senate. Reagan acknowledged that the economic recovery had not

---

Sioux Falls Argus Leader, September 7, 1986; "Abdnor Ads Add Sparks to Campaign," *Sioux Falls Argus Leader*, September 28, 1986.

147. Abdnor Commercial no. 2, Center for Political Communications, University of Oklahoma.

148. Todd Murphy, "Daschle Aides Assail Abdnor Ad," *Sioux Falls Argus Leader*, September 25, 1986.

149. "Abdnor Ads Add Sparks."

reached everywhere, and to show his concern, took two protesting farmers in his limousine for his ride back to the airport. The only strange part of the entire day's events was that Jim Abdnor was not in South Dakota with the president; he was back working in Washington, purportedly so that he would not miss votes on Philippine aid and a $550 billion continuing resolution to keep the government running until the budget passed. Some Democrats viewed his absence as an attempt to keep some distance from an unpopular incumbent president, but Abdnor, who had previously attacked Daschle for missing votes in Congress in order to attend fund-raisers, felt obliged to remain in Washington.[150] Abdnor responded to Democratic charges that he was avoiding Reagan as follows.

> That's a lie. President Reagan will tell you that and so will any guy in South Dakota. I happened to be chairman of a committee with a bill coming up that time and they can check it out if they want to. I made a big decision. Do I run off and do that or do I look like I'm really trying to accomplish something and taking care of business first. That was a tough decision. That appearance of Mr. Reagan helped me immensely.[151]

Present or not, Abdnor appeared to gain some momentum from the visit. Despite large protests, Reagan was well received. His personal visit with the protest leaders showed the Reagan touch at work. The South Dakota Poll, taken between October 8 and October 10, actually showed Abdnor with a narrow, 4 percentage point lead.[152] According to Stavrianos, the attacks were working on the undecided voters.

> [The series of advertisements] essentially said "this guy's not quite like you. He's gotten a little too much air. Maybe he's lost his way." The Fonda ad was effective. We didn't believe it. . . . But what we found, both in focus groups and in polling, was that a significant percentage of the undecided people they were aiming at said, "you know, I've always liked Daschle and Abdnor, but I think maybe it's true that Daschle is a little bit of an ambitious young politician, and we know Jim is a really solid guy," and that's what the whole race really was about. If voters

---

150. Todd Murphy, "Reagan Faces Farmers," *Sioux Falls Argus Leader*, September 30, 1986; Chuck Raasch, "Abdnor Skips Visit for Philippines Vote," *Sioux Falls Argus Leader*, September 30, 1986; David Kranz, "Reagan's Hour Puts Abdnor Back in the Race," *Sioux Falls Argus Leader*, September 30, 1986; Brenda Wade, "Democrats Welcome Reagan, But Not His Farm Program," *Sioux Falls Argus Leader*, September 30, 1986; Stavrianos interview.

151. Abdnor interview.

152. James Dickenson, "Candidates Reach for TV Saturation In the Dakotas' Close Senate Contests," *Washington Post*, October 23, 1986; "Poll Shows Senate Race to Be Tight," *Sioux Falls Argus Leader*, October 23, 1986.

focused on who is probably more capable of getting the job done, of standing up to the people and making a case for the state, then Daschle clearly won. If the question was, who right now do I feel is more exactly like me, who embodies South Dakota in a visceral sense, Abdnor won without question.[153]

Abdnor and Daschle met for the first of two debates on October 15. The campaign took a new turn as Daschle accused Abdnor of voting against Social Security and Medicare twenty-three times. Abdnor, for his part, accused Daschle of opposing red meat and supporting the Panama Canal "give-away."[154] The same issues reappeared at the second and final debate on October 18. The candidates also debated foreign policy. Abdnor, who traditionally voted against all foreign aid, defended his support for the Nicaraguan Contras by reiterating Reagan's line that they are the moral equivalent of our Founding Fathers. Daschle replied, "If they're freedom fighters . . . I have to look at a dictionary. That's absolutely poppycock. They're thugs in most cases."[155]

Two days after the second debate, Daschle presented a list of thirty-two votes in which Abdnor supported cuts in Social Security. Daschle also released a commercial featuring an 83-year-old constituent, Opal Finn. The advertisement repeated Daschle's accusations against Abdnor, and had Finn thanking Daschle for his support of Social Security.[156] The National Council of Senior Citizens joined the fight against Abdnor, claiming that the Senator was "taking a great leap from reality by saying he is a defender of senior citizens." Abdnor, who received only a 19 percent support score from the group, pointed to his 90 percent rating from the National Alliance of Senior Citizens, a more conservative organization representing a variety of conservative interests, and not particularly fond of the Social Security system.[157]

Social Security, according to Abdnor, became the primary issue in the last few days.

> They put out publicity galore and misleading statements. If we had done a better job of setting up our research we would have found out that the other side had voted the same way on these votes as we did, which I don't think was ever totally against Social Security. It was all concen-

---

153. Stavrianos interview.
154. Todd Murphy, "Sparks Fly in Senate Debate," *Sioux Falls Argus Leader*, October 16, 1986.
155. Todd Murphy, "Debate Smolders," *Sioux Falls Argus Leader*, October 19, 1986.
156. Daschle Commercial no. 16, Center for Political Communications, University of Oklahoma.
157. Chuck Raasch, "Elderly Group Hits Abdnor Vote Record," *Sioux Falls Argus Leader*, October 25, 1986.

trated on Social Security in the last few weeks like it had been in other previous elections around the country in other years. It's a great issue: you can scare the hell out of older people. It's one way to win an election I guess.[158]

The Social Security issue apparently shifted the votes of a large number of senior citizens in the closing weeks of the campaign, according to Republican party pollsters.[159]

With a close race on hand and partisan control of the Senate in the balance, President Reagan returned to South Dakota on October 29, combining partisan and personal appeals. "Will you choose the Democratic leaders who in 1980 weakened our nation and nearly brought our economy to its knees? Or will you choose to give the cleanup crew of 1980 a chance to finish the job?" Reagan then told South Dakotans that, in voting for Abdnor, "you'll be winning one for the Gipper," a reference to the legendary football star portrayed by Reagan in *Knute Rockne*.

This visit did not help Abdnor nearly as much as the first one, according to both camps. According to Daschle's campaign manager, the second visit showed South Dakotans that Abdnor wasn't tough enough to fight his own battles.[160] To Abdnor, the problem was that Reagan

> gave the same speech wherever he was. He kept talking about how prosperous this country is and how well we've done and how strong the defense is. Well that's fine, but when farmers and people are suffering it's not what they wanted to hear. If I could have had a speech out of him on Social Security like he gave on agriculture it would have been the greatest thing I could have had. But he didn't do that. It's not his fault. The guy who prepared him—it's like talking to the wall talking to that guy.[161]

In the final days of the campaign, Abdnor left behind the negative advertisements and tried to capitalize on his own personal popularity. According to *Congressional Quarterly*, "South Dakota has long found [Abdnor's] bumbling manner and inarticulate speaking style endearing rather than embarrassing, and he is a familiar and comfortable figure in small-town cafes from Sioux Falls to Rapid City."[162] As we showed in chapter 4, small-state senators have the advantage of truly having *personal* relationships with the voters. Abdnor tried to use this folksy persona to his advantage by releasing a commercial in

---

158. Abdnor interview.
159. Maralee Schwartz, "Politics," *Washington Post*, November 9, 1986.
160. Stavrianos interview.
161. Abdnor interview.
162. "South Dakota," *Congressional Quarterly Weekly Report*," October 11, 1986, 2486–87.

which he told viewers, "So I'm not a great speaker. Heck, I'm not a great dancer either. But I'm a great fighter for South Dakota."[163] Yet "the qualities that make Abdnor personally appealing . . . left a strong impression that he is not the most effective spokesperson for the state."[164] Abdnor lost the election by a 52 to 48 percent margin.

Survey Results

According to ABC exit polls (see table 7.2), Daschle defeated Abdnor by a 53 to 47 percent margin.[165] Males supported Daschle 51 to 49 percent, females, 55 to 45 percent. Abdnor did almost as well among Republicans (78 to 22 percent) as Daschle did among Democrats (83 to 17 percent), but Daschle swept the Independents, 67 to 33 percent. Daschle did better among liberals (86 to 14 percent) than Abdnor did among conservatives (72 to 28 percent), but liberals were only 12 percent of the electorate.

In terms of national issues, Abdnor did about as well among those who liked the status quo as Daschle did among those who were dissatisfied. The difference in the election demonstrates the importance of national political conditions: those who were dissatisfied with the economy far outnumbered those who were satisfied. Abdnor won 84 percent of those who thought the economy was excellent and 72 percent of those who thought the economy was good. But these were just 2 percent and 33 percent of the population, respectively. Alternatively, Daschle won 75 percent of those who thought the economy was poor and 63 percent of those who thought the economy was not so good. Fortunately for Daschle's campaign, these were 19 percent and 46 percent of the voters, respectively. Abdnor won 72 percent of those who considered themselves better off; Daschle won 74 percent of those who considered themselves worse off. But again, crucial for Daschle's campaign, those who were worse off outnumbered those who were better off by a four to three ratio. Of those who listed the state of the local economy as an important issue, 60 percent voted for Daschle. Had the economy of South Dakota not been in such severe economic straights, it is easy to imagine James Abdnor gathering far more than the two extra percentage points he needed to win reelection.

Conclusion

South Dakota in 1986 clearly illustrates the decline of partisanship in Senate voting. Though the state had a Republican plurality, and its voters are over-

---

163. Alan Ehrenhalt, "A Legislative Record: A Boon or Bane," *Congressional Quarterly Weekly Report*, October 25, 1986, 2719.
164. "South Dakota," 2487.
165. ABC News, *The '88 Vote*, 456.

TABLE 7.2. South Dakota Exit Poll Results (in percentages)

	All Voters	Daschle Voters	Abdnor Voters
Gender			
Male	53	51	49
Female	47	55	45
Race			
White	98	53	47
Black	2	47	53
Other	1	88	13
Ideology			
Liberal	12	86	14
Conservative	23	28	72
Party			
Democrat	42	83	17
Independent	11	67	33
Republican	45	22	78
Other	1	33	67
Better cope			
Democrats	53	84	16
Republicans	47	18	82
Personally better off than when Reagan took office			
Better off	28	28	72
About the same	36	50	50
Worse off	37	74	25
Reagan job performance			
Approve	53	29	71
Disapprove	47	79	21
State of economy			
Excellent	2	16	84
Good	33	28	72
Not so good	46	63	37
Poor	19	75	25
Important items (selected)			
National economy	47	57	43
Local economy	46	60	39
Reagan performance	28	47	52
Candidates' party	13	49	51

Source: ABC News, *The '88 Vote,* 456.

whelmingly more conservative than liberal, the wretched state of the farm economy led them to believe that Democrats were better able to handle the country's problems than Republicans. While President Reagan, who swept South Dakota in 1980 and 1984, was tolerated there in his 1986 visits, his farm policies were anathema to the state's voters. The ever-loyal Abdnor seemed more supportive of Reagan than he did of South Dakota's farmers. Though Daschle's campaign claims otherwise, Abdnor was no doubt hurt by the internecine campaign waged against him by Governor Janklow. According to the statistical estimates in chapter 4, this alone probably cost Abdnor more than 5 percent of the November vote.

In Congressman Tom Daschle, Abdnor faced a high-quality challenger whose district covered the entire state. Daschle was able to spend what for South Dakota was an enormous amount of money, much of it raised out of state. On the critical issue of government support for farmers, no one could outflank Daschle.

Conclusion

These four 1986 campaigns illustrate several salient characteristics of modern Senate campaigns.

1. The decline of partisanship—the declining attachment of U.S. voters to political parties and the increasingly candidate-centered nature of political campaigns means that no state can be considered safe for either party in a Senate election. Two-party competition is the norm, even in states such as Florida and South Dakota, which were once completely dominated by a single party. In Florida, the Democrat won in a Democratic state, but probably no Democrat other than Bob Graham could have defeated Paula Hawkins. In South Dakota, one of the most Republican states in the country, Democrat Tom Daschle defeated a popular incumbent Republican, due in large part to voter dissatisfaction with the state of the economy.
2. The role of television in modern Senate campaigns—television advertising played a major role in the California and Florida contests. Cranston put Zschau on the defensive from the day Zschau won the Republican primary, while Hawkins's negative advertisements cut substantially into Graham's large lead. Surprisingly, television also had an important effect in South Dakota, despite it being a sparsely populated state with no major media centers.[166] Abdnor, like Zschau and Hawkins, picked up when he launched his negative attacks on his opponent. On the other side of the ledger, it was Daschle's commercials that allowed South Dakota voters to view, over and over again, Abdnor's admission that lower farm prices might be necessary in the short run. In New York, an underfunded challenger necessarily underutilized television and thus was unable to effectively criticize the incumbent's record. Thus the *lack* of television advertising played a major role in the New York race.

---

166. See Dickenson, "Candidates Reach."

3. The role of money in modern Senate campaigns—money was very important in these 1986 campaigns in several ways. In order to criticize the incumbent's record effectively, a challenger must spend a substantial amount of money. The challenger's spending looms as one of the most important determinants of the competitiveness of Senate elections. Zschau, Graham, and Daschle were all well funded, Green was not. Moreover, the ability to raise money is influenced by the quality of the challenger. It is no coincidence that Governor Graham and Congressmen Zschau and Daschle were able to spend large sums of money, while private citizen and political unknown Green was not.

The incumbent's spending may not be as crucial in shaping voter attitudes in the campaign, since the incumbent has already had at least six years to make an impression on the public. Yet by amassing an enormous campaign war chest before the campaign even begins, an incumbent can deter potentially strong challengers from running. The effectiveness of this strategy was illustrated in 1986 by Alphonse D'Amato. Moreover, evidence from tracking polls suggest that campaign spending by incumbents was effective when used not to support the incumbent, but to attack the opposition. This was true in California and South Dakota. In contrast, Hawkins's attacks on the well-known and ever-popular Graham had less of an impact.

Money and television are tied together as the former is needed to purchase time on the latter. This can affect campaigns in ways that do not make headlines. For instance, in California, Alan Cranston did virtually no personal campaigning until the last week of the race. "He sat on the phone ten hours a day doing fund-raising. . . . It's an astonishing thing. That's what money is doing to political campaigns."[167] According to Paula Hawkins, "Money counts. That's what's so disgusting about this whole business."[168]

4. The influence of national issues on Senate campaigns—President Reagan's decision to campaign actively on behalf of Republican Senate candidates turned the 1986 Senate elections into a referendum on his administration's policies and performance, especially in handling the economy. Nevertheless, the impact of this issue on the outcomes of individual races depended on the condition of each state's economy. The depressed condition of South Dakota's agricultural economy was a major factor contributing to the defeat of James Abdnor; the prosperous condition of New York's service-based economy may

---

167. Greenaway interview.
168. Hawkins interview.

have contributed to the perception by many Democratic politicians that Alphonse D'Amato was unbeatable in 1986. In contrast, a strong Florida economy was not enough to help Paula Hawkins defeat Bob Graham, who was ideologically well positioned on the issues of crime, aid to Israel, and support for the Contras.

CHAPTER 8

Conclusions: Senate Elections, Senate Politics, and Electoral Accountability

The contemporary Senate is a very different legislative body than the one envisioned by the framers of the Constitution. Far from being insulated from public opinion, the modern Senate appears to be highly sensitive to changes in the public mood. During the 1960s, with liberal Democrats firmly in control, the Senate led the way in the development of progressive social legislation. Many of the policies that were adopted by Lyndon Johnson as part of his Great Society program and enacted by the Eighty-ninth Congress (1965–67), including civil rights legislation, federal aid to education, and the war on poverty, were first introduced and debated in the Senate during the 1950s and early 1960s.[1] During the 1980s, however, with conservative Republicans in the ascendency, the Senate was in the forefront of the Reagan revolution, reducing income tax rates and cutting spending on domestic social programs while dramatically increasing military spending. Like Lyndon Johnson, Ronald Reagan adopted many of the components of his initial legislative agenda from proposals first introduced and debated in the Senate.[2]

One of the most important reasons for the differences between the modern Senate and the Senate envisioned by the framers of the Constitution is the fact that, since the adoption of the Seventeenth Amendment to the Constitution in 1913, senators have been directly elected by the people instead of being appointed by state legislatures. But it is not only direct popular election that has altered the character of the Senate. It is also the nature of Senate elections.

Despite the six-year terms of Senators and the fact that only one-third of the Senate seats are up for election every two years, Senate elections have been characterized by greater volatility than House elections in recent years. This is true in two different respects. First, the average proportion of seats changing hands between the parties has been greater in the Senate than in the

---

1. For an excellent discussion of this period, see James L. Sundquist, *Politics and Policy: The Eisenhower, Kennedy, and Johnson Years* (Washington, D. C.: Brookings Institution, 1968).

2. See Charles O. Jones, ed., *The Reagan Legacy: Promise and Performance* (Chatham, N.J.: Chatham House, 1988); this anthology contains a number of articles analyzing the performance of the Reagan administration. See also B. B. Kymlicka and Jean V. Matthews, eds., *The Reagan Revolution?* (Chicago: Dorsey Press, 1988).

House. In addition, the average margin of control enjoyed by the majority party has been much smaller in the Senate than in the House.

In the five elections between 1980 and 1988, the average net change in party control in Senate elections was 4.4 seats, or 4.4 percent of the total membership and more than 13.0 percent of the seats at stake in each election; in these same five elections, the average net swing in party control in House elections was 16.4 seats, or 3.8 percent of the total membership. The main reason Senate elections resulted in larger swings in party control in comparison to House elections is that Senate incumbents were much more vulnerable to defeat than House incumbents. In the five elections between 1980 and 1988, more than 20.0 percent of Senate incumbents lost their races compared with less than 5.0 percent of House incumbents.

In addition to the fact that Senate elections were much more competitive than House elections during the 1980s, there was also a much more even division of seats between the parties in the Senate. The average plurality enjoyed by the majority party in the Senate was only 8.6 seats (8.6 percent of the total membership) compared with an average plurality of 77.6 seats (17.8 percent of the total membership) for the majority party in the House. Therefore, it took a much smaller seat swing to produce a shift in party control in the Senate than in the House. During the 1980s, there were two changes in party control of the Senate (in 1980 and 1986) but no changes in party control of the House. The closest the Republican Party came to taking control of the House of Representatives was in the 1980 election when it won 192 seats, still 26 seats short of a majority.

We believe that the greater competitiveness of Senate elections, which is due largely to the greater vulnerability of Senate incumbents, and the closer division of seats between the two parties in the Senate have contributed to important differences in leadership and decision making between the two legislative chambers. There appears to be a stronger sense of collective responsibility for policy outcomes in the Senate than in the House, because Senators realize that there is a real chance of a change in party control based on these outcomes. There is, in addition, a greater incentive for cooperation between the majority and minority parties in the Senate because each side realizes that its position could change after the next election. Before discussing the consequences of Senate elections for the leadership and decision-making processes of the Senate, however, we need to summarize the factors that, based on the analyses presented in the preceding chapters, appear to explain the competitiveness of recent Senate elections.

Explaining Competition

Without question, the most important factor contributing to the level of competition in recent Senate elections has been the quality of Senate challengers.

The opportunity to serve in this powerful and exclusive legislative body has attracted many ambitious politicians, including governors and other statewide officeholders, mayors of large cities, and numerous members of the House of Representatives. In contrast, virtually no members have left the Senate to seek any office except the presidency and vice presidency.

With its six-year term and membership of only 100, the Senate stands near the top of the opportunity structure of U.S. politics.[3] Moreover, at least two recent developments have enhanced the attractiveness of the Senate for ambitious politicians: the decentralization of the Senate's internal power structure since the 1950s and the continued role of the Senate as an incubator of presidential and vice presidential candidates.

Scholars who studied the U.S. Senate during the decade following the end of World War II portrayed it as an oligarchical institution dominated by an "inner club" of senior conservative Republicans and southern Democrats. Junior members were expected to serve a lengthy apprenticeship before wielding real influence, and mavericks who violated the Senate's informal norms were excluded from key positions.[4] By the mid-1960s, however, rules changes and an influx of new members had obliterated the old inner club and junior members were rapidly becoming full participants in the Senate's decision-making process. With more subcommittees than members and with rules that allowed any member to tie floor proceedings in procedural knots, every Senator had the potential to exert considerable influence over legislation.[5]

The democratization of the Senate has certainly enhanced the attractiveness of a Senate career for ambitious politicians. Moreover, since the 1950s, the Senate has been a leading incubator of presidential and vice presidential candidates. The reformed presidential nominating process that has existed since 1972 gives an advantage to candidates who can attract national media coverage—something that is usually easier for Senators than for members of the House of Representatives or governors. Although George McGovern (in 1972) was the last member of the Senate to win his party's presidential nomination, several strong candidates have emerged from the Senate since then, including Birch Bayh (D-Indiana) and Frank Church (D-Idaho) in 1976, Edward Kennedy (D-Massachusetts) in 1980, Gary Hart (D-Colorado) in 1984, and Albert Gore, Jr. (D-Tennessee) and Robert Dole (R-Kansas) in 1988. Moreover, successful presidential candidates have frequently looked

---

3. Joseph A. Schlesinger, *Ambition and Politics: Political Careers in the United States* (Chicago: Rand McNally, 1966), 22–36.

4. The classic study of the Senate during this period is Donald R. Matthews, *U.S. Senators and Their World* (Chapel Hill: University of North Carolina Press, 1960); see also William S. White, *Citadel: The Story of the United States Senate* (New York: Harper and Brothers, 1956).

5. For a comprehensive discussion of the changes in the Senate, see Barbara Sinclair, *The Transformation of the U.S. Senate* (Baltimore: Johns Hopkins University Press, 1989); see also Michael Foley, *The New Senate* (New Haven: Yale University Press, 1980).

to the Senate when choosing their running mates. Walter Mondale (D-Minnesota) and Robert Dole in 1976, and Lloyd Bentsen (D-Texas) and Dan Quayle (R-Indiana) in 1988 were sitting Senators when they were selected to run for the vice presidency. The role of the Senate as a springboard for presidential and vice presidential candidates has enhanced the attractiveness of a Senate career for ambitious politicians.

Although many successful Senate candidates have been experienced politicians, it has not only been experienced politicians who have found the Senate an attractive career option. A number of celebrities and multimillionaires have also run for the Senate in recent years, and several have been successful. The membership of the Senate has included former astronauts (John Glenn, D-Ohio, and Harrison Schmidt, R-New Mexico), professional athletes (Bill Bradley, D-New Jersey), and heirs to some of the nation's largest fortunes (John Heinz, R-Pennsylvania, and Jay Rockefeller, D-West Virginia).[6]

What all of the millionaires, celebrities, and officeholders who ran for the Senate had in common, and what, according to our results, primarily explains their success as Senate candidates, was their ability to amass large campaign war chests. The cost of running an effective Senate campaign varies considerably from state to state, depending on such factors as geographic size, population, and the number of major media markets in the state. By the late 1980s, however, a challenger in a small state such as Delaware or Rhode Island typically had to spend over a million dollars in order to have a realistic chance of winning, while a challenger in California, New York, or Texas had to spend at least ten times that amount in order to wage a creditable campaign against an entrenched incumbent.

The main reason for the rapid increase in the cost of running for the Senate during the 1980s was the increasing use and cost of television advertising. As our case studies of four 1986 Senate contests clearly demonstrated, television advertising has become the primary method by which Senate candidates communicate with the voters, even in such sparsely populated states as South Dakota.

Television advertising is especially important for Senate challengers, because it makes it possible for challengers to make themselves and their messages known to large numbers of voters. At the beginning of the campaign, the incumbent usually enjoys a large advantage in recognition over the challenger. The perquisites of incumbency make it possible for senators to conduct what amounts to a continuous campaign for reelection.[7] Especially

---

6. See David T. Canon, *Actors, Athletes, and Astronauts: Political Amateurs in the United States Congress* (Chicago: University of Chicago Press, 1990).

7. See David R. Mayhew, *Congress: The Electoral Connection* (New Haven: Yale University Press, 1974).

during the last two years of their terms, Senators are prone to make frequent trips home to "campaign" at taxpayer expense and to inundate their states with newsletters extolling their virtues. Senators are also inclined, during the final two years of their terms, to bring their voting records more closely in line with the views of their state's voters.[8] As Hubert Humphrey (D-Minnesota) once explained, "the first four years are for God and country, but the last two are for the folks back home."

For the first approximately five-and-a-half years of their terms, Senators enjoy a virtual monopoly in explaining their performance to the voters. Barring a scandal, little or no critical information is likely to reach the voters in their home states. It is only during the few months of the campaign that the voters are likely to receive any information critical of the incumbent's performance in office, and the challenger plays a crucial role in providing that information. One of the most important findings that emerged from our analysis of voters' evaluations of Senate candidates is that exposure to the challenger is by far the strongest predictor of negative evaluations of incumbent Senators.

You cannot beat a horse with no horse, and you cannot beat a congressional incumbent with an unknown challenger. Given a choice between a mediocre incumbent and an unknown challenger, the large majority of voters will choose the incumbent. One of the most important differences between Senate and House elections, and the major reason for the greater vulnerability of Senate incumbents, is the visiblity of the challenger, and the main reason Senate challengers are much more visible than House challengers is their ability to use television.

Not only can Senate challengers better afford to buy advertising time on television than their House counterparts, but they are also much more likely to receive free exposure in the printed and electronic media. A clever Senate challenger with a small campaign budget can use free media exposure to multiply the impact of his or her paid advertising, as Paul Wellstone demonstrated in his successful challenge to Senator Rudy Boschwitz (R-Minnesota) in 1990. With a total campaign budget of only $1.3 million, Wellstone was able to purchase only a few spots on Minneapolis television, but his advertisements were so clever that they were replayed numerous times on local news broadcasts, allowing Wellstone to reach a much wider audience.

The second major factor contributing to the competitiveness of Senate elections in recent years has been a decline in party identification and loyalty in the U.S. electorate that has led to increased interparty competition at the state level. During the 1940s and 1950s, there were many states whose Senate

---

8. Richard C. Elling, "Ideological Change in the U.S. Senate: Time and Electoral Responsiveness," *Legislative Studies Quarterly* 7 (1982): 75–92.

seats could be considered safe for one party or the other. Even after the demise of the solid South in presidential elections, that region's Senate delegation remained solidly Democratic for many years. The first Republican senator ever elected from a southern state was John Tower of Texas in a 1961 special election to fill the seat left vacant by Lyndon Johnson's election as vice president. During this period, many states in the Midwest and New England were almost as safe for the Republicans as the southern states were for the Democrats. States such as Maine, Vermont, New Hampshire, North and South Dakota, Indiana, Iowa, Kansas, and Nebraska consistently sent Republicans to the Senate. Between 1940 and 1956, only two Democrats were elected to the Senate from these nine states, and one of these Democrats served for only two months.

Between the 1950s and the 1980s, the decline of party loyalties in the electorate and the rise of candidate-centered, media-based Senate campaigns meant that the importance of party labels in determining the outcomes of Senate elections decreased dramatically. As a result, two-party competition spread to states that were once safely Democratic or Republican. By 1991, every southern State except Louisiana had elected at least one Republican Senator and the GOP held seven of the twenty-two Senate seats from the old Confederacy—down from a peak of eleven following the 1980 election. Similarly, every one of the nine once solidly Republican states listed in the preceding paragraph elected at least one Democrat to the Senate between 1958 and 1990, and Democrats held eight of the eighteen seats from these states at the beginning of 1991.

The fact that no state can be considered truly safe for either party has encouraged ambitious politicians, regardless of party affiliation, to run for the Senate in general elections. At the same time, this trend has probably contributed to a decline in competition in Senate primary elections. In the past, an ambitious politician in a one-party state had no choice but to seek office within the dominant party, even if that meant challenging an incumbent in the primary. Since the 1960s, however, competition has shifted from the primary of the once-dominant party—the Democrats in the South, the Republicans in the Midwest and New England—to the general election.

Our examination of recent Senate elections uncovered another factor that has contributed to competition—the impact of national issues such as the popularity of the incumbent president and the state of the economy. There is no question, for example, that voter discontent with economic conditions and with the Carter administration's handling of the Iran hostage crisis was largely responsible for the Republican takeover of the Senate in the 1980 election. Nine Democratic incumbents lost their seats in 1980 as the GOP scored a net gain of twelve seats in the Senate—the largest shift in Senate seats since 1958.

What has perhaps not been recognized by students of Senate elections is that national issues can strongly influence the outcomes of individual Senate races even when they do not strongly favor one party at the national level. In 1986, for example, neither economic conditions nor public evaluations of the Reagan administration gave a decisive advantage to either party. The Democrats' gain of eight seats in the 1986 Senate elections was largely a result of the vulnerability of a number of the first-term GOP incumbents who rode into office on Ronald Reagan's coattails in 1980. Without any help from the top of the ticket in 1986, seven of these Republican freshmen lost their seats.

National issues did have strong effects on the outcomes of several individual Senate contests in 1986, but these effects depended on local economic conditions and the positions taken by the Senate candidates. Our examination of data from a number of state exit polls in 1986 demonstrated that voters' evaluations of economic conditions and Ronald Reagan's job performance varied widely. In some states, such as Florida and California, rapid economic growth and the popularity of the Reagan administration helped GOP Senate candidates, even though the Republicans lost both of those contests. In other states, such as North and South Dakota, a depressed farm economy and poor evaluations of the president's job performance clearly hurt the chances of the Republican Senate candidate.

The effects of national issues on Senate elections depended not only on local economic conditions, but also on the positions taken on these issues by the Senate candidates. In the 1986 South Dakota Senate race, for example, the Republican incumbent, James Abdnor, was badly hurt by his support for the Reagan administration's farm policies and by his statement that farmers might have to sell their crops below cost for a period of time. Other Republican Senators from neighboring farm states with equally serious economic problems, such as Charles Grassley of Iowa and Robert Dole of Kansas, strongly criticized the administration's agricultural policies and breezed to victory.

One additional factor that contributed to competition in a number of Senate contests was ideological misrepresentation. Our analysis of the outcomes of Senate elections demonstrated that the distance between an incumbent's voting record and the views of the electorate in his or her state had a significant impact on the results of these contests: the greater the distance, the less support the incumbent received, with all other factors held constant. Although some senators did attempt to bring their voting records into line with the views of the voters during the last two years of their terms, there were a number of clear cases of ideological misrepresentation—senators whose ideological positions were far out of line with the views of a state's voters. A number of these ideological misfits, such as George McGovern (D-South Dakota) and Frank Church (D-Idaho) managed to survive for more than one term thanks to favorable national conditions at election time, weak opposition, or a reputation for effective constituent service. Eventually, however, almost all of them were defeated.

True ideological misfits are exceptional in the Senate. A less dramatic type of ideological misrepresentation appears to be fairly common, however. According to our results, the ideological positions of most senators were more extreme than the views of their state's voters. Most Republican senators were more conservative than their state's voters, while most Democratic senators were more liberal than their state's voters. Most incumbents could have improved their electoral prospects by taking a more moderate ideological position. This finding raises the question of what explains ideological misrepresentation.

A partial explanation for ideological misrepresentation may be provided by Fenno's model of the constituency.[9] According to this model, certain parts of a member's constituency are more politically significant than others. Fenno calls the most politically significant parts of the constituency the "reelection" constituency and the "primary" constituency: these consist of voters who support the member in a general election or a primary election. It is very likely that the views of voters who make up a senator's or House member's reelection and primary constituencies differ from those of the entire electorate. Most Republicans' reelection and primary constituencies will be more conservative than the electorate, while most Democrats' reelection and primary constituencies will be more liberal than the electorate.

In addition to the pull of the reelection and primary constituencies, there is an additional factor that appears to contribute to ideological misrepresentation in the Senate—presidential ambition. The reformed presidential nominating process requires candidates to obtain the support of party activists and presidential primary voters, especially in those states that hold early caucuses and primaries such as Iowa and New Hampshire, and these activists and primary voters tend to be more ideologically extreme than the general public.[10] This system appears to favor liberal Democrats and conservative Republicans over more moderate candidates in each party. Thus, ideologically moderate senators with presidential ambitions may be tempted to shift their positions to the left, in the case of Democrats, or to the right, in the case of Republicans, even if this increases their distance from their own state's electorate. Presidential ambitions appear to have contributed to some of the most extreme cases of ideological misrepresentation during the 1970s and 1980s.

Although the number of Senators actively pursuing the presidency at any

---

9. See Richard F. Fenno, *Home Style: House Members in Their Districts* (Boston: Little, Brown, 1978), 1–30.

10. See James I. Lengle, *Representation and Presidential Primaries* (Westport, Conn.: Greenwood Press, 1981): see also William Crotty and John S. Jackson III, *Presidential Primaries and Nominations* (Washington, D.C.: Congressional Quarterly Press, 1985).

given time may be fairly small, the number who have presidential aspirations will usually be much larger and the anticipation of a presidential campaign may cause some of these senators to adjust their ideological positions accordingly. Thus, at the beginning of 1991, there was considerable speculation that Senator Sam Nunn (D-Georgia) had shifted to a pro choice stance on abortion and adopted a relatively dovish position on the Persian Gulf crisis in anticipation of a run for the Democratic presidential nomination in 1992. (Ultimately, Nunn did not seek the Democratic nomination.)

Senate Elections and Electoral Accountability

Electoral accountability is essential to the well-being of a representative democracy. Unless leaders can be held accountable for their actions by the voters, they will have little reason to act in accordance with the wishes and interests of the public. To be meaningful, however, electoral accountability requires effective competition. Challengers must not only be allowed to criticize the performance of incumbent officeholders, but to communicate these criticisms to the public so that voters can make an informed choice.

In recent decades, U.S. congressional elections have fallen far short of the ideal of representative democracy when it comes to effective competition. During the 1980s, at least three-fourths of all House incumbents and close to half of all Senate incumbents were either unopposed or faced only token opposition in general elections. The basic problem was that the challengers in these races were financially uncompetitive.

By 1990, the cost of waging a serious challenge to a House incumbent was at least $500,000, but more than half of all challengers spent less than $50,000. The costs of running a campaign have increased more rapidly than the overall rate of inflation, but, between 1980 and 1990, average spending by House challengers actually decreased by more than 30 percent in real dollars.[11]

By 1990, the cost of waging a serious challenge to a Senate incumbent varied between a million dollars in the least populous states to ten million dollars or more in the most populous states. Senate challengers, at least until recently, have done far better than their House counterparts when it comes to keeping up with the rising costs of campaigning. According to the information presented in chapter 7, between 1980 and 1986, average spending by Senate challengers increased by more than 50 percent in real dollars. Nevertheless, many Senate challengers in recent elections have been woefully underfinanced, allowing potentially vulnerable incumbents to triumph by default.

---

11. Alan I. Abramowitz, "Incumbency, Campaign Spending, and the Decline of Competition in U.S. House Elections," *Journal of Politics* 53 (1991): 48–49.

The case of New York's Alphonse D'Amato, described in chapter 5, is an excellent example of this problem. D'Amato's challenger in 1986, consumer advocate Mark Green, spent slightly more than a million dollars—not enough to make much of an impression on the electorate in a state such as New York. Meanwhile, D'Amato spent over twelve million dollars on his campaign and breezed to victory with 57 percent of the vote. A better financed challenger might very well have defeated D'Amato or at least made the race competitive.

Until recently it appeared that Senate challengers, unlike their House counterparts, were at least keeping up with the inflation in campaign costs. This trend may not continue indefinitely, however. In 1988, average spending by Senate challengers remained at about the same level as in the previous two elections. In 1990, average spending by Senate challengers declined and a large number of challengers were woefully underfinanced. Lack of adequate financing certainly contributed to the difficulties experienced by challengers in both 1988 and 1990: only three Senate incumbents—Chic Hecht (R-Nevada), John Melcher (D-Montana), and Lowell Weicker (R-Connecticut)—were defeated in 1988, and only one incumbent—Rudy Boschwitz (R-Minnesota)—lost in 1990. In fact, Senate incumbents enjoyed a higher rate of reelection in 1990 than their House counterparts—97 percent of Senate incumbents were successful compared with "only" 96 percent of House incumbents. The large majority of these victorious incumbents won by decisive margins: nineteen of the thirty Senate incumbents running for reelection in 1990 won by a margin of at least 20 percentage points, and only six won by a margin of less than 10 percentage points.

It would be a mistake to read too much significance into the results of the 1988 and 1990 elections. These two elections may prove to be aberrations from the recent pattern of competition for Senate seats. In this regard, the 1992 Senate elections should be an interesting test. The Senate class that is up for reelection in 1992 has experienced high rates of turnover in its two most recent elections in 1980 and 1986. In 1992, the Democrats will be defending twenty of the thirty-four seats at stake—thirty-three regular seats plus a special election in California to fill the unexpired term of Pete Wilson, who resigned from the Senate after his election as governor. If national conditions are favorable, meaning that President Bush enjoys a high approval rating and the economy is growing, the GOP may have a chance of picking up the six seats necessary to regain control of the Senate. If the economy fails to rebound and the President's approval rating remains below 50 percent, however, the Republicans will be hard pressed to hold onto the seats that they now control.

Regardless of what happens in 1992, however, there are reasons for concern about the future of competition in Senate elections. The largest potential problem is that the rising cost of running for the Senate may deter potentially strong challengers from running. In order to raise the money required to wage an intensive media campaign in a populous state, even incumbent senators must begin raising money several years before the end of their terms. In recent years, several incumbents, such as Lawton Chiles of Florida, have cited the demands of almost constant fund-raising as a major deterrent to remaining in the Senate. The need to amass huge campaign war chests apparently also contributed to the willingness of five members of the Senate—Alan Cranston (D-California), Dennis DeConcini (D-Arizona), John Glenn (D-Ohio), Donald Riegle (D-Michigan), and John McCain (R-Arizona)—to engage in extraordinary efforts to assist Charles Keating, president of the notorious Lincoln Savings and Loan Association, in his dealings with federal regulators.

While fund-raising has become an increasingly onerous task for incumbents, the average challenger, even one who has held public office, cannot hope to match the incumbent's spending dollar for dollar. Fortunately, according to our results, this is not necessary. In fact, based on the findings reported in chapter 4, challenger spending, although subject to diminishing marginal returns, has a much stronger impact on the outcomes of Senate contests than incumbent spending. Nevertheless, a challenger usually must spend several million dollars in order to have a realistic chance of defeating an incumbent senator.

In order for Senate elections to remain competitive in the future, challengers must be allowed to raise and spend as much money as it takes to communicate with the electorate through the mass media. Ceilings on campaign spending, which have been proposed as a method of reducing the burden of fund-raising on Senate candidates, might well exacerbate the advantage of incumbency and reduce competition. The same thing is true of proposals to eliminate campaign contributions by political action committees (PACs). Democracy is expensive. In the absence of generous public financing, competition can best be insured by making it easier for challengers to raise money. When it comes to competition in congressional elections, in the words of Reverend Ike, "money is not the root of all evil—lack of money is the root of all evil."

Competitive elections are a necessary, but not sufficient, condition for effective accountability in a representative democracy. In a legislative body such as the Senate, competition between incumbents and challengers only insures that legislators can be held accountable by their constituents for their individual actions. It does not guarantee that legislators can be held accountable for the collective performance of the legislative body or the government as a whole. This sort of collective accountability requires some mechanism by which voters can assign responsibility for the overall performance of the legislature or the government. The principal mechanism that can provide collective accountability of this sort is the political party.

In a legislature whose members are elected separately from individual districts, there is inevitably a problem with enforcing collective accountability. Citizens can only vote for or against the incumbent from their own district, but their well-being depends on the decisions made by the entire legislature. The solution to this problem is for voters to judge their own incumbent as a member of a party team—either the government team or the opposition team.

In the U.S. political system, it is very difficult for voters to enforce collective accountability on members of Congress. In the first place, most voters know very little about what Congress has been doing collectively. Many do not even know which party controls the House and Senate.[12] Most voters do have meaningful opinions about the president's performance, but, in recent years, Congress and the presidency have frequently been controlled by different parties.

Despite these obstacles to collective accountability, however, national issues do affect the outcomes of congressional elections. Voters reward or punish the president by voting for or against his party's congressional candidates. According to the evidence presented in chapter 4, evaluations of presidential performance affect the fortunes of the president's party in Senate elections both directly and indirectly, through their impact on evaluations of party competence. Economic conditions also have an indirect effect on the outcomes of Senate elections through their influence on party competence evaluations. The stronger the performance of the economy and the more popular the incumbent president, the more seats the president's party can expect to win.

Economic conditions and the popularity of the incumbent president also affect the outcomes of House elections.[13] However, because of the overwhelming advantage of incumbency in House elections, the magnitide of this effect appears to be much smaller. That is, the proportion of the seats at stake that would be expected to change parties as a result of a specific increase or decrease in the president's approval rating or the gross national product is much smaller in the House than in the Senate. Furthermore, because the division of seats between the parties has been much closer in the Senate than

---

12. See Donald E. Stokes and Warren E. Miller, "Party Government and the Saliency of Congress," in *Elections and the Political Order*, ed. Angus Campbell, Philip E. Converse, Warren E. Miller, and Donald E. Stokes (New York: Wiley, 1966), 194–211.

13. See Edward R. Tufte, "Determinants of the Outcomes of Midterm Congressional Elections," *American Political Science Review* 69 (1975): 812–26; see also Alan I. Abramowitz, "National Issues, Strategic Politicians, and Voting Behavior in the 1980 and 1982 Elections," *American Journal of Political Science* 28 (1984): 710–21.

in the House, national issues are much more likely to produce a change in party control in the Senate.

All of this means that senators are likely to experience a stronger sense of collective responsibility for national policies than members of the House. Not only does their individual survival depend more on national political forces, but their status as members of the majority or minority party in the Senate depends on those forces. In the House of Representatives, the Democratic party has been in the majority since 1955. At the beginning of 1991, not a single Republican member of the House of Representatives had ever had the opportunity to chair a committee or subcommittee, and there appears to be little chance that any of them will get that chance in the near future. In the Senate, in contrast, most of the members had experienced at least one change in party control and many had experienced two such changes. Another change in control in the near future is a real possibility.

Senate Elections, Leadership, and Decision Making

In our opinion, the characteristics of Senate elections have had important consequences for the style of leadership and the decision-making processes that have characterized the Senate in recent years. Specifically, we believe that alternation in party control and a sense of collective accountability for national policies have contributed to the development of a more consensual style of leadership and a more responsible approach to legislative decision making in the Senate than in the House of Representatives.

While the Senate and House both experienced fairly high levels of partisan conflict on major issues and increased party-line voting during the Reagan and Bush years, the styles of leadership practiced in the two chambers differ markedly. In the House, the Democratic leadership has used its control of the rules and procedures to minimize the influence of the minority party. The Republicans, for their part, have responded by engaging in legislative guerilla warfare—seeking to undermine Democratic policies rather than trying to shape those policies to their own liking. This strategy was epitomized by the selection, in 1989, of Newt Gingrich of Georgia as the chief GOP whip, the second-ranking Republican leader, in the House. Gingrich is known as the leading advocate of a confrontational approach in dealing with the Democrats. The result of all of this is that, since Ronald Reagan's initial legislative successes during 1981, both Reagan and his successor, George Bush, have had great difficulty getting their legislative proposals considered, let alone enacted, by the House of Representatives. Even when Democratic and Republican leaders have agreed on a compromise, they have not always been able to bring their respective party's rank and file along.

In the Senate, in contrast, the leaders of the majority party—the Republicans between 1981 and 1987 and the Democrats since 1987—have generally followed a policy of consulting with the minority leadership with regard to such matters as scheduling and setting the rules for debate. As a result, partisan rancor has been kept to a minimum and legislative compromises have been facilitated. Furthermore, agreements between majority and minority party leaders have generally been supported by the members.

A stronger sense of collective accountability appears to have contributed to a greater sense of personal responsibility for legislative decisions among Senators than among members of Congress. Senators, no less than members of Congress, are concerned about the consequences of national policies for their own constituents, and some Senators place a great deal of emphasis on constituent service. New York's Alphonse D'Amato was given the nickname "Senator Pothole" because of his reputation for constituent service. In dealing with major issues, however, Senators do appear to be more willing than House members to look beyond the immediate reaction of the voters in their own state and to weigh the consequences of their actions for the well-being of the nation.

A good example of the difference in the way the two chambers deal with national issues was provided by the outcome of the 1990 budget agreement with the Bush administration. After weeks of difficult negotiations, House and Senate leaders from both parties reached an agreement with the administration on a plan to reduce the deficit that included both tax increases and cuts in popular domestic programs. On the House side, however, neither party's leaders could keep their troops in line and the agreement was overwhelmingly defeated. Newt Gingrich, the second-ranking GOP leader in the House, voted against the agreement. After it was defeated in the House, the initial budget resolution never came to a vote in the Senate. There was little question that the resolution would have passed easily, however, and a watered-down resolution later sailed through the Senate after barely receiving a majority in the House.[14]

Faced with a semipermanent Democratic majority and Republican minority, members of both parties in the House have little motivation to consider the national consequences of their actions. In the absence of any sense of personal responsibility for legislative results, individualism tends to run rampant. While localism and individualism abound in the Senate as well as the House, the real possibility of a change in party control means that senators must be concerned about the reputations of their parties. Ironically, the competitiveness of Senate elections may force senators to consider the consequences of their actions for the nation as well as for their own constituents.

---

14. For an analysis of the politics of the 1990 budget negotiations, see *Congressional Quarterly Weekly Report*, October 6, 1990, 3183–204.

Appendixes

APPENDIX A

Measuring Senate Campaign Spending

Incumbent and challenger campaign spending were adjusted in order to correct for both inflation and differences in state population and to allow for diminishing returns on expenditures.

To correct for inflation, spending was measured in constant (1974) dollars.

To correct for differences in state population, we first estimated the impact of population on spending in Senate elections by regressing both challenger and incumbent spending on state population. We found that both challenger and incumbent spending were highly responsive to differences in state population, but that they also reflected costs that are relatively constant across all states. Therefore, we corrected for differences in state population by dividing each candidate's inflation-adjusted spending by a state-specific cost factor equal to the number of House districts in a state plus a constant (10) derived from the regression analyses. The state cost factor thus ranged from 11, for the least populous states, to 55, for California. According to this approach, a Senate campaign in California costs about five times as much as an equivalent campaign in Delaware or Wyoming.

To allow for diminishing returns on spending, we used the natural logarithm of incumbent and challenger spending, after adjusting for inflation and differences in state population.

In open seat races, our spending variable was the difference between the natural logarithm of the Democratic candidate's spending and the natural logarithm of the Republican candidate's spending, after adjusting both figures for inflation and state population.

APPENDIX B

Special Conditions Affecting Incumbents in Senate Elections, 1974–86

Year	State	Party	Candidate	Type	Description
1974	CO	R	Dominick	H	Difficulty walking due to back injury
1974	CO	R	Dominick	C	Handling of contributions from milk producers while chairman of Republican Senate Campaign Committee
1974	KA	R	Dole	C	Outspoken support for President Nixon while chairman of Republican National Committee
1974	SD	D	McGovern	C	Disastrous presidential campaign
1976	IN	D	Hartke	C	Excessive foreign travel
1976	MD	R	Beall	C	Secret $250,000 campaign contribution from White House in 1970
1976	NV	D	Cannon	C	Gifts and campaign contributions from corporations concerned with subcommittee
1976	NM	D	Montoya	S	Use of staff to manage business properties; space leased to post office in shopping center owned by senator; tax audit blocked
1978	MA	R	Brooke	S	Lied about financial worth in divorce proceedings; mother received $72,000 in fraudulent medicaid payments
1978	MI	R	Griffin	C	Announced retirement from Senate, then changed his mind
1978	WV	D	Randolph	C	Waffling on Panama Canal Treaty
1980	AZ	R	Goldwater	H	Hip ailment, difficulty walking
1980	GA	D	Talmadge	S	Financial misconduct and alcoholism
1980	WA	D	Magnuson	H	Difficulty walking and inability to campaign actively
1984	IA	R	Jepsen	S	Membership in "health spa" used for prostitution
1984	OR	R	Hatfield	C	Wife received $55,000 for real estate work for Greek financier backing African oil pipeline supported by senator
1986	ID	R	Symms	C	Personal eccentricities; alleged drunkenness on Senate floor

(*continued*)

Year	State	Party	Candidate	Type	Description
1986	NY	R	D'Amato	C	Contributions from brokerage firms while chairman of securities subcommittee
1986	ND	R	Andrews	C	Use of private detectives to investigate opponents; controversial medical malpractice lawsuit
1986	SD	R	Abdnor	C	"Misstatements" regarding farm problems
1986	WA	R	Gorton	C	Vote trading on judicial appointments
1986	WI	R	Kasten	S	Arrest for drunken driving; association with fraudulent real estate deal; failure to file income tax returns

Note: C = controversy; H = health problems; S = scandal.

APPENDIX C

Celebrity Challengers in Senate Elections, 1974–86

Year	State	Party	Candidate	Previous Activities
1974	SD	R	Thorsness	Vietnam POW
1976	CA	R	Hayakawa	President of San Francisco State University involved in highly publicized confrontation with student demonstrators
1976	NM	R	Schmitt	Astronaut
1976	NY	D	Moynihan	White House advisor, ambassador to India, UN ambassador
1984	MI	R	Lousma	Astronaut

Index

ABC News, 67, 148, 162–63, 166, 180–81, 187, 203–4, 206, 222–23
Abdnor, James, 44, 87n, 103, 145–46, 185, 207–25, 233
Abortion, 156, 178, 188, 209
Abourezk, James, 208
Abraham, Henry, 71n
Abramowitz, Alan, 87n, 93n, 95n, 101n, 108n, 139n, 238n
Abrams, Robert, 171
Abramson, Paul, 164n
Abzug, Bella, 168
ADA scores. *See* Americans for Democratic Action (ADA) scores
Adair, John, 20–21
Adams, Ansel, 155, 157
Adams, Brock, 195n
Adams, John, 14
Adams, John Quincy, 14
AFL-CIO, 4, 80–81, 150
Age, 28–29, 32
Ailes, Roger, 174
Air Force One, 195
Alabama Democratic Office, 73
Alabama Power Company, 71
Aldrich, John, 164n
Allen, James, 71–72
Allen, Maryon, 56, 71
Alliance for Justice, 3
Almanac of American Politics, 79, 123n, 142n, 147, 186
Altman, Robert, 154
Alvarez, R. Michael, 53

Ambition, 52–54, 229–30, 232, 234–35
American Civil Liberties Union, 4
American Conservative Union (ACU), 62
American Electronics Association, 150
American Independent Party, 79
Americans for Democratic Action (ADA) scores, 57–58 (Fulbright), 61–62 (Case), 66–67 (Javits), 72 (Stewart), 75–76 (Gravel), 79–80 (Stone), 86, 91 (Hatfield), 150 (Cranston), 167–68 (D'Amato), 169 (Bill Green), 188 (Hawkins), 208 (Abdnor)
Amlong, William, 81n
Anchorage Times, 76
Anderson, Jack, 73–74
Anderson, Paul, 191n, 192n, 193n, 194n, 195n, 197n, 200n, 202n
Andrus, Cecil, 76
Antonovich, Mike, 153–55, 157
Apple, R. W., 2n
Arkansas Gazette, 57n, 58n, 59, 61
Articles of Confederation, 8
Ashbrook, John, 62
Asher, Herbert, 28n
Asians, 147, 165
Associated Press, 64
AWACS, 150

Bacon, Augustus, 22
Bafalis, Skip, 189
Baldwin, Abraham, 9
Bale, Richard, 211, 216n

247

248   Index

Balzar, John, 153n, 154n, 155n, 156n, 157n, 159n, 160n, 161n, 162n
Bancroft, George, 8n, 9n, 11n
Banks, Jeffrey S., 53n
Baron, Dempsey, 189
Barone, Michael, 57n, 58n, 61n, 66n, 72n, 75n, 76n, 79n, 147n, 148n, 149n, 165n, 166n, 168n, 185n, 186n, 189n, 206n
"Bartles and Jaymes," 162
Bartlett, Charles, 21
Bartlett, E. L., 74
Basile, Philip, 177
Baucus, Max, 56n
Bauman, Robert, 62
Bayh, Birch, 137, 229
Beatty, Warren, 174
Behr, Roy, 216
Belafonte, Harry, 170–71
Bell, Jeffrey, 56, 61–65, 68, 83–84
Bentsen, Lloyd, 230
Berke, Richard, 4n
Berkman, Michael, 58n
Bernard, Charles, 60
Bevill, Tom, 72
Biden, Joseph, 1, 3–4, 155
Bird, Rose, 148, 152, 158, 160–62
Birmingham News, 72, 74n
Birmingham School of Law, 72
Blacks, 5–6, 29, 32–33, 57, 73, 147, 161, 163–65, 181–82, 203–4
Blanket primary, 51
Blumenthal, Sidney, 196n
Borah, William, 22
Boren, David, 125
Bork, Robert, 1–6
Boschwitz, Rudy, 70n, 119, 231, 236
Bowman, Tom, 202n
Boyd, Gerald, 1n, 162n
Brace, Paul, 53
Bradley, Bill, 65, 107, 119, 191, 230
Brady, David W., 58n
Bragdon, Peter, 211, 213n
Brandes, Sara L., 102n
Braun, Carol Mosely, 84

Brearly, David, 7
Breaux, John, 5–6
Bridges, Lloyd, 155
Bristow, Joseph, 22–23
Brody, Richard, 58n
Brokaw, Chet, 213n
Brooke, Edward, 88–89, 104–5, 111
Brooks, J. R., 73
Brown, Jerry (Edmund G.), 106–7, 148
Browne, Moan Z., 192n
Brown v. Board of Education, 57
Broyhill, James, 2–3
Bryan, William Jennings, 17, 25
Buckley, James, 62, 103, 166
Buckley, William F., 62, 168
Buckley v. Valeo (1976), 124–25, 137
Buenker, John D., 23n
Buffalo, 166
Bumpers, Dale, 56, 58–61, 71, 83–84
Burdick, Quentin, 116, 118
Burkart, Michael P., 108n, 139n
Burke, Edmund, 111
Burks, Edward C., 64n
Bush, George, 60, 63n, 99–100, 138, 239–40
　California Senate election (1986), 159
　Florida Senate election (1986), 191, 194–95
　New York Senate election (1986), 173–74
Byrd, Robert, 1, 74

Caldeira, Gregory A., 31n
California, 1986 (Cranston vs. Zschau), 145–65
　abortion rights, 156
　Asians, 147
　Bird, Rose, 148, 152, 158, 160–62
　blacks, 147, 161, 163–64
　Bush, George, 159
　campaign finance, 145, 152, 154–55, 158–61
　capital gains differential, 150
　challenger quality, 145, 152–53, 157, 165

Contras, 156, 158
Cranston, Alan (background), 149–50
death penalty, 152, 161
debates, 160–61
economic conditions, 149, 162
environment, 152, 157, 160, 164
gender, 163
Hispanics, 147, 161
ideology, 148, 150–52, 156–57, 159, 161–64
incumbent advantage, 152, 160, 165
Israel, 150, 159–60
issues, 159–60, 162–64
Jews, 159
mass media, 145, 154–57, 158
MX missile, 156, 158
national political conditions, 164–65
nuclear arms control, 156, 158
partisanship, 148, 163–64
party competence, 149
personal controversies, 155, 164
personal popularity, 164
presidential approval/popularity, 149
Proposition 65, 159
Reagan, Ronald, 146, 149, 159–62
Republican primary campaign, 153–57
Saudi Arabian arms sales, 159
South Africa, 160
state political characteristics, 147–49, 164
Strategic Defense Initiative, 156
television, 145, 155–57, 161–62, 165
whites, 163–64
Zschau, Ed (background), 150–51
California Democratic Council (CDC), 149
California Poll, 160–61
Call, Wilkinson, 13
Cameron, Charles M., 57n, 86n
Campaign finance, 6, 87–92, 107–9, 113–14, 123–43, 235–37
  California Senate election (1986), 152, 154–55 , 158–61

candidate self-financing, 132–34
coordinated expenditures by party committees, 123, 132
finance laws, 124–25
Florida Senate election (1986), 191, 194–96
fund-raising for candidates, 123, 126–27, 131–37
independent expenditures, 123, 137–39, 143, 213
New York Senate election (1986), 169–74, 183
partisan spending ratio, 128–31
political action committee spending, 131–37
sources of campaign funds, 131–39
South Dakota Senate election (1986), 210, 212–14, 217
spending limits (reforms), 141–43, 237
strategic decision making by parties, 128–30
Campaign intensity, 30–31
Campbell, Angus, 238n
Campbell, James E., 94n
Candidate preference, 33–43
Candidate quality, 54, 84, 89–92, 100–101, 106–9, 111–13, 231, 235–37
Cannon, Howard, 88–89
Cannon, Lou, 57n, 60n, 162n
Canon, David T., 53, 230n
Carroll, Maurice, 68n, 69n, 70n
Carswell, G. Harrold, 57
Carter, Jimmy, 1–2, 71, 150, 186–87, 200, 202, 207, 213–14
Carter Administration, 75–76, 130, 232
Case, Clifford, 54, 56, 61–66, 83, 92
Catholics, 203
Chaffee, John, 70n, 188
Challenger (space shuttle), 193
Challengers, 235–37
  celebrity challengers, 100–101, 107, 109, 112–13
  spending, 107–9, 113, 126, 128–37, 237

250 Index

Challengers (continued)
 challenger quality, 100–101, 107,
  109, 112–13, 145, 152–53,
  157, 165, 171–72, 177, 183,
  190, 205, 209
Chiles, Lawton, 237
Christian Voice, 4
Church, Frank, 111, 137, 229, 233
Civil Rights Act of 1964, 57
Civil Rights-Civil Liberties Law Review,
 168
Clark, William, 17
Clarke, Paul, 153–54
Clarke, Peter, 100n
Cleveland, Grover, 17
Closed primary, 51
Clymer, Adam, 65n
Coffey, John, 80
Cohen, William, 70n
Collective accountability, 239–40
Columbia University, 66, 75, 78
Commerce Department, 168
Communicating for Agriculture, 215
Congress Watch, 66, 168
Congressional Quarterly, 19n, 54, 213,
 221
Congressional Quarterly Weekly Report,
 33, 120n, 159n, 211n, 212n,
 221n, 240
Congressional Record, 20n, 21n, 22n,
 23n, 75
Conklin, Ellis, 76n, 77n
Connecticut Compromise, 9–10
Conservative Party (of New York), 66n,
 68, 103
Constituency groups, 6, 234
Constituency service, 169, 178, 182
Constitution of the United States, 6, 12,
 15
Constitutional Convention of 1787, 6–
 10, 19
Contras, 151, 154, 156, 158, 178, 193,
 220
Converse, Philip E., 238n
Cornell University, 168

Court of Appeals, 195
Cover, Albert D., 57n, 86n, 95n
Cranston, Alan, 137, 145–46, 148–53,
  155–65, 183, 185, 224–25,
  237
Crime, 146, 173, 193, 198–99
Crosby, Stills and Nash, 180
Crotty, William, 234n
Cuban-Americans, 201
Culver, John, 137
Cunningham, Doug, 210n
Cuomo, Mario, 166, 170, 173, 175–76,
 180

Dallas Morning News, 82
D'Amato, Alfonse, 56, 65–70, 83, 87n,
  145–46, 166–83, 185, 203,
  225–26, 236, 240
Danforth, John C., 70n
Daschle, Thomas, 145–46, 171, 185,
  207–25
Davis, Ed, 153–54, 156–57
Death penalty, 146, 152, 161, 198–99,
 203
Decker, Cathleen, 157n
DeConcini, Dennis, 159n, 237
Democratic Party political machines,
 23–24
Democratic-Republican Party, 14
Democratic Senate Campaign Commit-
 tee, 213
Deng Xiaoping, 197–98, 200
Denholm, Frank, 208
Dennis, James, 73
Denton, Jeremiah, 35, 74, 107
Detente, 60
Dewar, Helen, 66n, 67n, 77n, 152n
Dickenson, James, 212n, 213n, 216n,
 217n, 219n, 224n
Dickenson, John, 7
Dinkins, David, 175
Dionne, E. J. Jr., 4n, 162n
Direct popular elections, 227
Direct primary, 49–50
Dixon, Alan, 25, 54, 84

Doig, Stephen, 81n, 82n
Dole, Robert, 66n, 173, 197, 229–30, 233
Dominick, Peter, 112
Doonesbury, 107
Douglas, Helen Gahagan, 148
Douglas, Stephen, 19
Downey, Thomas, 146, 170
Drexel Burnham Lambert, 176
Driscoll, John, 91
Drug Enforcement Caucus, 188
Drugs, 169, 173, 180, 183, 188, 191, 193, 196–203, 205
Dukakis, Michael, 100, 119, 199
Dumas, Ernest, 59n
Durenberger, David, 87n
Dyson, John, 170–75, 177, 179–80

Eagleton Institute, 63–64
Eaton, Jim, 199
Eckerd, Jack, 79, 189
Economic conditions, 2, 95–99, 146, 238
　California Senate election (1986), 149, 162
　Florida Senate election (1986), 203–5
　New York Senate election (1986), 166, 180–82
　South Dakota Senate election (1986), 208–10, 221
Education, 28–29, 32
E. F. Hutton, 176
Ehrenhalt, Alan, 147n, 149n, 150n, 151n, 165n, 186n, 187n, 189n, 207n, 208n, 209n, 212n, 222n
Eichel, Larry, 3n
Ekirch, Arthur, 18n, 50n
Electoral College, 19
Electoral competition, 31–33
Elling, Richard C., 231n
Ellsworth, Oliver, 9
Environment, 152, 157, 160, 164, 172, 192–94
Environmental Impact Act, 75
Equal Rights Amendment, 68, 188

Erikson, Robert, 164n
Evans, Rowland, 63n, 156n, 201n
Evans, Susan, 100n

Fallows, James, 168
Farrand, Max, 7n, 8, 9n, 10n
Faubus, Orval, 58
Federal Election Campaign Act of 1971 (FECA), 124
Federal Election Commission (FEC), 73, 87, 123n, 124, 134
Federal Housing Administration (FHA), 79
Federalist Party, 14
Fein, Esther, 179n
Feldman, Paul, 154n
Fenno, Richard F., 100n, 101n, 234
Fenwick, Millicent, 107
Ferejohn, John A., 58n
Ferraro, Geraldine, 146, 169, 171
Fiedler, Bobbi, 153–54, 156
Fiedler, Tom, 190n, 191n, 193n, 195n, 201n, 202n
Finn, Opal, 220
Fiorina, Morris, 83n
Fitzgerald, James, 77
Florida, 1986, 145–47, 185–205
　abortion, 188
　blacks, 203–4
　budget deficit, 203
　Bush, George, 191, 194–95
　campaign finance, 146, 191, 194–96
　Catholics, 203
　challenger quality, 146, 190, 205
　Contras, 193
　crime, 146, 193, 198–99
　death penalty, 146, 198–99, 203
　debate, 200–201
　Drug Enforcement Caucus, 188
　drugs, 146, 188, 191, 193, 196–203, 205
　economic conditions, 203–5
　elderly, 193
　environment, 192–94
　Equal Rights Amendment, 188

252   Index

Florida, 1986 (*continued*)
  gender, 203–4
  Graham, Robert (background), 189–90
  Hawkins, Paula (background), 187–89
  Hawkins Amendment, 197
  Hispanics, 193, 201
  ideology, 146, 186, 188
  Israel, 193
  Jews, 193, 203
  Latin America, 191
  Manion, Daniel, 195
  mass media, 146, 201
  missing children, 188, 196
  Missing Children Act of 1982, 188
  MX missile, 188
  partisanship, 186–87, 204–5
  party competence, 204–5
  personal controversies, 188, 190–91, 194–95, 205
  presidential approval/popularity, 187, 203–4
  Protestants, 203
  race, 203–4
  Reagan, Ronald, 146, 187, 189, 191, 195–96, 200–205
  school prayer, 188
  social security, 189
  state political characteristics, 185–87, 200
  television, 192–93, 196–201
  Transgulf pipeline, 192
  whites, 203–4
Florida Audubon Society, 192
Florida Sierra Club, 192
Florida State Public Service Commission, 187
Florio, James, 119
Foley, Michael, 229n
Folsom, James "Big Jim" Sr., 72
Folsom, James Jr., 56, 70, 72–74, 83–84
Fonda, Jane, 174, 217–19
Ford, Gerald, 62, 69, 130, 192

Foster, David, 21
Fox, Al, 72n, 73n
Foundation, 62
Free Congress, 156
Freeman, Mike, 212
Frey, Lou, 187
Friends of Alaska Committee, 77
Fritchey, Clayton, 59n
Fuerbringer, Jonathan, 1n
Fulbright, William, 54, 56–61, 67, 83, 92

Gaer, Bernard, 61
Gallup, George, 60
Gallup Poll, 96, 98n, 100
Gann, Paul, 150
Gant, Dr. Robert, 4
Garth, David, 177
Gates, Mireille, 210n
Gingrich, Newt, 239–40
Glantz, Stanton A., 108n, 139n
Glenn, John, 56n, 107, 159n, 230, 237
Goldwater, Barry, 66, 69, 94, 112, 148, 167, 206
Goldwater Youth, 62
Goodell, Charles, 103
GOPocrats for Cranston, 152
Gore, Albert Jr., 229
Gorton, Slade, 105, 195n
Gottstein, Barney, 77
Graddick, Charles, 74
Grady, John, 79
Graham, Phil, 189
Graham, Robert, 106, 145–46, 185, 188–205, 209, 224–26
Grassley, Charles, 233
Gravel, Mike, 56, 74–78, 84, 87n, 92
Great Society program, 227
Greely, John, 78n
Green, Bill, 168–69
Green, Mark, 145–46, 168–83, 225, 236
Greenaway, Roy, 150–51, 153n, 157, 159n, 162, 225n
Griffee, Carol, 59n

Grimes, Alan, 19n
Gruening, Clark, 56, 74–78, 83–84
Gruening, Ernest, 74–75
Gubernatorial election, 31–33
Gulf of Tonkin Resolution, 75
Gunter, Bill, 56, 78–83, 187
Gurney, Edward, 79

Hamilton, Alexander, 10n
Hanna, Mark, 18
Hart, Gary, 155, 229
Harvard Law Review, 168
Harvard Law School, 168, 189
Harvard University, 62, 78
Hatch, Orrin, 188, 192
Hatfield, Mark, 61, 88, 91
Hatfield, Paul, 56n
Hawkins, Bert, 88
Hawkins, Paula, 79, 83, 106, 145–46, 185, 187–205, 224–26
Hawkins Amendment, 197
Hayakawa, S. I., 106, 112, 151
Hayden, Tom, 105
Haynes, George, 12–13, 14n, 15n, 16n, 19n, 20n
Hecht, Chic, 236
Heflin, Howell, 6, 91
Heinz, H. John, III, 70n, 230
Helms, Jesse, 113, 157
Hempstead Township, 167
Herman, Robin, 69n
Herschensohn, Bruce, 153, 156–57, 162
Heymann, Philip, 74
Hibbing, John R., 102n
Hinckley, Barbara, 101n
Hispanic Officers Association of Florida, 199
Hispanics, 147, 161, 165, 193, 201
Hobson, Richmond, 21
Hofeld, Albert, 84
Hoffman, Dustin, 65
Hofstadter, Richard, 16n, 17n
Holm, John D., 102n
Holmes, Ralph, 74n

Holtzman, Elizabeth, 70, 146, 167, 169, 171
Homestead Act, 16
Horton, Willie, 174, 198–99
House elections, 11, 32–33, 93–95, 235–36, 238–39
  compared to Senate elections, 6–9, 11–12, 14, 25, 27, 31–43, 54–55, 93–95, 100–101, 126, 227–29, 231
House of Representatives, 12, 14–15, 20, 239
H. R. 39 (race rider), 20–24
Humphrey, Hubert, 231
Hunt, James, 113

Ideology, 30, 32–33, 41–43, 85–86, 89–91, 94, 101, 101–2, 109–10, 140, 233–40
  California Senate election (1986), 148, 150–52, 156–57, 159, 161–64
  Florida Senate election (1986), 186, 188
  New York Senate election (1986), 166–69, 175, 180–82
  South Dakota Senate election, 206, 208
Imrie, Bob, 216n
Incumbency
  incumbency advantage, 12, 34–38, 45–46, 54–55, 72, 87–89, 152, 160, 165, 167–70, 183, 213, 227–28, 230–31
  incumbent performance, 102–12
    health, 105, 109, 112
    intraparty opposition, 105–6, 109, 112
    political controversies and scandals, 104, 109, 111
    voting record, 103, 109
  incumbent spending, 126–37, 139–43
  incumbent vote margin, 89–91
  incumbent vulnerability, 24–27, 35, 54–55, 83–84, 227–28

Independent expenditures, 123, 137–39, 143
Information Associates, 216
Israel, 59, 150, 159–60, 168, 169, 172, 193, 217
Issues (impact of national), 232–33, 238
Issues and Answers, 60

Jackson, Andrew, 49
Jackson, John S., III, 234n
Jacksonians, 14
Jackson State University, 72
Jacobson, Gary, 85n, 93n, 108n, 127n, 128, 139n, 169n
Jacobson-Kernell hypothesis, 128–31
Janklow, William, 208, 210–15, 224
Javits, Jacob, 54, 56, 61, 65–70, 83–84, 87n, 92, 112, 167, 169
Jefferson, Thomas, 10, 14
Jepsen, Roger, 65, 111
Jewell, Malcolm, 50n, 51n
Jewish Federation Council of Los Angeles, 159
Jews, 59–60, 77–78, 159, 193, 203
John Birch society, 160
Johnson, Andrew, 16
Johnson, Lyndon, 57, 94, 206, 227, 232
Jones, Charles O., 227n
Jones, John Harris, 61
Joyce, Fay, 81n, 83n
Justice Department, 56, 73, 82, 169

Kassebaum, Nancy, 70n
Katosh, John P., 28n
Kean, Thomas, 65
Keating, Charles, 159, 237
Keating, Kenneth, 166
Kemp, Jack, 62–63
Kemp-Roth tax cut, 63, 79
Kennedy, Edward, 3, 137, 155, 161, 213–14, 218, 229
Kennedy, John, 180
Kennedy, Robert, 148, 155, 166
Kennedy Institute, 62
Kenney, Patrick J., 105n
Kepple, David, 74n
Kernell, Samuel, 93n, 96n, 98, 128, 169n
Kerr, Peter, 171n
Key, V. O., 49n, 50n, 83n, 186
Kiewiet, D. Rod, 53n
Kilpatrick, Andrew, 73n
King, Martin Luther Jr., 208
Kissinger, Henry, 60
Klibanoff, Hank, 213n
Knute Rockne, 221
Koch, Edward, 166, 168, 173–75
Korologos, Tom, 1
Kosen, Bill, 77n
Kramer, Gerald H., 93n, 95n
Kramer, Michael, 168n, 177n, 178n
Kranz, David, 219n
Kuchel, Thomas, 149, 152
Kunst, Bob, 190n
Kuttner, Robert, 60n
Kymlicka, B. B., 227n

Laffer, Arthur, 153–55
LaFollette, Robert, 50
Lamm, Richard, 191
LaRouche, Lyndon, 89
Lautenberg, Frank, 107
League of Women Voters, 160
Ledbetter, Stewart, 89
Lefkowitz, Louis, 68
Lehrman, Lewis, 180
Lengle, James I., 234n
Lescaze, Lee, 66n, 67n
Levitin, Teresa E., 102n
Levitt, Arthur Jr., 170
Lewis, C. R., 75
Lewis, William, 60n, 61n
Liberal Party (of New York), 66n, 68, 167, 169, 174–75, 179
Libertarian Party (Alaska), 75
Lincoln, Abraham, 16, 19, 205

Lincoln Savings and Loan Association, 159, 237
Link, Arthur, 16n, 17n, 18n
Lobbying organizations, 6
Lorimer, William, 19
Los Angeles Times, 153–54, 156, 160, 162
Love, Keith, 152n, 153n, 155n, 156n, 157n, 158n, 159n, 160n, 161n
Lugar, Richard, 191
Lungren, Daniel, 153
Luttbeg, Norman, 164n
Lynn, Frank, 68n, 169n, 170n, 171n, 172n, 173n, 174n, 175n, 176n, 177n, 178n, 179n
Lystad, Robert, 194n

McCain, John, 159n, 237
McCarthy, Joseph, 57, 201
McCloskey, Paul, 151
McCormick, Stanley, 16n, 17n, 18n
Macdonald, Katharine, 154n
McFadden, Robert, 177n
McGovern, George, 57, 86n, 103, 111, 137, 148, 206–7, 209, 211, 217, 229, 233
Mack, Connie III, 190
MacKay, Kenneth (Buddy), 81–82
MacKenzie, Don, 80
McKinley, William, 17
Madison, James, 7, 9, 10–11
Magnuson, Warren, 105, 112
Malbin, Michael, 123n, 129n, 132n, 135n
Manion, Daniel, 195
Mann, Thomas, 123n, 129n, 132n, 135n
Marcos, Ferdinand, 156
Margiotta, Joseph, 67–68, 167, 180
Marist Institute, 179
Martin, James, 72
Martin, Luther, 9
Mason, George, 7
Mason, Tom, 217

Mass media, 41, 44, 47, 100–101, 229–32, 237
 California Senate election (1986), 145, 154–58
 Florida Senate election (1986), 192–93, 196–201
 New York Senate election (1986), 172–74, 176–77
 South Dakota Senate election (1986), 211, 213, 216, 218–19, 222
Mathias, Charles, 61
Matthews, Donald R., 229n
Matthews, Douglas, 57n, 58n, 61n, 66n, 79n
Matthews, Jay, 154n, 157n, 158n, 160n, 161n
Matthews, Jean V., 227n
Mattingly, Mack, 35, 104
Maxwell, Robert, 88
Mayhew, David, 55n, 230n
Medicare, 220
Melcher, John, 116, 236
Metzenbaum, Howard, 56n, 118–19, 137
Mexican immigrants, 201
Miami Herald, 191n, 193, 193n, 194n, 195, 196n, 199–200
Midterm elections, 96–98, 109, 114–15
Miller, Jim, 80
Miller, Judith, 83n
Miller, Warren E., 102n, 238n
Miller, Zell, 104
Mills, Betty, 76n
Missing children, 188, 196
Missing Children Act, (1982), 188
Mondale, Walter, 86n, 215, 230
Montoya, Joseph, 111
Moral Majority, 217
Morgan, Dan, 59n, 60n
Morgan, Dick, 22
Morin, Richard, 193n, 195n
Morris, Gouverneur (of Pennsylvania), 10
Mother Hale, 174

Moynihan, Daniel Patrick, 88–89, 103, 113, 166
Mugwumps, 17
Murkowski, Frank, 77–78
Murphy, George, 149
Murphy, Todd, 210n, 211n, 212n, 213, 214n, 217n, 218n, 219n, 220n
MX missile, 151, 156, 158

Nader, Ralph, 66, 146, 168, 177, 180
Nassau County Republican Party (of New York), 70, 167, 178
National Abortion Rights Action League (NARAL), 3, 5n
National Alliance of Senior Citizens, 220
National Association of Realtors, 213
National outcome of senate elections, 93–100
  prediction of future elections, 99–100
National Conservative Political Action Committee (NCPAC), 101, 103, 137, 207
National Council of Senior Citizens, 220
National Election Studies (NES), 27–47
National Republican Senatorial Committee, 195
National Review, 62
National Rifle Association, 176
Naylor, Robert, 153
Neas, Ralph, 1
Nelson, Avi, 88
New Jersey Plan, 8
New Republic, 177
New York, 1986, 145–47, 165–83
  abortion, 178
  Asians, 165
  balanced budget, 193
  blacks, 165, 181–82
  Bush, George, 173
  campaign finance, 146, 169–74, 183
  capital gains differential, 150
  challenger quality, 146, 171–72, 177, 183

constituency service, 169, 178, 182
Contras, 178
crime, 173
D'Amato, Alphonse (background), 167–68
debates, 178
Democratic party primary, 169–73
drugs, 169, 173, 180, 183
economic conditions, 166, 180–82
environment, 172
gender, 181–82
Green, Mark (background), 168–69
gun control, 178
Hispanics, 165
ideology, 166, 167–68, 169, 172, 175, 180–82
incumbent advantages, 169–70, 183
Israel, 169
issues, 180–82
mass media, 172–74
Nassau County Republican Party, 167, 178
New York Times endorsement, 178–79
partisanship, 166, 181–82
party competence, 181–82
personal controversies, 167, 169, 176–77, 183
personal popularity, 183
presidential approval/popularity, 166, 181–82
race, 181–82
Reagan, Ronald, 166, 173
Reaganomics, 172
representation, 168
senior citizens, 180
social security, 180
South Africa, 172, 178
Soviet Jews, 183
state political characteristics, 165–66
Strategic Defense Initiative, 178
television, 172, 174, 176–77
turnout, 173
unemployment, 180
whites, 181–82

New York Democratic State Committee, 171
New York State Power Commission, 170
New York Times, 5, 59n, 63n, 64n, 67, 69, 70n, 72n, 82n, 169n, 172, 173n, 175, 176n, 177n, 178–79, 180n
Nicholson, Jack, 65, 217
Niemi, Richard, 186, 206n
Nixon Administration, 60, 107
Nixon, Richard, 59, 62, 79, 130, 148, 151, 156, 192
Noble, Kenneth, 4n
Nonpartisan primary, 51
Norcross, David, 65
Norpoth, Helmut, 95n
Norris, George, 21
North Vietnam, 217
Novak, Robert, 63n, 156n, 201n
Nuclear Freeze movement, 150, 156, 158
Nunn, Sam, 155, 235

Oates, Marylouise, 159n
Olson, David, 50n, 51n
Open primary, 51n, 74, 77
Open seats, 108, 127
O'Reilley, Barbara, 81n
Oreskes, Michael, 169n
Ornstein, Norman, 123n, 129n, 132n, 135n
Ottinger, Richard, 103
Overman, Lee, 14

Packwood, Robert, 54, 134
Palm Beach Post, 196
Panama Canal Treaty, 79–80, 83, 220
Partisanship, 30, 32–37, 86, 89–91, 101–2, 109–10, 115, 140, 148, 163–64, 166, 181–82, 186–87, 204–6, 222–23, 231–32
Party competence evaluation, 95–100, 109, 113–15, 238
Party defections, 34–37

Party identification, 33–35, 41–43, 101–2, 109–10, 115, 231–32
Paterson, William, 8
Patterson, Samuel C., 31n
Peck, Gregory, 5
Pentagon Papers, 75
People for the American Way, 3, 5
Percy, Charles, 61
Personal controversies, 155, 164, 167, 169, 176–77, 183, 188, 190–91, 194–95, 205, 213, 217
Personal popularity, 164, 183, 207, 219, 221–22
Peters, John G., 104n
Peterson, Bill, 71n, 194n, 197n, 199n, 200n
Pettigrew, Richard, 80–81
Philippines, 156
Planned Parenthood, 5
Political action committees (PACs), 6, 78, 124, 131–37, 171–72, 176
Political controversies, 18–19, 86–87
Pollock, Howard, 75
Polsby, Nelson, 173n
Population size of state, 102, 109–11
Populist Movement, 16–17
Powell, Lewis, 1
Presidential approval and popularity, 2, 94–100, 109, 114–15, 130, 149, 166, 181–82, 187, 203–4, 187, 206, 233, 238
Pressler, Larry, 208
Primary Elections, 49–92, 105–6, 109, 112
  Alabama, 1978, 56n, 71
  Alabama, 1980, 56, 70–74, 83–84
  Alaska, 1980, 56, 74–78, 84
  Arkansas, 1974, 56–61, 83–84
  California, 1986, 153–57
  Florida, 1980, 56, 78–84
  New Jersey, 1978, 56, 61–65, 83–84
  New York, 1980, 56, 65–70, 83–84
  New York, 1986, 169–75
  1990 primaries, 91–92
  South Dakota, 1986, 210–15

Princeton University, 150
Progressive Movement, 16–20, 22–24, 49–50
Proposition 13, 63, 65, 148
Proposition 65, 159
Proxmire, William, 88n
Public opinion polls, 4–5, 67, 96, 100, 148, 160–63, 166, 180–81, 187, 203–4, 206, 219; 222–23
Pure Food and Drug Law, 18
Purnick, Joyce, 70n, 169n
Putney, Michael, 199

Quayle, Dan, 230
Quinn, Sally, 71n

Raasch, Chuck, 217n, 219n, 220n
Race, 29, 32–33, 181–82, 203–4
Raczkoski, Richard, 198–99
Rafferty, Max, 148–49, 152
Ralph, James Walter, 63
Rasmussen, Jim, 217n
Reagan, Ronald, 1–2, 5–6, 12, 35, 62–63, 65, 69, 94, 100, 130–31, 137–38, 145–51, 154–56, 159–64, 166, 172–73, 182, 187, 189, 191, 195–96, 200–211, 213–14, 216, 218–21, 223, 225, 227, 233, 239
    California, 1986, 145–51, 154–56, 159–64
    Florida, 1986, 145–47, 187, 189, 191, 195–96, 200–205
    New York, 1986, 145–47, 166, 172–73, 182
    South Dakota, 1986, 145–47, 209–10, 218–21
Reagan Administration, 118, 150, 233
Reaganomics, 63, 172
Reaves, William, 198–99
Reed, Nat, 192
Reed, Roy, 59n, 60n
Region (of NES respondent's residence), 29, 32
Reid, T. R., 63n, 64n

Reiner, Ira, 154
Representation, 7–11, 43–46, 54–57, 85–86, 168, 233–40
    collective accountability, 239–40
    Fenno model of the constituency, 234
Reston, James, 3n
Rice, Tom W., 105n
Richardson, Bill, 148, 150
Riegle, Donald, 159n, 237
Right-to-Life Party (of New York), 66n, 68
Rivers, Ralph, 75
Roberts, Clint, 209
Roberts, Steven, 5, 6n
Robertson, Peggy, 61n
Robinson, John P., 102n
Rockefeller, Jay, 230
Rockefeller, Nelson, 148
Rockefeller, Winthrop, 58
Rohde, David, 52–53, 164n
Roosevelt, Franklin D., 25, 180
Roosevelt, Franklin D. Jr., 66
Roosevelt, Theodore, 17–18, 155
Rosenstone, Steven J., 28n, 29n
Roth, William, 63
Rucker, William, 20, 22
Runoff primary, 52n, 74
Rural Electrification Administration, 210
Rutgers University, 63
Ryan, Robert, 80n

Safire, William, 64n
St. Petersburg Times, 81, 189
Salinger, Pierre, 149
Sanford, Terry, 6
Santini, James, 89
Sarbanes, Paul, 137
Saudi Arabia, 150, 159
Scarrit, Tom, 71n, 72n, 73n, 74n
Scarrow, Howard, 171n
Schlesinger, Joseph A., 52, 229
Schmalz, Jeffrey, 176n
Schmitt, Harrison, 107, 113, 230
Schneppie, Richard, 88

Schwartz, Maralee, 159n, 160n, 161n, 174n, 177n, 196n, 212n, 217n, 221n
Segal, Jeffrey, 57n, 86n
Sellers, Patrick J., 53
Senate
  Aging Committee, 188
  Agriculture Committee, 79, 188
  Appropriations Committee, 167, 207
  Banking Committee, 150, 167, 188
  committee (and subcommittee) chairs, 2
  compared to House, 12, 15
  democratization, 229
  Environment Committee, 207
  Ethics Committee, 168
  Foreign Relations Committee, 79, 150
  Housing and Urban Affairs Committee, 150, 167
  Indian Affairs Committee, 207
  Joint Economic Committee, 167, 207
  Judiciary Committee, 2–6, 13
  Labor and Human Resources Committee, 3, 188
  majority party advantages, 2
  origins of, 6–8
  party control, 1–2, 227–28
  political theory of Framers, 10–12
  Select Intelligence Committee, 150
  Small Business Committee, 167
  Subcommittee on Securities, 176
  Veteran Affairs Committee, 150
  Watergate Committee, 79
  Water Resource Subcommittee, 207
Senate elections
  candidate characteristics, 102–9, 111–14, 145
  challengers, 34–47, 54–55, 85, 87–92, 100–101, 106–8, 113, 126, 128–37, 139–43, 145, 228–31
  compared to House elections, 6–9, 11–12, 14, 25, 27, 31–43, 54–55, 93–95, 100–101, 126, 227–29, 231, 235–36, 238–39

general elections
  California, 1986, 145–65
  Florida, 1986, 145–47, 185–205
  New York, 1986, 145–47, 165–83
  South Dakota, 1986, 145–47, 205–25
history of, 7–8, 11–26
incumbency advantage, 12, 34–38, 45–46, 54–55, 72, 87–89, 152, 160, 165, 167–70, 183, 213, 227–28, 230–31
incumbent performance, 102–12
incumbent vote margin, 89–91
incumbent vulnerability, 24–27, 35, 54–55, 83–84, 227–28
indirect election of senators, 7–8, 11–15
national political conditions, 93–100, 114, 140, 145
partisanship, 30, 32–35, 36–37, 86, 89–91, 231–32
party control, 1–2, 227–28
political controversies, 86–87, 89–90
prediction of results
  1988 Senate Elections, 116–20
  1990 Senate Elections, 116–20
primary elections, 49–92, 105–6, 109, 112
  Alabama, 1978, 56n, 71
  Alabama, 1980, 56, 70–74, 83–84
  Alaska, 1980, 56, 74–78, 84
  Arkansas, 1974, 56–61, 83–84
  California, 1986, 153–57
  Florida, 1980, 56, 78–84
  New Jersey, 1978, 56, 61–65, 83–84
  New York, 1980, 56, 65–70, 83–84
  New York, 1986, 169–75
  1990 primaries, 91–92
  South Dakota, 1986, 210–15
state characteristics and effect on Senate elections, 101–2, 114, 145
typical office-seeker, 52–54

260 Index

Senate Republican Campaign Committee, 174
Senior citizens, 180, 193, 221
Seventeenth Amendment, 12, 15, 19–26, 49, 227
"race rider" (H. R. 39), 20–24
Sex (of NES respondent), 29
Shanard, George, 217
Shapiro, Catherine R., 58n
Shaw, Robert, 80n, 81n, 82n
Shaw, Robert Jr., 81n
Shelby, Richard, 6
Shenon, Philip, 5n
Sherley, Joseph, 21
Sherman, Roger, 8
Shevin, Robert, 189
Shudlick, John Larsen, 190n
Sikes, Robert, 81–82
Simon, Paul, 1, 65
Simon, William, 62
Simpson, Alan, 70n
Sinclair, Barbara, 229n
Sioux Falls Argus Leader, 210n, 212n, 213, 215, 217, 218n, 219n
Skelton, George, 156n, 160n, 161n
Smathers, Bruce, 189
Smith, Hedrick, 134
Smith, Patti, 65
Smothers, Ronald, 172n
Social Security, 180, 189, 220–21
Solarz, Steven, 171
Sorauf, Frank J., 124n, 143
South Africa, 160, 172, 178
South Dakota, 1986, 145–47, 205–25
  Abdnor, James (background), 207–8
  abortion, 209
  budget deficit, 206
  campaign finance, 146, 210, 212–14, 217
  challenger quality, 209
  Daschle, Thomas (background), 208–9
  debates, 211–12, 216–17, 220
  economic conditions, 146, 205
  farm policy, 146, 206, 208–10, 215–18
  ideology, 146, 206, 208
  incumbent advantages, 213
  Israel, 217
  mass media, 216
  Medicare, 220
  native American, 205
  partisanship, 206, 222–23
  party competence, 222–23
  personal controversies, 213, 217
  personal popularity, 207, 219, 221–22
  presidential approval and popularity, 206
  primary challenge, 210–15
  Reagan, Ronald, 209–10, 218–21
  Republican primary, 210–15
  right-to-work laws, 209
  senior citizens, 221
  social security, 220–21
  state political characteristics, 205–6
  television, 146, 211, 213, 216, 218–19, 222
  whites, 205
South Dakota Poll, 219
South Dakota State University, 208
South Dakota University, 213
Southern Democrats, 5–6, 20–21
Southern Manifesto, 57
Soviet Union, 156, 201, 211
Sparkman, John, 71
Spears, Gregory, 190n, 194n, 195n, 198n, 201n
Squier, Robert, 197
Stafford, Robert, 70n, 88–89
Stanford University, 149–50
Stanley, Harold, 186n, 206n
State party nominating convention, 49–51
State size, 43–46, 53, 102, 109–11
Statile, Anthony, 65
Stavrianos, Peter, 207, 211n, 214–15, 219, 220n, 221n
Stennis, John, 6
Sternberg, Steve, 194n
Stevens, Ted, 70n, 75–78

Stewart, Donald, 56, 70–74, 83–84, 87n, 92
Stewart, Robert, 153n
Stockton, John, 13
Stokes, Donald E., 238n
Stone, Richard, 56, 78–84, 87n, 92, 187
Storrs, Henry, 15
Story, Joseph, 12n
Strategic Defense Initiative (SDI), 156, 178
Strategic spending, 128–31
Streisand, Barbra, 217
Strinden, Earl, 116
Sullivan, Joseph F., 62n, 63n, 64n, 65n
Sulzer, William, 21
Sundquist, James L., 227n
Supreme Court, 1, 124, 137
Syracuse University, 66, 167
Systems Industries, 150

Taft, William Howard, 17
Talmadge, Herman, 104–5, 111
Tammany Hall, 23, 66
Tampa Tribune, 196
Taylor, Elizabeth, 101
Taylor, Paul, 161n
Tedin, Kent, 164n
Television, 64–65, 82, 87, 101, 146, 230–31
　California Senate election (1986), 155–57, 161–62, 165
　Florida Senate election (1986), 192–93, 196–201
　New York Senate election (1986), 172, 174, 176–77
　South Dakota Senate election (1986), 211, 213, 216, 218–19, 222
Terry, William, 59n, 60n
Thieman, Frank, 217–18
Thomas, Clarence, 84
Thorsness, Leo, 209
Thurmond, Strom, 3, 105, 186
Toner, Robin, 5n, 6n
Tower, John, 232

Transgulf pipeline, 192
Traugott, Michael W., 28n
Tsongas, Paul, 104
Tufte, Edward R., 93n, 238n
Tunney, John, 105–6
Turley, Thomas, 13
Turner, Wallace, 76n, 77n, 78n
Turnout, 27–33, 73, 161

Ueberroth, Peter, 153
Ujifusa, Grant, 57n, 58n, 61n, 66n, 72n, 75n, 76n, 79n, 147n, 148n, 149n, 165n, 166n, 168n, 185n, 186n, 189n, 206n
Unemployment, 180
United States Bureau of the Census, 28
University of Alabama, 71
University of Florida, 78, 189
University of Michigan Center for Political Studies (CPS), 27
University of Nebraska, 207
University of South Dakota, 210
Utah State University, 187

Van Nostrand, Maurice, 65
Vietnam War, 217
Vinich, John, 118
Vinocur, John, 179
Virginia Plan, 7–9
Voinovich, George, 119–20
Voter familiarity (with candidates), 36–39, 44–46

Wade, Brenda, 210n, 216n, 219n
Wadler, Joyce, 68n, 70n
Wagner, Robert, 23, 66
Walker, Jack, 173n
Wallace, George, 71, 79, 81, 186
Wallop, Malcolm, 118
Warner, John, 107
War Powers Act of 1973, 66
Warren, Earl, 155
Washington, George, 10, 14
Washington Post, 67n, 71, 72n, 74n, 177, 189, 194n

Watt, James, 208
Weicker, Lowell, 61, 116, 236
Welch, Susan, 104n
Wellstone, Paul, 119, 231
WESH-TV (Florida), 190
Westlye, Mark C., 101n
Whig Party, 14–15
White, William S., 229
White House Conference on Small Business, 151
Whites, 163–64, 203–5
Whitman, Christine Todd, 119
Who Runs Congress, 168, 170
Williams, Jim, 189
Williams, Lena, 3n
Williams, Robin, 217
Wilson, James, 8
Wilson, Malcolm, 68
Wilson, Pete, 107, 148
Wilson, Woodrow, 17
WNBC-TV, 64
Wolfinger, Raymond E., 28n, 29n
Women, 29
Women's Legal Defense Fund, 3
World Bank, 217
Wright, Gerald, 58n

Young Communists League of America, 201
Young, Horace, 21–22

Zaldivar, R. A., 190n, 196n, 198n, 199n, 200n, 201n, 202n
Zilm, Martha, 153–54
Zorinsky, Edward, 99n
Zschau, Ed, 145, 148, 150–51, 153–65, 185, 209, 224–25
Zwick, David, 168